P9-DMZ-666

EIGHT STEPS TO SEVEN FIGURES

EIGHT STEPS TO SEVEN FIGURES

THE INVESTMENT STRATEGIES OF EVERYDAY MILLIONAIRES AND HOW YOU CAN BECOME WEALTHY TOO

CHARLES CARLSON, CFA

CURRENCY

DOUBLEDAY

New York   Toronto   London   Sydney   Auckland

A CURRENCY BOOK
PUBLISHED BY DOUBLEDAY
a division of Random House, Inc.
1540 Broadway, New York, New York 10036

CURRENCY and DOUBLEDAY are
trademarks of Doubleday, a division of Random House, Inc.

Book design by Donna Sinisgalli.

Library of Congress Cataloging-in-Publication Data
Carlson, Charles B.
Eight steps to seven figures: the investment strategies of everyday millionaires
and how you can become wealthy too / Charles Carlson.—1st ed.
p.   cm.
Includes index.
1. Portfolio management. 2. Investments. 3. Stocks. 4. Wealth.
5. Finance, Personal. 6. Portfolio management—Case studies.
I. Title: Eight steps to seven figures. II. Title.
HG4529.5.C37 2000
332.6—dc21
99-053845
CIP

ISBN 0-385-49731-8

1   3   5   7   9   10   8   6   4   2

To

Tom and Barbara

Thanks for your courage, inspiration, and friendship.

And, of course, the food.

ACKNOWLEDGMENTS

I owe a debt of gratitude to many people for this book. First, a big thank you goes to my editor, Roger Scholl, for his guidance and patience. I'd also like to thank my agent, Wesley Neff, who helped shape the original idea for this book. Special thanks go to Avis Beitz, Elberta Miklusak, Gloria Proctor, Tanya Habzansky, David Wright, and especially Mike Gutierrez, whose work "in the trenches" is greatly appreciated. My undying gratitude also goes to Denise Weaver, who had to tolerate me during the writing of this book. I'd also like to thank my parents, Leonard and Frances Carlson, for their help on this project.

Lastly, I'd like to thank the organizations that helped me connect with many of the everyday millionaire investors in this book—the National Association of Investors Corporation, American Association of Individual Investors, Horizon Publishing (publisher of *DRIP Investor* and *Dow Theory Forecasts* newsletters), and the Motley Fool online service—as well as the everyday millionaire investors who were kind enough to participate in this project. No you, no book. It's that simple.

Contents

PREFACE

Too many people in this world settle for less. They settle for less because they don't know more is possible.

More *is* possible. More money. More financial freedom. More peace of mind.

But in order to have more, you'll have to get down to the doing of creating wealth. Unfortunately, most Americans either don't know how to go about building wealth or aren't willing to make the necessary sacrifices. Instead, people would rather moan about the wealth of others.

For example, people decry the fact that the rich get richer in this country. The rich *are* getting richer. Money begets money. Simple mathematics.

Fortunately, getting rich in America is not a zero-sum game. The rich don't take what's yours. They build on what's theirs. They build on what, in most cases, took them much effort and many years to create. In their bestselling book, *The Millionaire Next Door,* Thomas J. Stanley and William D. Danko claim that 80 percent of the millionaires in this country are first-generation millionaires. They didn't inherit their wealth. They created it.

Make no mistake, you can create wealth, just like the rich. *You can have a seven-figure investment portfolio.* If you don't believe me, believe the everyday millionaire investors who share their recipes for success in this book.

Believe Rex Trotter, who built a seven-figure investment portfolio by age forty, without an inheritance and without any special expertise in investing.

Believe Will Robinson, a retired metallurgist who didn't start investing until age fifty-five but who still built a portfolio worth $1.4 million before his eightieth birthday.

Believe Jeff Tolstoy, who retired before the age of fifty-five with a portfolio worth $3.6 million.

Believe schoolteacher Bob Sutton, age fifty-six, who started investing at age seventeen and now has an investment portfolio worth $1.3 million.

THE RICH WEREN'T ALWAYS RICH

It should be reassuring to know that many of the millionaire investors discussed in this book started out in straits similar to yours.

They had little or no money. Little or no knowledge. A fear of failure. Barely a plan.

So how did these average Janes and Joes build their seven-figure portfolios?

They started the process.

They had a goal.

They invested for growth.

They reduced risk by maintaining a long-term focus.

They kept at the process.

They focused on their strengths.

They took advantage of what Uncle Sam offered.

They limited shocks to the process.

In short, they took measures available to *anyone,* including you.

EIGHT STEPS TO SEVEN FIGURES

I've always been fascinated by regular people who built not-so-regular fortunes solely by investing. I believed much could be learned from these successful individual investors.

Little did I know just how much.

Every one of the 170 or so millionaire investors participating in my study provides insights that can benefit virtually any investor. These millionaire investors know what works on Wall Street and, perhaps more important, what doesn't work. They know the hardships and the hurdles you face starting and maintaining an investment program. They faced the same hardships and hurdles.

My challenge was to distill these 170 individual investor success stories to their common denominators. By finding common threads responsible for investment success, I could create a blueprint, an action plan so simple to follow that any investor—regardless of income, age, and investing expertise—could create personal wealth in the financial markets.

In your hands is such an action plan.

Eight Steps to Seven Figures is the definitive, step-by-step plan for investing your way to a seven-figure portfolio.

Eight steps. That's all it takes. Eight simple steps.

But simple doesn't necessarily mean easy. You'll need discipline. Patience. Persistence. Perseverance. You have to change the way you think about money and spending. You may have to sacrifice today for a better tomorrow. But if you're up to the task, following these eight steps will make you a better investor. And a wealthier one, too.

You have more than just my word on that. You have the words of 170 everyday millionaire investors, people, in many respects, a lot like you.

Charles Carlson

INTRODUCTION

Our nation has two national pastimes: baseball and Warren Buffett.

Indeed, it's difficult to go a day without hearing the name Warren Buffett.

"Buffett is buying silver."

"Buffett likes real estate investment trusts."

"Buffett says the market is overvalued."

"Buffett . . . Buffett . . . Buffett . . ."

Whole industries have been spawned in recent years around the sayings and doings of this man. Books, newsletters, mutual funds, television specials . . . all attempting to capitalize on the popularity of this unassuming gent from Nebraska.

Why the public fascination? You're probably saying it's because he's rich. Yes, Mr. Buffett is rich. Very rich—$30 *billion* rich.

But that's only part of it. A lot of people are mega-rich. Athletes, movie stars, financiers, politicians. Few capture our interest like Mr. Buffett. No, our fascination with Mr. Buffett goes much deeper than merely his rather sizable bank account.

We're intrigued with Mr. Buffett because he's one of us. Warren doesn't have a ninety-five-mile-an-hour fastball. He can't dunk a basketball. He's not a scratch golfer. He can't do Hamlet. He doesn't know a motherboard from a Mother Hubbard.

Warren loves McDonald's and Dairy Queen. He drinks a lot of Coke. He's a meat-loaf-and-mashed-potatoes kind of guy. Heck, he's from Omaha. Not Los Angeles or New York or Washington, D.C., or Silicon Valley.

Omaha, for crying out loud.

And one more thing, and this is a biggie: Warren made his billions doing something that's available to *anyone.*

He got rich buying stocks.

Washington Post.

American Express.

Coca-Cola.

Wells Fargo.

Gillette.

That Warren Buffett made his loot investing in common stocks gives him a certain accessibility that doesn't exist with other rich people. I can't be like Mike (Jordan). I can't be like Bill Gates. I can't be like Dustin Hoffman.

I *can* be like Warren. I can buy Coca-Cola stock. I can buy Wells Fargo. I can buy American Express. That's why we're fascinated with Warren Buffett. *His* path to wealth could be *our* path to wealth.

Now I'm not saying that, if you buy stocks, you'll eventually count commas like Warren Buffett counts commas. (That's three commas—$1,000,000,000—for your garden-variety billionaires.) What I am saying is that there's no reason Warren has to have all the fun, or all the commas.

In fact, while Warren Buffett is the most obvious example of an individual investor who made good, *real* good, he's not alone. Many individual investors have built two-comma (that's seven figures) investment portfolios.

You can build a seven-figure portfolio.

This book shows you how.

What's different about this book, however, is that it won't tell you how Warren Buffett made his billions in the market. Plenty of books tell you that. I tell you how Sally Finn made her millions. Never heard of Sally Finn? She lives with her husband in the Upper Midwest. Sally has an investment portfolio of $2.1 million despite being only fifty years old. How did she do it? She bought good growth stocks—Merck, Dell, Intel. She bought stock every month. She held her stocks, on average, for five years. And she put the maximum each year into her employer's 401(k) retirement program.

I tell you how A. J. Wright made his seven-figure ($1.7 million to be exact) portfolio. Never heard of A. J. Wright? A.J., age fifty-five, lives on the East Coast with his wife. He started investing at age twenty-five. A.J. built his seven-figure portfolio by following this adage (these are his words): "Save ten percent, give ten percent, and spend the rest [after taxes]."

Sally and A.J. are just two of the 170 everyday millionaire investors who share their money making investment secrets in *Eight Steps to Seven Figures*.

In fact, these 170 millionaire investors share much more than just their investment secrets. In Chapter 1, we learn more about these people—their ages, incomes, education, etc. In Chapter 2, we learn about their investment mistakes. Interestingly, the same mistakes come up time and again. You can avoid these mistakes by listening to these voices of experience.

We start the eight steps in Chapter 3. These eight steps, which run from Chapters 3 through 10, distill the success formulas of all 170 everyday millionaire investors. It is my firm belief that these eight steps provide a blueprint for *any* investor—regardless of age, income level, or investment acumen—to build great wealth over time.

Chapter 11 looks at the best of the best, the most successful millionaire investors. This chapter also includes my own two cents on ways to maximize the power of these eight steps.

The material I obtained from these millionaire investors is so rich that I simply could not include all of it in the first eleven chapters of the book. In order that you don't miss any of the wit and wisdom of our everyday millionaire investors, Chapter 12 provides especially noteworthy stories, opinions, and advice from our millionaire investors.

It's always dangerous for people like me to tell people like you that a million-dollar portfolio is within your reach. We sound like just one more of those slick pitchmen hustling the latest can't-miss, get-rich-quick scheme. That's what makes this book unique. *Eight Steps to Seven Figures* isn't about some "guru" telling you how to make millions. It's not about *me* telling you how to make millions in the stock market. It's about ordinary people, just like you, telling you how they won big on Wall Street, people with no agenda other than to help others duplicate their successes.

That purity of motive alone should get you to listen to what they have to say.

You'll be glad you did.

AUTHOR'S NOTE

To protect the privacy of the millionaire investors who participated in this project, I have substituted pseudonyms in place of the investors' real names. The quoted material from the investors was taken from their handwritten or typed responses to in-depth questions on an investor survey in which they volunteered to participate. In some cases, the quotes were cleaned up grammatically or shortened to improve clarity. All other information from the surveys has remained unchanged.

EIGHT STEPS TO SEVEN FIGURES

1

You Can Be a Millionaire Investor

I think my experience proves that you don't have to be smart or have any special talent. Time and consistency are the key factors.

—JOHN CONMED, NEW YORK,
$5.5 MILLION INVESTMENT PORTFOLIO

There are some eight million millionaires in the United States.

My guess is that you are not one of them.

That doesn't have to be the case. Anyone can invest his or her way to a million dollars.

Anyone.

How? By following the eight simple steps in this book.

You Don't Have to Kill Bugs to Be a Millionaire

Notice I said anyone can *invest* his or her way to a million dollars. A lot of books have been written in recent years about millionaires. Where they live. What they wear. What they drive. In short, we know a lot about *who* they are. We know less, however, about *how* they got their millions. Oh sure, the books tell us that typical millionaires live below their means. They make building wealth a priority. They possess college degrees. Still, at the end of the day, many of these millionaires gained their wealth partly through means not available to most of us.

For example, in their bestselling book *The Millionaire Next Door*, Thomas J. Stanley and William D. Danko write that two thirds of millionaires are self-employed. More than one fifth of the typical millionaire's wealth is tied to his or her private business. These millionaire entrepreneurs are welding contractors, auctioneers, rice farmers, and paving contractors. They own mobile-home parks and pest-control services.

So there you have it. In order to be a millionaire, you have to be a bug killer.

Fortunately, that's not the case. You can be a retired college professor, like Millie S., fifty-eight years old and single, who has an investment portfolio worth $1.6 million. How did she do it? Simple.

Millie started investing at age fourteen.

She bought industry leaders, such as McDonald's, Walgreen, and Exxon.

Stocks everyone knows. Stocks everyone could own.

She held her stocks for ten years or longer.

Or you can be an engineer, like Pat J. Pat, fifty-seven, lives with his wife in Virginia. He's worked for the same company for thirty-seven years. Pat, who began investing at age thirty-two, has an investment portfolio of nearly $2 million. How did Pat do it?

He bought quality stocks. Pat's largest stock holdings are such familiar names as AT&T, Dell Computer, Lucent Technologies, and Bristol-Myers Squibb.

Stocks everyone knows. Stocks everyone could own.

Pat also took full advantage of his employer's 401(k) retirement program.

In short, Millie and Pat got rich using vehicles and strategies available to anyone, including yourself.

You Can Be a Millionaire Investor

How do I know *anyone* can invest his or her way to a million dollars? Because I've seen it done over and over again by individuals who are probably a lot like you. Individuals like Millie and Pat.

Or like my friend Saul. Saul is seventy-six years old. Saul has $2 million in stocks and bonds—a nice portfolio by any yardstick. What is especially noteworthy about Saul's seven-figure portfolio is that Saul didn't start investing until he was in his sixties.

"I didn't have any money to invest prior to that," says Saul.

Saul built his portfolio using basic approaches that you'll find in this book.

Saul focused on quality stocks that were leaders in their industries—Procter & Gamble, Exxon, General Electric, Intel. Nothing fancy, just solid companies with solid prospects.

Saul reinvested dividends.

He bought stocks on a regular basis.

He held them for a long, long time.

"Sometimes I wondered if I knew what I was doing. Sometimes I still wonder," says Saul.

His $2 million portfolio is evidence that Saul knew enough.

Or consider Sam B., age fifty. Sam, an attorney, has more than $3 million in his portfolio. How did Sam, at such a relatively young age, amass such an impressive portfolio?

He started investing at age twenty.

He took advantage of his employer's 401(k) retirement by contributing the maximum permitted by law.

He held his stocks, on average, for ten years.

He invested regularly, especially during market declines.

He bought quality stocks. "Almost all the stocks I own are blue chips, with the majority paying dividends, and no acquisition is made with the intention of disposal," says Sam.

Now I know some of you probably are saying that, sure, Sam has a seven-figure portfolio because he makes a lot of money as an attorney. Yes, Sam's income obviously gives him a leg up in the investing game. But a high income is no guarantee of a seven-figure portfolio. More than 25 million households in the United States have annual incomes in excess of $50,000; more than 7 million have annual incomes over $100,000. Yet the number of American households with a net worth of more than $1 million is around 3 million.

You might also be saying that Sam, because he is a lawyer, has some special expertise in investing.

Wrong.

Sam knew nothing about investing when he started. He educated himself via investment courses in college and publications such as *The Wall Street Journal*. But he was hardly born with a silver ticker tape in his mouth.

Nor does Sam spend a lot of money every year on fancy investment tools. On the contrary, Sam spends less than $250 per year on investment research.

Sounds simple, right? Listen to A. J. Wright, whose investment portfolio totals $1.7 million. "Investing doesn't have to be rocket science," says A.J. He ought to know.

A.J. was a rocket scientist.

If it is so simple to have a seven-figure portfolio, why doesn't everyone have one? Because investment success doesn't happen overnight. If you start investing today, you won't be rich tomorrow. Or a month from now. Or a year from now. Or five years from now. You will be rich twenty or thirty years from now. Most people don't want to wait that long. They want it now. And if they can't have it now, they don't bother.

Most people are not millionaire investors because investing now means delaying gratification. We live in a world where many people feel *entitled* to the good life right now, not when they're sixty years old. We want to consume today *and* have our seven-figure retirement savings waiting for us tomorrow. Unfortunately, spending today and saving tomorrow won't get you a million bucks.

Yes, successful investing is simple. But it isn't easy. Doing one sit-up is simple. Doing one sit-up every day for the rest of your life may be simple, but it isn't easy. You'll forget. You'll make excuses. You'll get bored. The upshot is that it's easier *not* to do one sit-up every day even though the effort to do so would be minimal. Why? Because doing the sit-up is new behavior. It's outside the norm. It's not habit.

What Saul and Sam and A.J. and other everyday millionaire investors have done successfully is incorporate simple investing strategies into their daily lives. Investing in General Electric each month is like paying the utility bill. Saving 10 percent of your salary in your employer's 401(k) plan is like brushing your teeth. Reinvesting dividends is like grabbing that cup of coffee every morning.

Investing practices become so interwoven into the fabric of your everyday life you can't imagine *not* doing them. It's not an option.

WHO ARE THESE EVERYDAY MILLIONAIRES?

Millie, Saul, Pat, Sam, and A.J. are 5 of the 170 everyday millionaires I surveyed for this book. In order to participate in the project, an individual must have at least $1 million in investable assets, including money in 401(k) plans but excluding the value of his or her home.

The millionaires were asked a series of questions about their finances and investment strategies:

- How did they get started investing?
- What hurdles did they overcome to invest?
- What types of stocks did they buy?
- What mistakes did they make?
- Do they feel individual investors are disadvantaged in the financial markets relative to large investors?

- What does investment risk mean to them?
- What resources did they use to educate themselves?
- What investment strategies did they follow?
- What are their best stocks?
- How long do they typically hold investments?
- How long have they been investing?
- Have they ever followed a "hot" tip?

The millionaires also provided a wealth of demographic data—age, income, marital status, number of children, employment history, and education.

MEET THE EVERYDAY MILLIONAIRE INVESTORS

Here's what our survey results tell us about everyday millionaire investors:

- Approximately 80 percent are male.
- Average age of the everyday millionaire investors is sixty.
- The millionaire investors have been married, on average, for thirty-two years.
- Average annual income for these millionaires is $151,500.

Perhaps a more relevant figure is the median income of our millionaires, which is $115,000. That means half of our everyday millionaires had incomes below this level, while half had incomes above this level. Keep in mind a few things about this number. First, many of the millionaire investors I surveyed are retired. Their annual income is not a result of their employment wages but comes from several areas, not the least of which are the dividends and interest earned on their seven-figure investment portfolio. In other words, these millionaire investors have six-figure incomes primarily because they have seven-figure investment portfolios. Second, these millionaire investors began investing long before they had six-figure incomes.

- Only one in five of the millionaire investors has been divorced. This is well below the national average of around one in two.
- The average number of kids per millionaire household is just under two.
- Judging from our millionaire investors, getting a good education is strongly correlated with financial success. More than 80 percent of our millionaire investors have a college undergraduate degree, with nearly half having an advanced degree.
- Our everyday millionaire investors have stable employment histories. The average number of jobs held by our millionaires is three. That compares to the average of roughly thirteen different employers the typical worker has in his or her career. The average number of years our millionaire investors have been at their current job is nineteen.
- Most people would expect that millionaire investors have a definite budget to which they adhered each month. Not true. Less than 30 percent of the millionaire investors surveyed said they maintained a monthly budget.
- About 40 percent of everyday millionaire investors do their own taxes.
- Creating a seven-figure portfolio, contrary to what's purported by television infomercials and day-trading advocates, does not occur overnight. Our millionaire investors have been investing, on average, for thirty years.
- The average size of the investment portfolios of those surveyed was $2.17 million.
- Despite their impressive portfolios, millionaire investors didn't start out as investment experts. More than 85 percent of the millionaire investors said they had no investment expertise when they started.

THE FABULOUS BAKER BOYS

THEODORE AND HARVEY BAKER WERE NEVER CONFUSED with a couple of Wall Street rich guys. The two boys grew up on a farm in Wisconsin. Harvey, the older brother, took care of Theodore, who was mentally disabled. Neither of the boys had any particular job skills other than farming. When their dad died, the boys sold the farm for what was estimated to be around $50,000 (it was the late 1950s) and moved into town. Each took a job as an unskilled laborer in a factory. The two boys never married and lived together for the rest of their lives. Why do I mention Theodore and Harvey? When the two boys died (Theodore in 1989 and Harvey in 1994), they had amassed combined estates totaling $6 *million.*

How did they do it? According to the boys' lawyer, Bill Engler, Jr., Theodore and Harvey saved religiously. Engler says that the two boys did not turn on lights at night, cooked in bacon grease, and walked everywhere they went—they didn't own a car. And they invested. (Harvey was in charge of investing.)

What happened to their money when they died? The Baker brothers, neither of who completed the ninth grade, bequeathed their $6 million estate to scholarships for students from their area who attend the University of Wisconsin.

SOURCE: JANE BIRNBAUM,
NEW YORK TIMES/DETROIT FREE PRESS, JULY 15, 1996.

- Our everyday millionaire investors, on average, hold forty-four stocks in their portfolios.
- As you would guess, only 3 percent of our millionaire investors have ever declared bankruptcy.
- In many cases, millionaire investors developed their penchant for savings and investing from their parents. Indeed, 60 percent of them said that their parents were "important" or "very important" influences on their investing. More than 80 percent classified their parents as "frugal."
- Millionaire investors maintain good financial records. Only 18 percent classified their financial records as "average" or "below average."
- For the most part, millionaire investors stay away from non-standard investments or investment strategies. Only 19 percent have ever bought options; only 6 percent have ever bought futures; less than 30 percent own gold; only 15 percent have ever sold stocks short.
- Although these investors are primarily do-it-yourselfers, more than 60 percent do use outside advice. This advice comes primarily in the form of brokers (48 percent) and investment newsletters (15 percent).
- For the millionaire investors who use a broker, more than 40 percent use a traditional full-service broker.
- About one in five belongs to an investment club and has belonged to the club, on average, for eight years.
- Even millionaire investors can't resist hot tips. Roughly 60 percent admitted to acting on a "hot tip." As is usually the case with hot tips, however, the tip was a bummer. Indeed, the tips panned out only about 20 percent of the time for these millionaire investors.
- Two thirds of everyday millionaire investors track their investments with a personal computer.
- About a third of the millionaire investors inherited money. In most cases, the inheritance had little impact on their financial

positions. In fact, an overwhelming percentage of millionaire investors used money saved from their paychecks to start their investment programs.

- Millionaire investors don't spend thousands of dollars each year on investment research. Nearly 70 percent spend $500 or less per year on investment research. More than 35 percent spend $250 or less. Only 9 percent spend more than $1,000 per year.

- Millionaire investors spend, on average, twelve hours per week tracking their investments. That's less than two hours per day, or about half the time the average American spends watching television each day.

- Nearly half of our millionaire investors classify themselves as "growth" investors. Around 25 percent call themselves "value" investors. About 16 percent call themselves both growth and value.

- Millionaire investors understand the importance of maintaining regular investment programs. Well over half of our millionaire investors invest at least once a month. Another 28 percent invest at least quarterly.

- A slight majority of millionaire investors consider themselves to be "conservative" investors. About 26 percent classify themselves as "aggressive." Interestingly, 14 percent classify themselves as both aggressive and conservative.

- When asked what they fear most, millionaire investors not surprisingly said a prolonged bear market. Many of them also mentioned Uncle Sam's ability to tax away their wealth.

- You won't find day traders among the millionaire investors I surveyed. Indeed, 75 percent said they held their investments on average for at least five years. Nearly 40 percent said they held investments for ten years or longer. Only 8 percent said they held investments for one year or less.

- Millionaire investors aren't necessarily daredevils, but they understand that you must accept some risk in an investment program to generate decent returns. Approximately 48 percent said they had an "average" tolerance for risk. Approximately 38 percent said they had an "above average" tolerance for risk. Only 13 percent said they had a "below average" tolerance for risk.

- For the most part, millionaire investors are buy-and-hold investors. Only one in four attempts any type of market timing.
- Millionaire investors understand the corrosive nature of taxes. Nearly 70 percent considered taxes "important" or "very important" in their investment program.
- More than three quarters of millionaire investors invest in "what they know."
- One out of two everyday millionaire investors doesn't believe individual investors can consistently beat the market.
- Millionaire investors know a good deal when they see one. An overwhelming percentage of the everyday millionaire investors who are eligible to participate in their employers' 401(k) plans do so. The majority invested the maximum permitted in the plans.

DOING THE STEPS

It's not enough to know about the investment habits of these everyday millionaires. My goal was to go beyond the data to devise a cohesive investment action plan that would allow all investors to duplicate the success of these investors. Fortunately, common success factors exist across virtually all millionaire investors. These common success factors comprise the eight steps to seven figures:

EIGHT STEPS TO SEVEN FIGURES

Step 1—Start investing NOW.
Step 2—Establish a goal—*any* goal—it doesn't matter what it is as long as it matters to you.

Step 3—Buy only stocks and stock mutual funds. Forget about asset allocation.

Step 4—Swing for singles. You'll strike out fewer times and hit some home runs in the process.

Step 5—Invest every month, no matter how small the investment.

Step 6—Buy and hold . . . and hold . . . and hold . . . and hold . . . and hold.

Step 7—Take what Uncle Sam gives you.

Step 8—Limit shocks to your finances.

The remainder of this book explores each of these steps in detail. For now, let me make two points. First, these steps are not especially exotic or complicated. I'm sorry if that disappoints you. If you were looking for some revolutionary investment "secret" to propel you to instant riches, look elsewhere.

But don't let the simplicity of these steps fool you. In their simplicity lies their power. For example, Step 1—*Start investing NOW*—seems rather obvious. Yet, the power of this step cannot be overstated. Just by doing step 1, you put a seven-figure portfolio within your grasp. That's *power.*

Look at step 7—Take what Uncle Sam gives you. Uncle Sam gives a tax break to investors who hold stock for twelve months or more. Uncle Sam also makes available retirement programs such as 401(k) plans and Roth IRAs. You should take advantage of these in your investment program. You get it, right? What you may not "get" is that this simple step has probably created more everyday millionaire investors than anything else. That's *power.*

This leads me to my second point. These simple-sounding steps are so powerful that you don't even need to follow all of them in order to become a millionaire investor. I know successful investors who have done nothing more than follow steps 1 and 7. I know successful investors who ignored steps 3 and 8 and still have seven-figure portfolios. The upshot is that by following just a couple of steps, you can truly become a millionaire investor. By following *all* of the steps, an investment portfolio of several million dollars is within your grasp.

The following millionaire investor profile—a profile is featured at the end of each chapter—is of P. F. Turner. I profile Mr. Turner because he did a good job at following most of the steps.

He started investing at age fourteen (step 1).

He bought stocks (step 3).

He focused on high-quality, dividend-paying issues such as BellSouth and Exxon (step 4).

He held stocks for ten years or longer in most cases (step 6).

He invested the maximum in his employer's 401(k) plan (step 7).

He had one job for thirty years and one wife for forty years (step 8).

Mr. Turner made a few mistakes along the way. He bought gold. He sold too early. (Chapter 2 discusses these and other common millionaire mistakes and how to avoid them.) Still, Mr. Turner did a lot of things right. The reward for his efforts?

A $3.5 million investment portfolio.

NAME: P. F. Turner

AGE: 66

HOME: Southeast

MARITAL STATUS: Married (never divorced)

CHILDREN: 2

EDUCATION: College (undergraduate) degree

OCCUPATION: Retired telephone company manager

CURRENT INCOME: $108,000

FIVE-YEAR AVERAGE INCOME: $75,000

HIGHEST ANNUAL INCOME: $108,000

HOW MANY DIFFERENT JOBS SINCE AGE 25? 1

HOW LONG DID YOU WORK AT YOUR EMPLOYER? 30 years

DO YOU HAVE AN ANNUAL HOUSEHOLD BUDGET THAT YOU FOLLOW? No

HAVE YOU EVER DECLARED BANKRUPTCY? No

WOULD YOU CONSIDER YOUR PARENTS TO BE FRUGAL? Yes

HOW IMPORTANT WERE YOUR PARENTS IN DEVELOPING YOUR DISCIPLINE AND EXPER-
TISE IN INVESTING (VERY IMPORTANT, IMPORTANT, NOT IMPORTANT)? Important

DO YOUR CHILDREN INVEST REGULARLY? Yes

HOW GOOD ARE YOUR FINANCIAL RECORDS (GOOD, AVERAGE, BELOW AVERAGE, DISAS-
TER)? Good

DO YOU DO YOUR OWN TAXES? Yes

AT WHAT AGE DID YOU START INVESTING? 14

HOW MANY YEARS HAVE YOU BEEN INVESTING? 52

WHAT IS THE SIZE OF YOUR ENTIRE INVESTMENT PORTFOLIO (INCLUDING ALL STOCKS,
BONDS, IRAS, 401(K) PLANS, ETC., BUT NOT INCLUDING THE VALUE OF REAL ES-
TATE)? $3.49 million

WHAT IS THE BREAKDOWN OF THESE ASSETS? Stocks (82 percent), IRA (11
percent), bonds (7 percent)

HOW MANY INDIVIDUAL STOCK DO YOU OWN? 40

NAME YOUR 5 LARGEST HOLDINGS: BellSouth, CCB Financial, Duke
Energy, Exxon, GTE

HOW MANY INDIVIDUAL MUTUAL FUNDS DO YOU OWN? 0

HOW MANY INDIVIDUAL BONDS DO YOU OWN? 14

HAVE YOU EVER PURCHASED STOCK/INDEX OPTIONS? Yes

HAVE YOU EVER PURCHASED STOCK/INDEX FUTURES? No

DO YOU OWN GOLD OR PRECIOUS METALS? Yes

HAVE YOU EVER SOLD STOCK SHORT? Yes

DO YOU RECEIVE ADVICE ON YOUR INVESTMENTS FROM AN OUTSIDE SOURCE? No

ARE YOU A MEMBER OF AN INVESTMENT CLUB? No

DO YOU INVEST ONLINE? No

DID YOU HAVE SPECIFIC INVESTMENT GOALS WHEN YOU STARTED INVESTING? Yes.
Invest in high-grade stocks that pay 5 percent yield and regularly
increase their dividends.

WHAT ARE THE PLANS FOR YOUR ESTATE? Two daughters each receive half. I
will give to them equally each year to reduce my estate to non-
taxable at my death.

WHAT HURDLES, IF ANY, DID YOU OVERCOME TO BEGIN INVESTING? My father was an investor. I grew up thinking you were supposed to save your money in the bank and draw interest. When you have enough saved to buy 100 shares of a stock at the right price then you withdrew the money and bought the stock.

HOW, PSYCHOLOGICALLY SPEAKING, DID YOU DEAL WITH THE NOTION OF PUTTING OFF CONSUMPTION TO SAVE FOR A BETTER FINANCIAL FUTURE? I did not knowingly deal with it. I suppose you could say I did not know any better. I just always saved part of what I earned. I don't remember applying a set percentage. Just save something most of the time.

WHERE DID YOU GET THE MONEY TO START INVESTING? Christmas and birthday presents and odd jobs as a youngster. As a teenager, I almost always had a summer job or two and also after school.

WERE THERE ANY SPECIFIC EVENTS, LIFE-CHANGING MOMENTS, ETC., THAT SPURRED YOU TO BEGIN INVESTING? The event did not spur me to begin, but it did spur me to work harder at investing whereas before I didn't spend too much time and did it as a hobby or sideline. The event was my demotion at the company where I was working because I was overweight and didn't belong to the country club. At the same time my job rating was excellent. I realized I wanted to keep the retirement benefits I'd earned but I needed to become self-sufficient.

HAVE YOU INHERITED WHAT YOU THOUGHT WAS A LARGE AMOUNT OF MONEY? No

DID YOU START INVESTING WITH A SPECIFIC PLAN IN MIND? Yes. When I started my regular permanent job, we made enough so that we could live on 53 to 55 percent of my income. That is my gross income minus taxes, stock purchases, IRAs, savings, etc. As money accumulated, I bought more stock.

DID YOU KEEP TO YOUR PLAN? Yes

HOW DID YOU EDUCATE YOURSELF ABOUT INVESTING? DID YOU FIND THIS EDUCATION PROCESS DIFFICULT? FUN? I attended 2 classes in college. Before and after that I read everything I found that was remotely related to investing. I talked to anyone successful to get them to tell me how they operate. It is probably 50 percent boring and repetitious and 50 percent fun in learning.

DID YOU HAVE ANY SPECIAL EXPERTISE IN INVESTING WHEN YOU STARTED? I thank my mother and father for a high IQ and common sense. I thank my teachers for putting up with me and teaching me to become good at reading, writing, arithmetic.

WHAT MAGAZINES, NEWSLETTERS, TELEVISION/RADIO SHOWS, INTERNET SITES, ETC., DO YOU FIND THE MOST USEFUL FOR INVESTMENT RESEARCH? *Barron's, Investment Quality Trends* newsletter, *Income Digest* newsletter, *Personal Finance* newsletter

HOW MUCH DO YOU SPEND PER YEAR ON INVESTMENT RESEARCH RESOURCES? Between $251 and $500

DO YOU USE A COMPUTER TO KEEP TRACK OF YOUR INVESTMENTS? No

HOW MANY HOURS PER WEEK DO YOU DEVOTE TO YOUR INVESTMENTS AND INVESTMENT STRATEGIES? 30

WHAT CRITERIA DO YOU USE TO PICK STOCKS/MUTUAL FUNDS? The stock must be listed on the New York Stock Exchange or be so compelling as to make an exception—too hard to keep track of otherwise. Must be S&P (Standard & Poor's) rated B+ or better or Value Line safety rating of 2 or better—this avoids most of the financial comparison drudgery and screens out stocks you don't need to waste your time on. Must pay a dividend of 5 percent or better or 3.5 percent if dividend growth will get to 5 percent in a year. Dividend must be increased almost every year. Price must be in lower quarter of the latest 52-week range.

WHAT TYPE OF INVESTOR DO YOU CONSIDER YOURSELF TO BE? Income investor based on value

WHAT TERM BEST DESCRIBES YOUR INVESTMENT STYLE (CONSERVATIVE, AGGRESSIVE, OTHER)? Conservative

HOW OFTEN DO YOU BUY INVESTMENTS? Sporadically

ON AVERAGE, HOW LONG DO YOU HOLD AN INVESTMENT BEFORE SELLING? 10 years or longer

DO YOU "MARKET TIME"? IN OTHER WORDS, DO YOU TRY TO TIME PURCHASE/SALE OF IN-

VESTMENTS BASED ON YOUR EXPECTATIONS FOR MARKET MOVEMENTS AND/OR MOVEMENTS IN THE INDIVIDUAL STOCKS? Yes

DOES YOUR INVESTMENT APPROACH DIFFER DEPENDING ON WHETHER THE MARKET IS CLASSIFIED AS A "BEAR" OR A "BULL" MARKET? Yes. I become more selective and cautious in bear markets.

HOW IMPORTANT ARE TAXES IN YOUR INVESTMENT PROCESS (VERY IMPORTANT, IMPORTANT, NOT IMPORTANT)? Important

WHAT HAVE BEEN YOUR 3 BEST-PERFORMING STOCKS? Sturm, Ruger; Exxon; and CCB Financial

WHAT HAVE BEEN YOUR 3 WORST-PERFORMING STOCKS? Citizens Utilities, Schweitzer-Mauduit International, International Paper

WHAT WERE SOME OF YOUR BIGGEST INVESTMENT MISTAKES? I sold what I thought were overpriced stocks prior to 1987 and went to about a 50 percent cash position. The stocks I sold were my regular blue-ribbon stocks and they did go down some. Still thinking they were overpriced, I delayed rebuying them. They have been going up ever since. Moral: If you choose well in the beginning, don't worry about the market going down. Stay in the market buying undervalued, good stocks. Over the long run (5 plus years), good stocks will continue to go up regardless of the overall market.

DO YOU INVEST IN "WHAT YOU KNOW"? Yes

HAVE YOU EVER FOLLOWED A "HOT TIP"? No

HOW WOULD YOU BEST DESCRIBE YOUR INVESTMENT APPROACH? I continually watch about 120 pick-of-the-litter stocks by name. These are "no brainers." When the price is 10 percent to 25 percent from the 52-week low and I can't find a reason for it being down, I buy generally in $20,000 to $30,000 batches.

DO YOU FEEL INDIVIDUAL INVESTORS ARE DISADVANTAGED IN THE FINANCIAL MARKETS RELATIVE TO LARGE INVESTORS? No

DO YOU FEEL INDIVIDUALS HAVE ANY ADVANTAGES IN THE INVESTMENT PROCESS? No

DO YOU THINK IT IS POSSIBLE TO BEAT THE MARKET ON A CONSISTENT BASIS? Yes, although I don't think that I do it and I don't keep track of numbers to tell.

WHAT MADE YOU THINK YOU COULD BE A SUCCESSFUL INVESTOR? I never thought
   I would be unsuccessful. I have always been successful making
   money. I have had a few losses, maybe 6 stocks and not much
   money.

WHAT DOES THE TERM "RISK" MEAN TO YOU AS IT PERTAINS TO INVESTING? Risk
   means the chance of losing money.

WHAT IS YOUR RISK TOLERANCE? Average

HOW DO YOU DEFINE DIVERSIFICATION AS IT RELATES TO YOUR PERSONAL INVESTING
   STYLE? More or less equal investments in each of our basic
   needs—food, shelter, health, etc., or the things equivalent and
   add other stocks until you have 10 to 20.

HOW MANY INVESTMENTS DO YOU BELIEVE ARE NECESSARY TO BE PROPERLY DIVERSI-
   FIED? 1 checking account, 1 savings or money-market equivalent,
   1 stock conglomerate like GE, and perhaps 10 to 20 other
   stocks.

WHAT DO YOU THINK ARE SOME OF THE GREATEST MYTHS OF INVESTING? The
   greater the yield, the more the risk. Instead of paying dividends
   or increasing them, we are increasing your stock value by splitting, buying back stock, increasing executive compensation to
   draw better management. You are losing money to inflation by
   leaving your money in a 5 percent guaranteed money market.

WHAT IS YOUR GREATEST FEAR AS AN INVESTOR? I don't believe I have a fear.
   I'm confident in my choices at the prices I paid. I guess I fear a
   dividend cut or elimination.

WHAT IS THE BIGGEST BENEFIT OF HAVING A 7-FIGURE PORTFOLIO? Being able to
   afford good reference material like *Value Line,* S&P reports,
   Moody's, etc. But they are available free at the library. Probably
   the biggest benefit is to buy $50,000 of 20 diversified great
   stocks and not be concerned about it.

IF YOU COULD GIVE JUST ONE PIECE OF ADVICE TO INDIVIDUAL INVESTORS, WHAT
   WOULD THAT PIECE OF ADVICE BE? Buy and sell with your head, not
   with your heart. Use your own criteria. Don't fall in love with a
   stock. The company you own doesn't give a darn about you. You

are the owner. The executives are workers employed by you the same as the rest of the employees. If you don't like what they are doing or not doing, tell them and vote your proxy accordingly. If you don't get a response to a reasonable letter, sell 'em. You don't owe them anything. Remember—it's your money.

DOES (DID) YOUR EMPLOYER OFFER A 401(K) (OR SIMILAR) PLAN? Yes

DID YOU USE THE PLAN? Yes, I invested the maximum. I invested for growth and income.

IF YOU WOULD, PLEASE SHARE WITH ME YOUR FAVORITE PERSONAL INVESTMENT STORY: I shoot handguns and long guns at targets. Because of my interest, I had been watching stocks that made guns, powder, and reloading equipment. About 1990, Sturm Ruger, which makes guns, and Hercules, which makes reloading powder, fell into the lower quadrant of their 52-week price ranges. This was the case of buying with my heart after determining that the stocks met my criteria for ownership. I bought 100 shares of each. Remember this was for fun—a hobby interest—not a serious income, money-making investment. After a few months, the prices had increased faster than reasonable expectations. I called the broker. I called the companies. Nobody really knew anything. In less than a year, for no reason, Hercules doubles. I sell it to a greater fool. A year later, they sell the powder-making group to another company. The gun company kept plodding along with the price rising and continuing with dividend increases. Am I smart considering today's attitudes toward guns? I don't know. I also own Philip Morris, of which the breakup value is about $1\frac{1}{2}$ times the current price. I'll buy some more when the price gets a little lower.

ANY FINAL THOUGHTS? I don't think Social Security should be invested in the stock market. The large, well-thought-of mutual funds are buying stocks at inflated prices, which causes the snowball to get bigger. By charter, management, public, and peer pressure, funds are forced to stay invested. They continue to buy overpriced stocks . . . I don't have a computer and don't intend to get one. You don't need one for investing unless you want to spend more time playing with an unnecessary toy. I can key in trades with a regular telephone and secure information . . . I do miss the conversations I used to have with my broker.

2

MILLIONAIRE MISTAKES:

TEN COMMON INVESTMENT GOOFS MADE BY MILLIONAIRE INVESTORS, AND HOW YOU CAN AVOID THEM

A winner only has to be right 51 percent of the time. If you're right 75 percent to 80 percent of the time, you're a big winner.

—SAM STEVENS, MICHIGAN,
$1.8 MILLION INVESTMENT PORTFOLIO

Perfection is not a prerequisite for a seven-figure portfolio. Just ask Jack Tyson.

Jack, a retired salesperson, lives in the Southeast. Jack has built an investment portfolio worth nearly $2 million. His portfolio is stocked with a number of quality blue-chip stocks—General Electric, BellSouth, Bristol-Myers Squibb, and BP Amoco. Given his seven-figure portfolio, you would think Jack made all the right investment moves during his fifty-seven years of investing. Jack, like most millionaire investors, achieved his success despite making some common investment gaffes. I'll let Jack tell you about a big one he made:

My accountant had a friend who told him he was making a lot of money investing in Treasury bill futures with a firm in the Midwest. My accountant (super conservative) and I both invested a fair amount with this firm, for the monthly reports were glowing and we were all generating super profits in the monthly reports we got. I told a friend about my great fortune one day, and he simply asked, "Have they sent you any money?" I said no, that I was just letting the profits ride. He suggested I write them requesting they send me part of my accumulated profit. It turned out that there was none. The company had fictitious statements, and all the money was lost or in the pockets of the company owners. It turned out that it was a complete fraud that had taken in securities dealers, banks, and the security governing bodies. The principals went to prison, and one large investor, who had lost millions, committed suicide. There was a class action suit, which cost us more in legal fees, and we got back just a few pennies on the dollar. A good lesson!

Everyone makes mistakes, even millionaire investors like Jack. Some investing mistakes are unavoidable. You do your homework, you buy the stock at the right price, and it still goes south.

The trick to successful investing, however, is avoiding the avoidable mistakes. Such mistakes are usually caused by emotion, personality traits, or human psychology. In their book, *Why Smart People Make Big Money Mistakes* (Simon & Schuster), Gary Belsky and Thomas Gilovich give a number of factors that cause investors to make bad decisions. Three of the most common are:

- "The ego trap." Investors make poor judgments due to overconfidence. This classic investment mistake occurs after an investor has tasted success. The investor believes that he or she is a genius and can do no wrong. Overconfidence leads to abandoning sound investment principles to pursue higher-risk strategies. Overconfidence also causes investors to refuse to admit mistakes. Given the huge investment gains of recent years, most investors probably believe they have become stock-market experts, immune to bad decisions. Be warned—don't confuse genius with a bull market. Trust me—you are not as smart as you think. Millionaire investors approach investing with a healthy dose of humbleness. "I've always taken the attitude that I'm stupid," says Cal Akers, forty-eight. Cal has an investment portfolio worth $1.4 million. "I know I am not, but that mentality helps me because if I start with the assumption that I know nothing, I have to acquire knowledge. So I read everything I can get my hands on. I'm always asking probing questions. I never am afraid to ask why."

- "The herd mentality." Conformity is a strong human emotion. We usually feel comfortable in a crowd of similar people. The herd mentality has an extremely strong pull on Wall Street. If large numbers of investors say a particular stock is a good one, then everyone can't be wrong. Unfortunately, following the herd often leads to lazy investment decision making. You buy this "hot" stock without doing your homework. Sure, chasing "hot" stocks can make you money in the short term. But you better know when to sell. Over the long term, it's a tough way to make a buck.

- Reacting to what Belsky and Gilovich call "information cascades." Our tendency is to act on new information. The problem is that much new investment information is irrelevant to a company's long-term prospects. And even if new information is relevant, chances are you'll be the last to know. By the time you read something in *The Wall Street Journal* or on some Web site, everyone on Wall Street has probably read it, too. If you react to news in the financial media, you're reacting too late. The news is already reflected in the stock price.

Let me add a few of my own reasons why investors make mistakes:

- The "get-rich-quick" mentality. Most millionaire investors get rich slowly. Indeed, the millionaires we surveyed have been investing on average for three decades. Most people don't want to wait thirty years to get rich. Most don't want to wait thirty weeks. This "Las Vegas" mentality clouds people's judgments. I'm sure you think what happened to Jack Tyson couldn't happen to you. You're much too smart. The fact is *anyone* can get sucked in by get-rich-quick schemes. Have you ever played the lottery?
- "Paralysis from analysis." Some people don't make decisions until they have the facts. That's fine, as long as you realize you'll never have *all* the facts. You can't possibly know everything there is to know about a certain subject. Unfortunately, too many investors fail to do anything because they fear what they don't know. Consequently, they do nothing. Paralysis from analysis is one reason some investors never start an investment program.
- The "grass is greener" mentality. People make decisions because they don't believe that their current situation is optimal. Writers want to be lawyers. Lawyers want to be writers. Actors want to be athletes. Athletes want to be actors. Doctors want to be artists. Artists want to be doctors. The stocks I don't own are better than the stocks I do own. Rarely is the grass greener elsewhere. That's especially true in investing.

MILLIONAIRE MISTAKES

I asked the millionaire investors to describe their biggest investment mistakes. Not surprisingly, many stories were similar and had their roots in the above-mentioned human traits and characteristics. The following are ten of their most common mistakes. By being aware of these mistakes, you can avoid them in your own investment program.

MISTAKE #1: FAILING TO START EARLY

Millionaire investors know how powerful time can be in an investment program. They've benefited from that power. They also know just how much money they've left on the table by not starting their investment practices earlier. They know that if they could make a million after starting at age forty-five, who knows how much money they could have accumulated had they started at age twenty-five or fifteen?

Starting an investment program early is important for the following reason: The earlier you start, the more mistakes you can make and still be a successful investor. Time forgives a multitude of investment sins. And you will make mistakes. If you start investing at age fifty, those mistakes may be lethal. If you start investing at age twenty-five, those mistakes are manageable.

Another reason to start an investment program early is because it may be easier to invest when you are twenty-five than when you're thirty-five or forty-five. You probably have yet to experience life's big shocks at age twenty-five—marriage, children, tuitions, weddings, etc. You have fewer financial responsibilities, fewer real demands on your pocketbook.

Let's say there are twin brothers, age twenty-two. The first twin begins investing immediately and invests $2,000 per year for nine years until age thirty. At the end of nine years, the first twin stops investing. He gets married. He has kids. He buys a house he can't afford. He never invests another penny again.

The second twin, unlike his brother, waits until age thirty-three to start investing. The second twin invests $2,000 per year until age sixty-five. Thus, the second twin invests more than three times the amount of the first twin ($66,000 versus $18,000).

Which twin do you think has more money at age sixty-five (assuming a 10 percent average annual return)?

Surprisingly, even though he invested for only nine years, twin number one had $840,000 at age sixty-five versus $489,000 for twin number two. What accounted for the $351,000 difference? The nine-year head start.

Bottom line: If you avoid mistake #1, you virtually guarantee yourself investment success. Chapter 3 discusses more fully the importance of starting an investment program early and provides useful strategies for jump-starting your efforts.

MISTAKE #2: SELLING TOO SOON

Herb Evans knows well the dangers of selling stock too soon, although it was Herb's brother-in-law who felt the sting of selling early. Herb, whose investment portfolio is worth $1.6 million, was the beneficiary.

"My brother-in-law sold me thirty shares of AT&T because he needed cash at the time," says Herb. "I reinvested the dividends while making regular investments. In 1984, the breakup of AT&T gave birth to the Baby Bells, and I received fifty-one shares of each one. Today, with the spin-off of AirTouch, Lucent, MediaOne, and NCR, the initial investment in AT&T is now worth over a half million dollars."

Needless to say, Herb's brother-in-law sold AT&T too soon.

Selling stocks too soon is a common mistake because it's so easy to do. Nobody wants to lose a gain on a stock. So you sell to lock up profits. The problem is that you're basing your sell decision on irrelevant information. You have a gain in the stock. Therefore, you sell. You don't consider the stock's potential. You don't consider the company's fundamentals. You don't consider that maybe the company is an even better bargain now than when you bought because of new products or new technology.

You sell because you bought at a lower price and now have a profit.

When you consider how people make sell decisions, it's not surprising that stocks often keep rising long after they're sold.

MICROSOFT MILLIONAIRE BENEFITS
FROM BUY AND HOLD

FRED HOUSEL HAS EXPERIENCED BOTH THE DANGERS OF selling too soon and the joys of buying and holding. And he's experienced it with the same stock—Microsoft.

Most of us dream about finding the next Microsoft. That's because we missed the original. Fred Housel didn't miss the original.

Fred, a commercial photographer who lives in Microsoft's backyard in Seattle, began buying stock in the software giant in October 1986. His first purchase: 100 shares. The stock promptly went from $30 to $40. Fred sold his 100 shares for a $1,000 profit. "I thought I was one hot stock picker," says Fred. Luckily for Fred, he decided to buy 150 shares in June 1987. Microsoft stock was trading for $108. Then came the market crash of 1987. Although he sold other stocks, he held his Microsoft, even though the stock fell by a third. "It wasn't that significant to me yet," he says. Over the years, Fred continued to buy and sell Microsoft stock. Fortunately, his buys outweighed his sells. Today, his 14,000 Microsoft shares are worth about $1.2 million, or roughly 115 times what he paid for them. Had Fred held on to all of his Microsoft shares over the years, his holdings would be worth nearly $4 million.

"If there is one thing I've learned in investing in the last fifteen or eighteen years, it is to try not to sell your winners," says Fred. "Sell the losers. It's hard to sell the losers, because you feel, 'I am going to be justified in the stupid decision I made, and I will sell the winners and take the profits.' But every time I have sold Microsoft, I have regretted it, because every time it has been worth more afterward."

SOURCE: E. S. BROWNING, *THE WALL STREET JOURNAL*, JUNE 30, 1999

One way to avoid selling too soon is to refuse to set "target prices." Conventional wisdom says that you should set a sell price when you buy a stock. The reality is, however, that things change. I've seen too many investors sell a stock because it reached their target price only to regret it later when the stock moved sharply higher. I buy stocks with the hopes that they rise a minimum 300 percent or more over ten or fifteen years. If you sell stocks after they reach twelve-month price targets, you'll never own the stock that rises 500 percent or 1,000 percent.

One reason millionaire investors are millionaire investors is that they don't commit mistake #2 too often. The majority of the millionaire investors surveyed hold stocks for at least five years. Many hold for ten years or more. Millionaire investors understand that great investment ideas don't grow on trees. They also understand that good investment ideas usually remain good investments for several years.

MISTAKE #3: SELLING TOO LATE

One unfortunate by-product of not selling too early is that you might sell too late. Actually, I count on selling late. Why? Because I know that the odds of selling at exactly the best price are slim.

Several strategies exist to limit the impact of this mistake. One strategy is to buy growth stocks and avoid cyclical stocks. Growth stocks have rising earnings streams. Since stock prices follow earnings, growth stocks are "one-decision" stocks for long-term investors. You buy and hold growth stocks. Cyclical stocks—stocks that are extra-sensitive to swings in the economic cycle—run up and down, up and down. You don't make much money buying and holding cyclical stocks because of the erratic nature of their profit patterns. You trade them. For that reason, I own only one cyclical stock in a portfolio of more than twenty stocks. If you worry about holding stocks too long, don't buy cyclical stocks.

Another way to limit selling too late is to know why you bought the stock in the first place. I think it is easier to know when to sell if you know why you bought. If the reasons you bought don't pan out, it makes it much easier to dump a stock.

Owning a manageable number of stocks makes it much easier to follow each of your holdings. Unfortunately, too many investors own forty or fifty stocks. If you own that many stocks, you're likely to hold the bad ones too long simply because you can't keep track of all of your stocks. The fewer stocks you have—you can have a reasonably diversified portfolio with fifteen to twenty stocks—the easier it will be to know when it's time to sell one.

Bottom line: You are never going to call consistently peaks in stock prices. So don't worry if you sell late. If you buy right, selling late may mean making "only" a 300 percent profit instead of a 400 percent profit.

MISTAKE #4: BLINDLY FOLLOWING THE ADVICE
OF FRIENDS, COWORKERS, AND ESPECIALLY BROKERS

Thelma Boor lives in the Southwest with her husband of seven years. Thelma has been investing for twenty-three years. Thanks to her contributions in a 401(k) and Individual Retirement Account, Thelma possesses an investment portfolio worth $1.1 million. To say Thelma is a successful do-it-yourself investor is an understatement. Her self-reliance, however, did not come naturally. As is the case with many millionaire investors, she became a do-it-yourself investor after having a rough experience with a broker.

"For years my broker would call me with stock recommendations," says Thelma. "There was always a great story. I would say, 'Do you think I should invest in this?' He would say, 'yes,' and eventually I would lose money. Only many years later did I learn he was putting me in every new initial public offering. Finally, in October 1987, after the market tanked, he called me to invest in something. I had enough and said, yes, I was going to invest in a stock. I had always wanted to own Disney. I still own it today. I fired my broker and learned to follow my own head. Today, I do it all by myself. And guess what—I'm pretty good."

When starting an investment program, it's only natural to seek advice. The problems develop when you accept as gospel everything others tell you without doing your own homework.

Most people are truthful. But that doesn't mean their opinions are correct. I think brokers and financial planners are honest, hardworking people. That doesn't mean that all of them are knowledgeable advisers.

Make no mistake, brokers are not investment analysts. They are salespeople. Brokers usually recommend what the firm's analysts tell them to recommend. Brokers succeed because they are good salesmen. Yes, many sharp brokers exist. As a small investor just starting out, you won't end up with the sharpest brokers. You don't matter enough. Small investors get "green" brokers. That's the catch-22 facing many new investors. You want help. But because you are a beginner with a tiny investment stake, the help you're likely to receive may do you more harm than good.

I recommend a do-it-yourself style of investing for several reasons. First, nobody cares more about your money than you. You should be intimately involved in how your money is managed. In my experience, it's easier to become a self-reliant investor than it is to find a good broker. The millionaire investors I surveyed are largely do-it-yourself investors. They call their own shots. I'm sure many millionaire investors exist who are millionaires because they found smart brokers. Unfortunately, your odds of finding that superior broker are a lot higher than of your being able to do a credible job on your own.

A problem with new investors using a broker is that new investors don't know enough to manage the relationship. Millionaire investor Fran Marcus (investment portfolio: $2.8 million) says his biggest investment mistake has been "getting involved with a full-service broker without knowledge of the investing world."

In order for any relationship to be successful, checks and balances must exist. Power must reside in the hands of both parties. Unfortunately, investment newcomers abdicate all responsibility. Brokers shouldn't be treated any differently than any other person you employ for personal services. You don't tell your hairstylist to just "do his or her thing." It's a collaborative effort. You should have a similar relationship with your broker or planner. But you can't manage the relationship without knowledge. Fortunately, with the plethora of financial information available via the media and the Internet, it's never been easier to become a more knowledgeable investor.

It's just not brokers and planners who need to be evaluated. The hot tip that comes from your coworker needs to be evaluated thoroughly. Perhaps the coworker is the second coming of Warren Buffett. More likely, he or she is not.

I asked our millionaire investors if they acted on a "hot tip." Those that had usually got burned. I'm not saying you should never follow a tip from a friend or relative. I am saying you should do your homework before investing.

Laziness has no place in building a seven-figure portfolio.

MISTAKE #5: MARKET TIMING

The biggest risk of investing is not being in the market when it declines; it's being out of the market when it advances. Markets move in bursts. You need to be in the market to capitalize on those bursts. If you constantly move money in and out of the market based on market timing, you'll miss much more than you hit.

Don't be seduced by the potential riches of market timing. You won't get it right consistently. You need to make too many right decisions. You need to know when to get out *and* when to get back in the market. And if you mess up just one time, it can undo all your previous good trades.

On average, stocks rise three out of every four years. Any time you sell and pull money out of the market, you buck a long-term upward trend in the market. Millionaire investors don't buck the odds. They go with the percentages. And the percentages say timing the market is a losing bet.

MISTAKE #6: "MICRO" TIMING STOCK PURCHASES

Ask Jeremy Stauffer (investment portfolio: $1.5 million) about his biggest investment mistake, he'll tell you the following: "Setting limit orders too low and missing a great opportunity by one or two points."

Sometimes we are our own worst enemy. A good example is choosing "buy" prices on stocks. We want to buy the stock at precisely the right price. Not one-quarter more. So we place a "limit" order. A limit order allows you to specify the exact price at which you're willing to purchase the stock—not a penny more. We think the limit order gives us complete control over the buy price.

Actually, limit orders may do more harm than good for long-term investors. What often happens is that the stock falls to one-quarter or one-eighth above our buy price and then skyrockets. By trying to save 25 cents per share, we lose thousands of dollars in potential profits. For long-term investors, it makes little difference whether you pay one-eighth or one-quarter more for a share of stock.

Another way micro timing your purchases can hurt you is by

avoiding a quality stock because it has already had a nice price run up. Again, the key is to remember that you buy stocks with ten-year time frames in mind, not ten minutes. If it's a quality stock with good long-term prospects, don't be afraid to pay up a bit to buy. I've never regretted paying up for quality. Of course, paying up a bit to buy an acknowledged industry leader is different than paying up to buy some Internet stock with no earnings and whose market position could be wiped out by the next "new thing." How do you know if you're paying too much for quality? You don't, until after the fact. Still, the longer your time frame, the less risky it is to pay a little more for a quality stock. If a quality stock is in your approximate buy range, don't nickel and dime your way into the stock. Buy at the market.

MISTAKE #7: SPECULATING IN FUTURES, OPTIONS, AND SPECULATIVE STOCKS

It's happened to me. It will happen to you.

Your investment program is going along quite nicely. You've made some nice gains on blue chips. But something is missing. You hear about friends making a killing on speculative stocks. Or that relative who bought a new house with proceeds earned from the futures market. Or that hot shot down at the country club whose broker is putting him in all the best new initial public offerings. You begin to get antsy. You don't want to wait twenty-five years to get rich. You want big profits *now*. So you soup up your portfolio by venturing into the options and futures markets. You buy limited partnerships to trim your taxes. You dabble in the new-issues market. You buy gold because it looks cheap and ready to skyrocket.

In short, you stray from your investment approach.

Big mistake.

Almost to a person, the millionaire investors I surveyed regretted forays into the options and futures markets. They regretted buying limited partnerships. They lost money in the new-issues market. They wasted time and money that could have been much more productive investing in blue chips.

Making money consistently in the futures and options markets is difficult because you have to be right about the investment *and* the timing. Buying stocks is an easier way to make a buck. As long as you're right on the stock, your timing needn't be perfect. You can wait until your reasons for buying the stock pan out. When you buy options and futures, the clock starts ticking immediately. You can't afford to be patient, hoping your investment thesis comes to fruition. With options, you have at most nine months for your idea to develop. That's not a long time. Most options expire worthless. You shouldn't think yours will be any different.

"I once put $25,000 in the options market," says Sandra Bally. Sandra, fifty-nine, has a portfolio worth $4.6 million. "One year later, I had $24,000. I got out and have never gone back. Stocks make more."

I'm not surprised many of the everyday millionaire investors I surveyed told me that they had bad experiences with limited partnerships. People of wealth usually try to trim their hefty tax bills, and limited partnerships promise to do just that. The problem is that I've yet to run into an investor who had a good experience with limited partnerships. One reason is limited partnerships are hard to sell. Some investors have gotten into hot water with the Internal Revenue Service over limited partnerships that were structured improperly or ones in which tax deductions were overruled.

"We had bank savings accounts in the 1960s and 403(b) accounts in 1970s and 1980s," says Mary Franklin, sixty-one, a widow living in Ohio. "Then we were seduced by large tax savings in four limited partnerships in real estate, oil, and cattle in the '80s. The tax laws were changed, and we lost most of our investments in them. Now that I have learned about investing wisely, whenever someone tries to sell a limited partnership to me, I say, 'No way.' I feel much safer researching stocks." Mary researched funds and stocks well enough to amass an investment portfolio of $1.1 million.

Buying initial public offerings (IPOs) usually is another losing proposition for individual investors. When a company wants its stock to begin trading on one of the stock exchanges, it files an initial public offering. The firm hires an investment bank to "take it public." The investment bank rounds up a syndicate of investment firms which pledges to sell shares in the company to investors.

The problem with buying IPOs is that the best IPOs are not available to individual investors. All those Internet IPOs you read about that went from $10 to $60 were never available at the $10 price for individual investors like you and me. Only the best customers of the investment firms taking the company public get a piece of the best IPOs. Oh sure, you can buy the stock after it goes public and has already jumped 300 percent. That's a bad idea, since many IPOs return to their initial offering price over time. And if you ever are approached by a broker who wants to sell you shares in the next "hot" IPO, run for the hills. Any IPO that's offered to you and me is usually the bottom of the barrel, one that none of the big guys wants. You don't want any IPO in which you can actually buy shares. It's usually junk, pure and simple.

Finally, low-priced, speculative stocks are rarely "one-decision" stocks. Speculative stocks are generally second- or third-tier companies in their industry groups hoping to rise through the ranks. The problem is that such companies tend to have erratic earnings streams. The loss of a few customers can be devastating. Their fortunes can change overnight if a much larger company enters their industry. Speculative stocks experience huge price swings. You have to know when to buy and sell speculative stocks to make any money. That's much different than buying and holding General Electric forever. Most investors are not good at making multiple investment decisions in a short period of time. Most people lose money on speculative stocks. You shouldn't expect to be any different.

MISTAKE #8: REACTING TO NEWS

I'm probably the only professional in the investment business who doesn't have CNBC, the business television network, blaring in the background in my office. I do have a television set in my office. I use it to watch sporting events, mostly. But I rarely tune into CNBC. One reason is that I'm afraid of what I'll do if I'm inundated with news all day.

I can see why people get caught up in short-term thinking watching CNBC. One day feels like a lifetime given all the stuff that is reported each day. This company's earnings. That company's lawsuit. This new CEO. That new product. This hot new IPO. That sexy new technology.

And the opinions. Oh, *the opinions*. Everybody has an opinion on Wall Street, and CNBC makes sure you know everyone's opinion. Every minute of every day.

It's enough to drive you nuts. Or at the very least, enough to make you do things in your investment program that you shouldn't.

If you asked the reporters at CNBC (I don't mean to pick on CNBC, but it is the most obvious instigator of the "Stepford Investor" syndrome I see on Wall Street) if what they're reporting has lasting significance, I doubt they could say yes, and mean it. So why do they report it? Because they have a bunch of time to fill. So they tell you what the producer price index did this month. They tell you that payrolls declined 2 percent for the month. They tell you that Merrill Lynch downgraded its opinion of Philip Morris. Does any of this truly matter in the long run? No.

CNBC now uses the tag line "Breaking News" on some of its stories. I remember when "Breaking News" meant a President had been shot or war had broken out somewhere on the globe. "Breaking News" on CNBC means Alan Greenspan has a bad case of flatulence.

Reacting to news on CNBC or any other financial media outlet is a loser's game simply because this information may be "news" only to you. You are not first on the information food chain. If you read about something in *The Wall Street Journal*, you're not alone. Millions of other investors also read it, and millions more investors knew about it twenty-four hours earlier when the "news" actually took place. It's silly to think that what you hear on CNBC gives you a leg up in the information game. Chances are, the stock already is reflecting the information by the time you decide to move on the "news."

Don't get chased out of stocks simply because of a single news event that the financial media trumpet as being important. Chances are, that news event is some trivial piece of data whose primary value is to fill air time.

MISTAKE #9: IGNORING THE "LITTLE THINGS" OF INVESTING

Great coaches will tell you that attention to detail is what truly matters. Detail and preparation.

It's no different with investing. The things that are often given little consideration have big impact on portfolios over time. Take commissions and fund expenses. Every commission you pay reduces your investment portfolio. Every mutual-fund fee you pay lowers your investment stash. Every fee you pay your financial planner is money that will never earn a dime for you. These fees may not seem like much—$15 or $20 per week in brokerage fees, a few hundred dollars a year in fund expenses. But they add up to big money over time. Even those "cheap" online brokerage fees add up if you are trading several times a day.

Taxes are one of the "little things" that matter to an investing program. Over time, the ability to defer taxes can have a huge impact on a portfolio. Deferring taxes may sound like a little thing, but it is a big deal if you are a long-term investor.

It's easy to ignore the little things of investing when your portfolio is pulling in big returns. What's losing 1.9 percent of my fund assets each year to fees if I'm making 25 percent on my money? What's paying $40 per week in brokerage commissions (that's $2,000 per year, by the way) if I'm making 40 percent on my money. Who cares if I paid some taxes on a capital-gains distribution last year; I made 35 percent in that fund. For many investors, the only markets they know are the ones that go straight up. Millionaire investors have been around long enough to know that to infer future market conditions from the last three years is probably a huge mistake. In years when market returns are more normal (around 11 percent per year), the "little things," such as taxes and fees, will matter more.

Ignore the little things at your peril.

MISTAKE #10: BUYING "CHEAP" STOCKS THAT GET CHEAPER AND CHEAPER AND CHEAPER AND . . .

Everyone wants to find the next great "crash stock," the stock that goes from $2.00 to $200, the next Chrysler. Millionaire investors are no different. They want to find those stocks, too. Finding the next Chrysler *can* make you a lot of money. The problem is that most investors, including our millionaire investors, are not very good at picking crash stocks that rebound.

The stock market is a reasonably efficient animal. Stock prices may run to extremes periodically, but in the main, most stocks trade at deserving prices. The market's efficiency is driven primarily by more and more investors having greater and greater amounts of information and time-sensitive data. In short, finding mispriced stocks is difficult. A stock that seems "cheap" is cheap for good reasons. Business may stink. Finances are weak. New competitors are eating its lunch.

When you invest in a "crash stock," you make a bet that you have better information, insight, or knowledge into that stock than the rest of Wall Street. Perhaps you do. My guess is, however, that you are just as likely to be missing or overlooking relevant data that explain why the stock is selling at such "cheap" prices.

Investing in "cheap" stocks works best when the stock under consideration is an industry leader, with a strong track record, that may be out of favor due to some short-term development. Health-care stocks in 1994 were cheap due to Clinton's attempt at reshaping the health-care industry. Buying Merck or Pfizer or Bristol-Myers Squibb at the time would have been buying a "cheap" stock. But there's a huge difference between buying Merck on a price decline and buying some small computer company that doesn't have a ghost of a chance competing with Dell or IBM or Microsoft.

If you choose to invest in turnaround stocks, choose stocks that have the critical mass, finances, and industry strength to hang in until a turnaround takes hold. Don't bottom fish in small, speculative, technology-oriented companies.

CONCLUSION

Mistakes are part of life. Learning from mistakes is what separates winners and losers.

Most millionaire investors made a plethora of mistakes over the years. Fortunately, these investors were smart enough to recognize the errors of their ways and adjust investment practices accordingly. Indeed, mistakes don't have to be lethal. In some cases, making a mistake, if it forces you to correct bad investing habits, might be the best thing to ever happen to your investment program.

There are more investment pitfalls than the ten addressed in this chapter. But these are the big ones. If you avoid or limit these mistakes in your investment program, you'll get to a seven-figure portfolio much quicker.

. . .

The everyday millionaire investor profiled in this chapter is Leonard Falk. Leonard lives with his wife and two children in New York. I chose Leonard because he made a number of common investment mistakes.

He missed big profit opportunities in stocks by using limit orders.

He refused to buy more of a stock because it had already moved higher.

Fortunately, Leonard did plenty of things right. He started investing as soon as he began earning a paycheck.

"My father became very successful in the '60s and lived high on the hog without saving or investing," says Leonard. "He lost it all, and the effect on our family was quite bad. I started out with nothing and had to make something out of myself. I got scholarships and loans for school. I got an entry-level job, paid off the loans, and proved myself to my employer to move up to management. I started saving and investing with my first paycheck. It did not matter how little it was in the beginning. I knew I had to do it because no one was going to do it for me."

Another thing Leonard did right was buy quality stocks—his five largest holdings are Dell Computer, Microsoft, Intel, Merck, and AT&T—and hold them, on average, for ten years.

"I look for companies which are in the fields that I have personal knowledge of and can judge what they are doing and how well they are doing it," says Leonard.

His efforts have paid off nicely. Still shy of his fiftieth birthday, Leonard has an investment portfolio worth $1.5 million.

NAME: Leonard Falk

AGE: 49

HOME: New York

MARITAL STATUS: Married for 8 years. I have been widowed. Never divorced.

CHILDREN: 2

EDUCATION: College (advanced) degree

OCCUPATION: Chief Information Officer

CURRENT INCOME: $123,150

FIVE-YEAR AVERAGE INCOME: $102,862

HOW MANY DIFFERENT JOBS SINCE AGE 25? 1

HOW LONG HAVE YOU WORKED AT YOUR CURRENT EMPLOYER? 25 years

HOW MANY YEARS HAVE YOU BEEN INVESTING? 32

WHAT IS THE SIZE OF YOUR ENTIRE INVESTMENT PORTFOLIO (INCLUDING ALL STOCKS, BONDS, IRAS, 401(K) PLANS, ETC., BUT NOT INCLUDING THE VALUE OF REAL ESTATE)? $1.52 million

WHAT IS THE BREAKDOWN OF THESE ASSETS? Stamps/coins (4.6 percent), 401(k) (3.6 percent), IRA (mutual funds) (7.6 percent), IRA (stocks) (16 percent), bonds (1 percent), stocks (63 percent), cash (4.2 percent)

HOW MANY INDIVIDUAL STOCKS DO YOU OWN? 45

NAME YOUR 5 LARGEST HOLDINGS: Dell Computer, Microsoft, Intel, Merck, AT&T

HOW MANY INDIVIDUAL MUTUAL FUNDS DO YOU OWN? 14

NAME YOUR BIGGEST FUND HOLDINGS: Invesco Equity Income, Invesco Health Sciences, Invesco Dynamics, MFS Emerging Growth

HOW MANY INDIVIDUAL BONDS DO YOU OWN? 2

HAVE YOU EVER PURCHASED STOCK/INDEX OPTIONS? Yes

HAVE YOU EVER PURCHASED STOCK/INDEX FUTURES? No

DO YOU OWN GOLD OR PRECIOUS METALS? Yes

HAVE YOU EVER SOLD STOCK SHORT? No

DID YOU HAVE SPECIFIC INVESTMENT GOALS WHEN YOU STARTED INVESTING? Yes. My goal was to try to amass as much wealth as I could for my retirement years, trying not to spend any of it until I retired.

WHAT ARE THE PLANS FOR YOUR ESTATE? Since I was widowed at age 39, you would think that I have estate plans. I do not. I've got life insurance to cover the family besides the portfolio, but that is as far as I've gone.

WHAT HURDLES, IF ANY, DID YOU OVERCOME TO BEGIN INVESTING? Finding the cash to invest. Prior to the current DRIPs, I had to save up from my paycheck until I had enough to buy something and cover commissions. In the '70s, it was not easy to invest a little at a time.

HAVE YOU INHERITED WHAT YOU THOUGHT WAS A LARGE AMOUNT OF MONEY? When I was widowed, I had $25,000 to invest. The year was 1989. Dell Computer was trading at $5.00 and change. The year before I had purchased 100 shares of Dell at $9³/₄. I wanted to put all the money into Dell. But let's face it, that would not be a prudent investment. So I purchased 100 additional shares of Dell; 100 shares of NYNEX, AT&T, SBC Communications, Eastman Kodak; 200 shares of Computer Associates; and kept the rest in cash. I sold the Kodak and Computer Associates when I remarried. Big boo boo on Computer Associates. I should have sold NYNEX. I thought NYNEX had better growth. I kept the rest of the shares including my Dell shares. Those 200 shares of Dell have grown to 9,600 shares worth over $1 million. In hindsight, I should have put it all in Dell.

DID YOU START INVESTING WITH A SPECIFIC PLAN IN MIND? Initial plan was $50 per paycheck on a bi-weekly paycheck of $370.

DID YOU KEEP TO YOUR PLAN? Yes.

HOW DID YOU EDUCATE YOURSELF ABOUT INVESTING? DID YOU FIND THIS EDUCATION PROCESS DIFFICULT? FUN? I read magazines, asked questions, listened to news and business radio, watched *Wall Street Week* and *Nightly Business Report*. It was very exciting and educational. I started trying to predict events based on what I had conceptualized. As time went by, I started to act on my analysis.

DID YOU HAVE ANY SPECIAL EXPERTISE IN INVESTING WHEN YOU STARTED? I invested in companies that were in my field of knowledge. At age 17, I was a stamp and coin collector. When the General Numismatics Corp. went public, I got my father to let me buy 10 shares for $67.50. The company changed its name to the Franklin Mint and was purchased by what is now Time Warner. That $67.50 grew to over $6,000 in value when I sold it.

HOW MANY HOURS PER WEEK DO YOU DEVOTE TO YOUR INVESTMENTS AND INVEST-
MENT STRATEGIES? 7

HOW OFTEN DO YOU BUY INVESTMENTS? Monthly

ON AVERAGE, HOW LONG DO YOU HOLD AN INVESTMENT BEFORE SELLING? 10 years

DO YOU "MARKET TIME"? IN OTHER WORDS, DO YOU TRY TO TIME PURCHASE/SALE OF IN-
VESTMENTS BASED ON YOUR EXPECTATIONS FOR MARKET MOVEMENTS AND/OR
MOVEMENTS IN THE INDIVIDUAL STOCKS? No

DOES YOUR INVESTMENT APPROACH DIFFER DEPENDING ON WHETHER THE MARKET IS
CLASSIFIED AS A "BEAR" OR A "BULL" MARKET? No

WHAT HAVE BEEN YOUR 3 WORST-PERFORMING STOCKS? Western Resource
Utah, American Telenet, Biogenetic Technology

WHAT WERE SOME OF YOUR BIGGEST INVESTMENT MISTAKES? Not buying more of
Dell. Trying to buy stocks at a limit instead of market and missing by a quarter or less on stocks that doubled or tripled soon
after. Not being aggressive enough to act on my instincts and
buy instead of not buying because it was not prudent. In the
case of Iomega in 1995 when it was around $2.00, I knew the
zip drive was coming. But I was under the impression it was
going to sell for $500 a drive, a price I thought too high to suc-
ceed. In April 1996 I saw the drive was $199. I bought an
Iomega zip drive on the spot, ran to the computer to see the
stock was at $7.00 and change, and thought, well, missed that
one. After the splits and even at its current price, $7.00 in April
1996 was a good price.

DO YOU INVEST IN "WHAT YOU KNOW"? Just about exclusively.

HAVE YOU EVER FOLLOWED A "HOT TIP"? Yes, on cheap stocks (usually under
$2.00). None of them ever paid off.

DO YOU THINK IT IS POSSIBLE TO BEAT THE MARKET ON A CONSISTENT BASIS? No. You
pick your investment because it meets your criteria to purchase
and go from there. Invest for the long term.

WHAT MADE YOU THINK YOU COULD BE A SUCCESSFUL INVESTOR? Nothing. I just
had to try something. I had to use my ability to analyze and recognize companies which, in my opinion, did things the way I

would or created things that I wanted and I figured others would want also.

WHAT DO YOU THINK ARE SOME OF THE GREATEST MYTHS OF INVESTING? The little guy cannot compete in the market.

WHAT IS YOUR GREATEST FEAR AS AN INVESTOR? Losing everything.

WHAT IS THE BIGGEST BENEFIT OF HAVING A 7-FIGURE PORTFOLIO? Some sense of security that by the time I'm ready to pay for college for the kids and I'm ready to retire, I'll be able to do so.

IF YOU COULD GIVE JUST ONE PIECE OF ADVICE TO INDIVIDUAL INVESTORS, WHAT WOULD THAT PIECE OF ADVICE BE? Invest where you know something about the field or company and stay the course long term.

DOES (DID) YOUR EMPLOYER OFFER A 401(K) (OR SIMILAR) PLAN? Yes

DID YOU USE THE PLAN? Yes. I invest the maximum.

ANY FINAL THOUGHTS? Investing is a means that anyone can use to try to create wealth for his/her family, which could not be accomplished without the market.

3

START INVESTING NOW!

People should just get started and not be afraid to make mistakes.

—EILEEN FUNK, CALIFORNIA,
$6 MILLION INVESTMENT PORTFOLIO

STEP 1: START INVESTING NOW!

Time is an investor's biggest ally. To understand why time is so important to investment success, you need to appreciate the power of compounding.

Einstein reportedly called the power of compounding "the eighth wonder of the world," for good reason. Over time, compounding turns a little money into a lot without any special effort on your part.

Here's an extreme example of the power of compounding. Let's say your rich Uncle Chuck, in his will, offers you the choice of the following two inheritances:

- $1 million.
- The value, at the end of thirty days, of starting with a penny and doubling the amount every day for thirty days. In other words, you start with a penny on day one. At the end of day two you have 2 pennies. At the end of day three, 4 pennies. And so on for thirty days.

Which would you take?

I think most people would take the $1 million. After all, how much can 1 penny add up to after thirty days?

Try more than $5 million.

Do the math.

Day	Amount	Day	Amount
1	$.01	16	327.68
2	.02	17	655.36
3	.04	18	1,310.72
4	.08	19	2,621.44
5	.16	20	5,242.88
6	.32	21	10,485.76
7	.64	22	20,971.52
8	1.28	23	41,943.04
9	2.56	24	83,886.08
10	5.12	25	167,772.16
11	10.24	26	335,544.32
12	20.48	27	671,088.64
13	40.96	28	1,342,177.28
14	81.92	29	2,684,354.56
15	163.84	30	5,368,709.12

At the end of ten days, the value of your inheritance is only $5.12. At the end of twenty days, the value jumps to $5,242.88, still a far cry from $1 million. But here's where the power of compounding kicks in. In the last ten days, that $5,242.88 becomes $5,368,709.12. Why? Because you begin doubling larger amounts of money.

In looking at this example, you probably believe that the last few days are the most important. I disagree. You would never have built up the amount of money to take advantage of the power of compounding if you hadn't started in the first place.

Here's a real-life case of compounding brought to us by one of our millionaire investors, Robert Cole. Robert, fifty-six, is a forest consultant living in the Pacific Northwest. Robert started investing at age twenty-eight. He currently has an investment portfolio worth $1.2 million. Roughly 90 percent of his portfolio is in his 401(k) rollover program, where he made contributions directly via payroll deduction. "I never saw it [the money]," says Robert. Now here's the part on compounding that I love: "It took me twelve years to reach $50,000 in my investments," says Robert. "It took me fifteen and a half more years to reach $1 million." Robert adds, "In forest economics, long-term investment and the time value of money are basic principles. I chose to use them in my own life."

Remember this—the most important dollar you invest is the one you invest today. You'll never fully exploit the power of compounding unless you start now. Not a year from now. Not a month from now. Not tomorrow. Start investing now.

You might not have a lot of money. You may not know much about investing. It doesn't matter. It is impossible to become a millionaire investor without investing. So start today.

The benefits of starting to invest as soon as possible are evident in the following example:

- A twenty-year-old can achieve a million-dollar portfolio by age sixty-five if he or she invests just $67 per month (assuming an average annual return of 11 percent). Said another way, that twenty-year-old will invest, over the course of those forty-five years, less than $37,000 in order to create a $1 million portfolio. That's the power of time. That's the power of compounding.
- If that twenty-year-old waits until age thirty, he or she will need to invest $202 per month to reach seven figures by age sixty-five.
- By waiting until age forty, an individual will have to invest $629 per month to reach $1 million by age sixty-five.

- And if you wait until age fifty to begin your investment program, you'll need to invest an average of $2,180 per month to
have $1 million by age sixty-five.

These scenarios make two important points. First, the sooner
you start investing, the easier it is to build a seven-figure investment
portfolio. Second, even if you start investing at age fifty, you still have
a shot at seven figures. But it will be much harder than if you had
started earlier.

THE CATALYST OF FEAR

Fear is a good thing if it makes you do the right thing. According to
the Bible (Hebrews 11:7), Noah, "moved with fear," built an ark.
Certainly Noah had great faith. But I'm sure the *fear* of swimming
upstream in a very, very, very big stream helped him hammer that
first nail.

For many of our everyday millionaire investors, the major cata-
lyst for starting an investment program was fear. Fear about not having enough at retirement. Fear of not having the money to put kids
through college. Fear of not maintaining an adequate lifestyle for
the family. Fear of working forever because you must.

Take Ginny R., a college professor living in the Southeast.
Ginny, at age fifty-five, has built a million-dollar portfolio on the
backs of such blue chips as BellSouth, the regional Bell company;
Merck, the pharmaceutical giant; IBM, the computer and computer
services company; Lucent Technologies, the telecommunications-
equipment leader; and Exxon, the leader in the oil industry.

What started Ginny on the path to a seven-figure investment
portfolio was a mixture of fear and self-reliance.

"When my husband went to Viet Nam in 1967, I was left with
two babies," says Ginny. "I realized I needed to educate myself about
finances and did so, though we had little money to invest for years."

What is especially impressive about Ginny's million-dollar portfolio is that she and her husband spent over $200,000 on three bachelor's degrees and helped with a law degree, a medical degree, and a master's degree. "Tuition made our early investments very small," says Ginny. But over time, as expenses declined, Ginny and her husband were able to save more. "The last five years, we have invested about 20 percent of our pretax income."

What made Ginny a successful investor? Was it the ability to save 20 percent of her and her husband's income the last five years? What made Ginny able to build a seven-figure portfolio were the steps she took in 1967 and the willingness to start an investment program even with small amounts of money. That discipline laid the foundation for later years, when the couple had more money to invest.

Consider Peter H. Peter didn't start investing in earnest until age forty-seven. Today, Peter, at age fifty-eight, has $1.2 million in his investment portfolio.

What got Peter to take investing seriously? "After having four children, we decided to adopt. I realized that with a wife fifteen years younger and now more children to educate—hopefully in private colleges—I needed to ratchet up my retirement."

What's Peter's advice for would-be starters? "Just write that first check."

Writing that first check began much earlier for Ken C. Ken, like Peter, is fifty-eight. Ken had a bit of a head start on Peter. Ken began investing at age fourteen. Forty-four years later, Ken now has an investment portfolio worth $3.2 million.

Ken built his portfolio on simple, time-tested investment principles.

Buy quality stocks, especially on weakness.

Invest regularly.

Avoid "fad" stocks.

"I have learned to find opportunities as things rise and fall," says Ken. "I love to dollar-cost average as the opportunity presents itself."

The beauty of investments is that they are blind to the age of their owners. For that matter, investments are also blind to the sex and race of their owners. A stock doesn't care whether you're fourteen or forty-one or eighty-four. Male or female. Caucasian, Hispanic, Asian, Indian, or African-American. Everyone gets the same return.

In a sense, Wall Street is the perfect democracy. A fifteen-year-old has exactly the same chance of reaching a seven-figure portfolio by age forty as a forty-year-old has by age sixty-five. Twenty-five years is twenty-five years, no matter what age you start.

The upshot is that, whether you're fifteen or forty, you can build a seven-figure investment portfolio. *You just need to start today.*

OVERCOMING HURDLES

I'm sure you have many reasons for not starting an investment program.

No money.

No knowledge.

No time.

No broker.

Too old.

Too young.

I'm sure you think these are legitimate reasons. They are not.

There are no good excuses for not investing. I don't care how young or not so young you are. How rich or not so rich you are. How much you know or don't know. It has never been easier or cheaper to invest.

Never.

If you have just $50, there are literally hundreds of investment opportunities awaiting you. If your employer offers a 401(k) plan (see Chapter 9 for more on 401(k) plans), you can invest as little as

1 percent of your salary. That means if you make $400 per week, you can invest as little as $4.00.

Four bucks.

And you don't need a broker to invest. You can buy some of the best companies in the world—General Electric, Exxon, Lucent Technologies, Merck, Sony, BP Amoco—without a broker and for little or no fees. (I'll show you how to do this in Chapter 5.) Nor do you need a broker to buy some of the best mutual funds in the business.

In short, there are no excuses for not investing. None.

Still don't believe me? Let's address popular excuses for not starting an investment program.

EXCUSE #1: I DON'T HAVE *ANY* MONEY TO INVEST

Paula Cass began investing at age fifteen. Her first job paid $2.00 per hour. She augmented that by baby-sitting, typing thesis papers for grad students, and tutoring geometry. Today, Ms. Cass has an investment portfolio worth more than $6 million.

Saving has always been a way of life for Ms. Cass. "We received 10-cent allowances each week but had to save half in a savings account," says Ms. Cass. "When I turned fifteen and had my first bank job, my father asked for the money back that had been saved thus far. It wasn't much, only about $72, but it was all the money I had ever had, and I had saved hard for it. I vowed I would create my own savings and investing."

Ms. Cass saved even though she made very little early in her career. "My plan was that I would try to save 25 percent of everything that I made. I have equaled or exceeded the plan every year."

Ms. Cass didn't wait until she had big money to invest. She invested what she had regardless of the size of the investment.

Most of our everyday millionaire investors didn't have the luxury of a six-figure inheritance to propel them to seven figures. Most, like Ms. Cass, started small. Where did they find the money to invest?

Stretch your paycheck. By far, the primary source of "start-up" funds for most millionaire investors was their regular paychecks. Ted G., sixty-nine, started an investment program by saving $10 per week. Once his money totaled $300, he would buy $300 worth of stock. His first stock investment? "Texas Instruments." Today, Ted, an investor for fifty of his sixty-nine years, has a portfolio worth more than $1.1 million.

"As a young boy, my father taught us to 'earn a savings' wage," says Ted. "He started me saving from my paper route when I was ten. Therefore, I never had the problem of not spending money. I've always felt that you must learn to live within your income."

Ted is an excellent example of the mentality that pervades virtually all millionaire investors. They squeezed investment dollars out of their paychecks by making those paychecks stretch. What were some of the more interesting money-saving schemes used by our everyday millionaires?

- Rather than spend money in a restaurant on drinks, appetizers, and desserts, Jesse Kahn would buy only dinner and put the money saved into stocks. Jesse, fifty-nine, has an investment portfolio worth $1.6 million. "I was always a saver," says Jesse. "Beginning with my very first job, I always 'paid myself' a little bit from each paycheck. This allowed me to blow the rest without worrying about it. Saving a little bit, on a regular basis over many years, really adds up." Jesse began working at age thirteen, "cutting grass, shoveling snow, selling magazines, and delivering newspapers. It taught me street sense as well as a desire to acquire wealth." Jesse adds that "acquiring wealth is *addictive*. As my stock portfolio began to increase, I began to fund it more and more." That's how $10 becomes $1 million. You find more money to invest. That $10 regular investment becomes $50 per month, then $100 per month. The process becomes infectious. It also becomes fun.

- Jim V. makes about $75,000 per year as a transportation logistics manager. Despite being just forty-two, Jim has an investment portfolio worth $1.5 million. How did Jim get so much so fast? Actually, he's been investing since age sixteen. His investing style is pretty simple—"great blue-chip companies with consistent long-term track records." Jim also invests the maximum in his employer's 401(k) plan. Where does Jim find the money to invest? "All clothing purchases are made at that season's end, at steep discounts, usually at Wal-Mart. Food items are purchased at sale prices." Says Jim, "The purchase philosophy is simple—never pay full price."

- Paul Fritzker decided never to purchase anything "unless we could pay cash." Says Paul, "It's a real leveler and eliminates 95 percent of impulse buying." Paul, sixty, is retired and lives with his wife of thirty-seven years in New York. He has an investment portfolio of $1.4 million. "Our initial plan was to invest 10 percent and every time we received a raise, we allocated an additional amount." True to his word, Paul bought his first home—with cash. "Start [investing] immediately," says Paul. "There are many different investment strategies that will result in wealth. But without the self-discipline to invest in your future, you'll find yourself with a pile of debt."

- Gil P. is a college teacher living on the East Coast. Gil, age fifty, has an investment portfolio of $1.5 million. He built this impressive portfolio in just twenty years even though his highest annual income was $75,000. How did he do it? "My tastes are spartan, except for food. I don't eat meat. As an academic, I can wear the shoddiest clothes imaginable. I drive a fifteen-year-old car. I live in an old farmhouse. No one cares."

- Early in his life, Kelly T., seventy-two, "Looked around and saw the haves and the have-nots. It was easy to see that the haves got that way because they saved where they could, spent wisely, and seldom if ever bought on time. The have-nots were mostly living payday to payday because they ate out too often, bought furniture on time payments, ran up big credit-card bills. Both my wife and I wanted to be different." Says Kelly, "Getting started is just a matter of looking at spending habits to see where one could cut down. Then cut down and save what you were spending foolishly. Too many people think big but never even start small. They would rather 'invest' in the lottery than to start putting some nickels and dimes in a solid investment."

- For several of our millionaire investors, the Depression had a profound effect on their savings habits. Tess G., seventy, knows this all too well. "It all goes back to growing up in the Depression era," says Tess. "You made do with what you had or could afford. Those habits are hard to break. To this day, we still do not waste. Today's generation wants everything yesterday, and it goes on a credit card, on which they pay the minimum payment allowed. Nothing against credit cards, I use them, too. But they are paid in full monthly." Tess, who has been investing for roughly forty years, has a portfolio worth $1 million. "Our very first stock purchase was ten shares of AT&T at $70 per share. That was a lot of money to us in the late '50s. We had a mortgage, two young children, thoughts of college for them. But we were determined not to be left without financial security as our parents were. I can't say that we ever really did without anything. We took nice vacations, had nice cars. But we always managed to save."

Notice our millionaire investors didn't bemoan the fact that they didn't eat dessert or drive fancy cars or wear fancy clothes. Each almost reveled in his or her abstinence. This is a common trait of most millionaire investors. They frame the practice of saving not so much as doing without today as deferring for a better tomorrow.

I'm sure if you looked long and hard at your spending habits, you could come up with a few extra dollars every month:

Do you really need all those premium cable channels? ($15)

Do you really need cable television at all? ($35)

Do you need to talk to Betty Sue long distance every Wednesday when you could call her on the weekend and save a few bucks? ($5)

Could you rent one less tape at Blockbuster each week? ($10)

Could you take some leftovers to work once a week for lunch? ($16)

Do you still need all those magazine subscriptions? ($5)

That's $86 saved each month. That's $86 you could invest. Do you know what $86 per month, earning on average 11 percent per year, grows to over twenty-five years? One hundred and thirty-seven thousand dollars. And I've probably just scratched the surface of what you could save each month.

And what about those major purchases? Saving and investing just a small part of the money that sloshes around in those big transactions can provide a huge payoff down the road.

For example, do you need that $500 watch when the $100 watch will do just fine? That savings of $400, earning 11 percent a year for twenty-five years, grows to approximately $6,000. That's the "real" cost of the watch. Not $500, but $6,000.

Understand I'm not recommending that you live like some miser who reuses tea bags fifty times and stuffs pillows with dust bunnies. I'm not suggesting some big austerity kick. What I am saying is that all of us waste money on things that provide very little, if any, lasting pleasure. Recognizing those instances of wasteful spending can go a long way toward shifting from a spending mentality to a saving mentality.

One of my favorite quotes from the millionaire investors I surveyed comes from Colleen Kemins, a retired court reporter with an investment portfolio worth $2.1 million. Her statement truly crystallizes the savings mentality of everyday millionaire investors:

I wanted a better financial future more than I wanted things.

Remember—money spent is money that will never earn a dime in interest or appreciation.

Payroll deduction. One way to stretch your regular paycheck is to leave some at the office. That's the beauty of savings and investment plans built around automatic payroll deductions. You never see the money, so you never miss it. Many millionaire investors utilize payroll deduction to fund 401(k) retirement programs. By far, the 401(k) plan is the investment vehicle most responsible for creating everyday millionaire investors. Many of the investors I surveyed generated at least 35 percent of their seven-figure portfolio from a 401(k) plan.

Second jobs. A few of our millionaire investors worked more than one job to gather funds for investment. The money from these second and sometimes third jobs went straight into investments, not a new car or boat. "I used to officiate college football and basketball as a hobby," says Alex Canter, a retired engineer. "The officiating fees were the seed money to start investing." Alex, seventy-one, has an investment portfolio worth $1.1 million.

"Found" money. Many millionaire investors got their start with what they called "found" money. Found money may be funds from working overtime, a raise, a bonus check, holiday/birthday gifts, or an unexpected inheritance. Some millionaires, such as Tiffany King, used their income tax refund checks. Tiffany, fifty-four, is an interior designer living in the Southwest. Her investment portfolio of $1 million includes such blue chips as IBM, Philip Morris, AT&T, Merck, and Cisco Systems.

Felix Peters started his investing with gifts from family and friends. "In Italian families, at events such as baptism, first communion, confirmation, ordinations, and weddings, there are 'envelopes.' In addition to a nice card, there's usually a nice check," says Felix. "From my confirmation in the 1960s, I cleared a few thousand. I used that for my first phase of investing." Felix, who is in his forties, has an investment portfolio of $1 million.

Proceeds from a property/real estate sale. A number of millionaire investors said they got start-up funds by selling a home. Ben Carlson used the proceeds from the sale of a "self-built yacht" to bankroll his investment program. Ben, who works in marine construction, has been investing for seventeen years. At the age of fifty-one, he has an investment portfolio worth $1.5 million.

Bottom line: You have the money to invest. You just have to be creative in capturing it.

EXCUSE #2: I DON'T HAVE *ENOUGH* MONEY TO INVEST

Just because you can't afford to invest $1,000 or $5,000 doesn't give you an excuse for sitting on the sidelines. Do you have $10 to invest each month? Then you can own any number of blue-chip stocks. Do you have $50 to invest each month? You can own any number of attractive no-load mutual funds. Does your employer offer a 401(k) plan? If so, you can contribute as little as 1 percent of your salary.

You *do* have enough money to invest. You just don't know it. Let me show you how to invest seemingly small amounts of money each month in solid long-term investments.

DRIPs

What are DRIPs? These are programs, offered by approximately 1,100 publicly traded companies, that allow investors to buy stock directly from the company, *without a broker.* Investors buy stock from companies in two ways. First, instead of receiving dividend checks, investors have the company reinvest dividends on their behalf to purchase additional shares. Second, most DRIPs permit investors to send money directly to the company to buy additional shares. In many cases, these "optional cash payments" may be as little as $10 or $50. If you have deeper pockets, most DRIPs permit investments of up to $100,000 or more per year.

I discuss DRIPs at much greater length in Chapter 5. What's important for our purposes here is to understand that DRIPs are an extremely friendly way for investors with just a little money to buy blue-chip stocks. For example, the minimum investments in the DRIPs of Coca-Cola and Johnson & Johnson are just $10 and $25, respectively. And you'll pay no commissions to buy Coca-Cola and Johnson & Johnson via their DRIPs. For nearly all DRIP programs, the minimums are rarely above $100 per investment.

NO-LOAD MUTUAL FUNDS

Mutual funds are investment companies that take in funds from many individuals, commingle the money, and buy a portfolio of stocks that they manage. Investors purchase mutual funds through a broker or directly with the fund family. No-load funds are sold to investors without a broker and without an up-front sales fee. To join most no-load funds, you call the fund family directly via a toll-free number. The fund group sends you the necessary enrollment information and fund prospectus. The prospectus explains the details of the fund—fees, management styles, and so on. Investors buy and sell shares in the fund at the "net asset value." This is the total of the fund's assets minus any liabilities. Many mutual funds list their net asset values daily in *The Wall Street Journal*. Popular no-load fund families include Strong, Vanguard, Fidelity, Janus, and T. Rowe Price.

Mutual funds offer three primary attractions for investors. First, most mutual funds allow investors to start with a relatively small amount of money—$2,500 or less. Second, funds allow investors with a relatively small amount of money to diversify their investments across a large number of stocks. Third, mutual funds provide an easy way for small investors to have professional management of their funds.

These benefits don't come without a price. All mutual funds have annual expenses they charge investors. These fees are usually a percentage of your assets in the fund. Annual expense ratios can be as low as 0.18 percent in some index funds (index funds mimic a particular market index, such as the Standard & Poor's 500) to more than 2 percent in certain specialized funds. These fees can add up over time. Let's say you have $50,000 in a mutual fund that charges 1.5 percent in annual expenses. You'll pay $750 per year in that fund ($50,000 times 1.5 percent). Obviously fees matter, so you need to consider the annual expense ratio when choosing mutual funds.

The good news for new investors is that several mutual funds allow investors to get started with minimal amounts of money if the investor agrees to automatic monthly investments via electronic debit of a bank account. For example, the no-load mutual fund that I comanage—**Strong Dow 30 Value Fund** (800-368-1030)—allows an investor to start with just $50 if that individual invests at least $50 every month via automatic monthly debit. Other fund families that have similar programs include **Invesco** (800-525-8085) and **T. Rowe Price** (800-638-5660).

I provide specific mutual-fund recommendations in Chapter 6. For now, it's important to realize that even if you squeeze just $50 a month out of your budget, you can still invest in a top-shelf no-load mutual fund.

401(K) PLAN

The 401(k) plan is an investment program established by an employer to assist employees in saving for retirement. Under a 401(k) plan, part of your pay is deposited into an account in your name. These contributions are made with pretax dollars. In other words, neither federal nor state income taxes are withheld from this money. Because the amount you contribute to your 401(k) is not included on your W-2 form as taxable wages or income, your 401(k) contributions reduce your yearly tax bite. Funds in your 401(k) grow tax deferred. You'll pay no taxes until the funds are withdrawn. Better still, in many 401(k) plans, the employer matches a portion of your contribution. That's *free* money.

Why 401(k) plans are especially relevant for our discussion here is that the investment minimums are incredibly tiny. You can invest as little as 1 percent of your salary in a 401(k) plan. If you make $100 per week, you can put just *$1.00* in your 401(k) plan.

I discuss 401(k) plans in much greater detail in Chapter 9. What's critical that you understand now is simply this:

The 401(k) plan is the best investment deal you will ever get.

The 401(k) single-handedly has created more everyday millionaire investors than any other investment vehicle. If you are not taking full advantage of your employer's 401(k), you are making a big mistake. You have no business investing in any other investment until you contribute the maximum allowed by law to your plan.

I just discussed several ways individuals can invest a little money to get started. Bottom line: If you have 10 bucks, you have enough money to start investing.

EXCUSE #3: I DON'T KNOW ENOUGH

"The first foray I made into the stock market—I had previously bought bonds, insurance, and mutual funds—was in 1994 when I saw an article in the paper where you could invest directly with Exxon," says Colleen Kemins. "So I invested $8,000 per month for thirteen months, and it is now worth more than double what I paid for it counting splits. At that time, I had not the foggiest idea what I was doing. But it proved to be my biggest and smartest investment."

Colleen, whose investment portfolio exceeds $2 million, claims she didn't have the "foggiest idea" what she was doing when she bought Exxon. I disagree:

- She knew Exxon was an industry leader.
- She knew putting money into the market was better than keeping it on the sidelines.
- She knew investing every month was the best way to use "time" diversification so that she didn't invest all her money at the top of the market.
- She knew to hold onto her Exxon stock to maximize the power of compounding.

Colleen knew more than enough to be a successful investor. She just didn't realize it.

You know more than enough to be a successful investor. You just don't realize it.

Actually, even if you truly have no investment expertise, it shouldn't stop you from starting an investment program. More than 85 percent of our everyday millionaire investors, when asked if they had investment expertise when they started investing, said "No." That didn't stop them from starting. It shouldn't stop you either.

EDUCATION TOOLS

Never before have there been so many inexpensive and convenient ways to educate yourself about the financial markets. Books, newsletters, magazines, television shows, radio programs, seminars, continuing education classes, the Internet, investment clubs—all of these are educational tools readily available to everyone.

Shelley Weaver has used almost all of them. Ms. Weaver, whose investment portfolio totals nearly $2 million, has purchased more than 100 books on investing in the past ten years.

She subscribes to three investment newsletters (*Dow Theory Forecasts, DRIP Investor,* and *Personal Finance*).

She reads seven financial magazines every month (*Forbes, Fortune, Money, Smart Money, Kiplinger's, Worth,* and *Better Investing*).

She watches *Nightly Business Report.*

What's particularly noteworthy about Ms. Weaver is that she didn't start the education process until her sixties. "At age sixty-two, I realized that my husband and I could not live well on Social Security," says Shelley. "Investing was the only way I knew to have more income." Shelley spends between $500 and $1,000 a year on investment research tools and about ten hours a week reviewing her investments. "We have made more money investing than we ever did working."

What are favorite research tools of everyday millionaires? The following tables list research resources mentioned most often by our millionaire investors. (Note: I found several of our everyday millionaire investors from the subscriber rolls of two newsletters I help write—*DRIP Investor* and *Dow Theory Forecasts.* Thus, it's not surprising that these newsletters show up among the top ten.)

The Wall Street Journal (800-568-7625/www.wsj.com)
Dow Theory Forecasts newsletter (800-233-5922/ www.dowtheory.com)
Forbes magazine (800-888-9896/www.forbes.com)
CNBC cable television network (check your cable listings/ www.cnbc.com)

Money magazine (800-633-9970/www.money.com)

Value Line Investment Survey (800-833-0046/www.value-line.com)

Kiplinger's Personal Finance (800-544-0155/www.kiplinger.com)

Investor's Business Daily (800-831-2525/www.investors.com)

Barron's (800-822-7229/www.barrons.com)

DRIP Investor newsletter (800-233-5922/www.dripinvestor.com)

I know what some of you are saying. Sure, you can be a knowledgeable investor if you're willing to spend thousands of dollars every year in research material. Actually, about 70 percent of our everyday millionaire investors spend $500 or less each year on investment research; 37 percent spend $250 or less. Only 9 percent spend $1,000 or more each year on research tools.

Many of the everyday millionaires selected some of my favorite research tools. Among financial newspapers, I love both *The Wall Street Journal* and *Investor's Business Daily.* I read them every day. I also read *Barron's* each week. Among daily newspapers, *USA Today* and *The New York Times* provide solid financial and market information. Among newsletters, I'm partial to the ones I help produce— *Dow Theory Forecasts, DRIP Investor,* and *No-Load Stock Insider.* Also, *Value Line Investment Survey* and *Morningstar Mutual Funds* are excellent research tools and available at many libraries. I read a lot of magazines every month. If I had to pick four "must reads," they would be *Forbes, Smart Money, Money,* and *Bloomberg Personal Finance* (I'm a periodic contributor to Bloomberg). Among television shows, *CNBC, CNNfn, Bloomberg Television, Nightly Business Report,* and *CNN Moneyline* do a credible job of reporting the day's financial news.

THE INTERNET

If I could choose only one investment tool, however, I would choose the Internet. It's hard to overstate the amount of good investment information available on the Internet. Best of all, much of it is *free*.

And the Internet is easy on your mailbox. Indeed, virtually every research tool mentioned by our millionaire investors has an Internet Web site. While you might have to pay a few dollars a month to access all of the information on those Web sites, the free information is usually sufficient for most investors.

Getting on the Internet is easy. The first thing you'll need to surf the Internet is the appropriate computer hardware (computer, modem, and printer) and software (a "Web browser," such as Microsoft Internet Explorer or Netscape Navigator). You'll also need an Internet Service Provider (ISP). An ISP is your gateway to the Internet. You connect to the Internet via the ISP. You'll connect to the ISP via a toll-free or local telephone number. I use AT&T and America Online as my Internet Service Providers. My guess is that your local phone company probably offers Internet access services, too. Pretty soon, most of the country will also be able to access the Internet via their cable-television systems. Most ISP fees are $15 to $25 per month.

One of the more interesting developments among ISPs is the "PC giveaway." A growing number of Internet access companies are giving free computers to individuals who sign up for their services. Be aware, however, that you'll have to give to get. In order to get the free computer, you'll probably have to sign a multiyear Internet service contract. You may also be required to provide certain personal information—age, income, buying habits, etc.—that will be used by marketers for developing electronic commerce strategies.

Navigating the Net

Once connected to the Internet, you'll probably need assistance in finding Web sites of interest. Web "search engines" are good for finding your way around the Net. Search engines allow you to type in key words or phrases that will help the search engine locate Web sites relevant to your topic of interest. Don't be frustrated if your initial searches pull up sites that have little to do with your topic. Over time, you'll become more adept at refining your search techniques. While finding a Web site of interest may take some doing initially, remembering the site is easy. Your browser software allows you to "bookmark" favorite Web sites for easy retrieval.

To save you some time in finding good investment sites, I've included the Web addresses for some of my favorite search engines and investment Web sites. Just type these addresses into the address box at the top of your browser software.

•SEARCH ENGINES

http://www.altavista.com

http://www.google.com

http://www.askjeeves.com

http://www.lycos.com

http://www.yahoo.com

http://www.infoseek.com

http://www.excite.com

http://www.goto.com

http://www.go2net.com

http://www.hotbot.com

http://www.searchengine-
watch.com

•STOCK SCREENING TOOLS

http://www.marketplayer.com

http://www.irnet.com

http://www.financialweb.com/
rapidresearch.com

http://www.wsrn.com

http://www.stock-
screener.com

http://www.market-
guide.com

•WEB AGGREGATORS

http://www.yahoo.com

http://www.dailystocks.com

http://www.quicken.com

http://www.stock-fever.com

http://www.investor.msn.com

•INVESTMENT RESEARCH/USENET GROUPS

http://www.nyse.com

http://www.nasdaq.com

http://www.lehman.com

http://www.ibbotson.com

http://wwwhamquist.com

http://www.dejanews.com

http://www.fool.com

•INSIDER TRADING

http://www.insidertrader.com

http://www.dailystocks.com

http://www.dailyrocket.com

•STOCK CHARTS

http://www.bigcharts.com

http://www.quicken.com

http://www.equis.com

http://www.iqc.com

•INVESTMENT NEWS

http://www.newsalert.com

http://www.bloomberg.com

http://www.cnnfn.com

http://www.dailystocks.com

http://www.yahoo.com

http://www.moneynet.com

http://www.wsj.com

http://www.cbsmarket-watch.com

•STOCK MONITORING/PORTFOLIO TRACKING

http://www.investor.msn.com

http://www.yahoo.com

http://www.dailystocks.com

http://www.quicken.com

http://www.newsalert.com

http://www.riskview.com

http://www.sec.gov

•MUTUAL FUNDS

http://www.morningstar.com

http://www.quicken.com

http://www.stockpoint.com

http://www.stocksmart.com

http://www.investor.msn.com

http://www.fundsinter-
active.com

http://www.fundalarm.com

http://www.strongfunds.com

http://www.smartmoney.com

•DRIPS/NO-LOAD STOCKS

http://www.dripinvestor.com

http://www.noloadstocks.com

http://www.netstockdirect.com

http://www.bankofny.com

http://www.equiserve.com

http://www.chase-
mellon.com

http://www.harrisbank.com

http://www.stai.org

http://www.enrolldirect.com

•INTERNATIONAL INVESTMENTS

http://www.adr.com

http://www.global-investor.com

http://www.nasdaq.com

http://www.ifc.com

http://www.bankofny.
com/adr

http://www.ft.com

http://www.newsalert.com

•INVESTMENT EDUCATION

http://www.aaii.com

http://www.better-investing.org

http://www.investorama.com

http://www.fool.com

•FINANCIAL CALCULATORS

http://www.financenter.com

The best thing about the Internet is that what is available today will
pale in comparison to what will be available for individual investors
a few months or years from now. With that much free or nearly free
information at your fingertips, you have no excuses for not becoming a more knowledgeable investor.

NAIC AND AAII

Another way to educate yourself about investing is to join an investment club. According to the **National Association of Investors Corporation** (877-275-6242), the nonprofit umbrella organization for many investment clubs in this country, the number of clubs has grown from 12,429 in 1994 to more than 37,000 today. The NAIC provides a lot of useful information about forming and running investment clubs. The group also provides a wealth of solid financial information and research.

One out of five of the everyday millionaires in this book belongs to an investment club. For some everyday millionaires, like Alice Barton, the clubs provided a friendly teaching environment to get them started down the road to a seven-figure portfolio. "General reading [about investments] did not help me at all," says Alice. "Though I read and read, I had a hard time internalizing the material. After reading about investment clubs in a financial magazine, I decided that this might be the way to go. It was the investment club that gave me a focus for learning." Alice, who has been in a club for six years, has an investment portfolio worth $2.1 million.

If you're interested in joining an investment club, call the NAIC for clubs in your area. You can also visit the NAIC on the Internet at **www.better-investing.org.**

Another nonprofit organization dedicated to investor education is the **American Association of Individual Investors.** The AAII and its local chapters provide investor educational seminars and conferences throughout the country. The group publishes a wealth of solid information for investors. To find out more about an AAII chapter in your area, call 800-428-2244 or check out the AAII on the Internet at **www.aaii.com.**

Over the last five years I've spoken to many NAIC and AAII chapters throughout the country. Without exception, I have found the groups' members to be friendly and genuinely interested in helping individuals become better investors. If you are one of those people who feels more comfortable learning in a group environment, I highly recommend both organizations.

Continuing Education Classes

A final avenue for investor education that was mentioned by several of our millionaire investors was continuing education classes at local colleges. You probably live near a college, either a branch campus of a major college, a junior college, or a community college. These institutions offer adult classes on investments, usually at a reasonable fee. If you don't have the time to attend, do what one of our everyday millionaires did—obtain the reading list and read all the books.

Excuse #4: I Don't Have the Time

How much time do you spend watching television each week? Don't know? I'll tell you.

The average adult spends roughly *twenty-eight hours* each week watching television. That's according to Nielsen Media Research.

Hard to believe? Not really. Think about it. You probably watch one of those morning shows to catch the weather and traffic. At night, you watch that favorite show or two. You probably watch the evening news before you go to bed. And you might sneak a peak at Dave or Jay or Conan when you're under the covers. It adds up.

And how about your computer? How long are you online every day? Thirty minutes? An hour? More?

Yes, I know you're busy. *Everyone* is busy. With kids. With work. With life. But let's face it, we waste a lot of time on things offering very little payoff.

That's why I cringe when someone tells me he or she doesn't

have enough time for investing. *You have enough time.* It's just a question of priorities. And what could be more important than your family's financial future?

Investing is not a full-time job. It's not forty hours a week with overtime. Among the millionaire investors I surveyed, the average amount of time each devoted to investments and investment strategies was twelve hours per week, or less than a couple of hours a day. And many of them spend a lot less time than that.

Hank Firestone, an engineer in Texas, spends about fifteen minutes a day on his investments. Hank, who's just forty-four, has been investing for twenty-two years. One reason Hank spends just fifteen minutes a day on his investments is that he understands the importance of keeping an investment program simple and efficient. Hank owns just five stocks (Procter & Gamble, Dell Computer, AT&T, Gillette, and Texas Instruments) and four mutual funds. He holds investments on average for five years. He invests the maximum in his 401(k) plan. Hank follows the K-I-S approach—Keep It Simple. How has this low-maintenance approach worked for Hank? His portfolio exceeds $1 million.

Hank is a good example of how you can control the amount of time necessary to monitor your investment program. Don't overdiversify your investments. If your portfolio is exclusively stocks, you can have a nicely diversified portfolio with just fifteen to twenty stocks. If you supplement your portfolio with mutual funds, the number of stocks can be reduced. Despite having only five stocks and four mutual funds, Hank's portfolio is reasonably diversified.

You also reduce the need for portfolio monitoring if you commit yourself to a long-term investment strategy. Hank holds investments on average for five years. According to our survey, 75 percent of our everyday millionaires held stocks for five years or longer. If you plan to hold investments for a long time, you are not forced to worry about every little blip in price or every little news item. You can focus your research efforts on the big picture and not the time-consuming minutiae of daily trading.

Focusing on simple, understandable investments also reduces the time required to track your investments. Hank doesn't own exotic derivative investments that require the math skills of Pascal to understand. He doesn't own complex limited partnerships that even the IRS doesn't get.

Finally, Hank reduces the time required to track investments by using a computer. That's not unusual for everyday millionaire investors. Roughly two thirds of those surveyed use computers to track their investments.

Admittedly, a few of our everyday millionaire investors spend much more than twelve hours per week on their investments. Jesse Kahn spends twenty-five to thirty hours per week on his investments. Jesse, fifty-nine, has an investment portfolio worth $1.6 million. He owns forty-seven stocks and two mutual funds. "People should spend at least the same amount of time on their financial future and well being as they do planning their next vacation," says Jesse.

For people like Jesse, tracking their investments is a hobby, like golfing or knitting. They *love* it. "I have found investing to be a fun-filled, rewarding experience," says Gio Mallard. "It [investing] has become my hobby. Needless to say, I am not always correct, but I am unable to resist the challenge that investing provides me." Gio has been correct enough to have a portfolio worth $1.1 million.

You don't have to spend thirty hours a week on your investments. I contend you don't have to spend twelve hours per week. If you keep your investment approach simple and focus on the long term, a few minutes each day is all it takes.

EXCUSE #5: I'M TOO YOUNG

If time is the most important factor in an investment program, then it's impossible to be too young to be an investor. Indeed, you should start an investment program as early as possible.

JUNIOR INVESTOR KNOWS
HIS ABCS AND P-E RATIOS

RICHARD ANDERSON, JR., IS A BIG FAN OF THE MARKETS.

He can name the thirty stocks that make up the Dow Jones Industrial Average.

He owns mutual funds.

He knows what makes a quality company—"good management, good products and services, good customer services."

Richard even had the good fortune of being asked to ring the opening bell for trading on the New York Stock Exchange.

In many ways Richard is a lot like the investors in this book, with one small exception.

Richard is five years old.

Richard began his financial education at age two when he began watching CNBC, the financial news show. Richard Junior quickly took an interest in things financial, an interest spurred by both parents.

"Every night after we do his regular homework from school, I go over the list of the Dow stocks with him," says Richard's mother, Michelle Anderson. "Children think money grows on trees. I think it's very important that children have an understanding of the economy and money."

SOURCE: PETER ALAN HARPER,
ASSOCIATED PRESS/*AKRON BEACON JOURNAL*, MAY 31, 1998

If your youngster shows an interest in investing, it has never been easier to get him or her started regardless of age. Once an individual reaches the age of majority (eighteen in most states), he or she may have an investment account registered solely in his or her name. Youngsters under the age of eighteen are not permitted to have their own brokerage accounts. However, several ways exist for parents to introduce interested youngsters to investing.

Dividend reinvestment plans provide an interesting investment vehicle for kids. Many child-friendly companies offer DRIPs—Coca-Cola, Walt Disney, Wrigley, Mattel, just to name a few. Since many DRIPs permit very small investments, the programs are a good way for a youngster with limited funds to start investing in the stock market.

Another investment vehicle for kids is a good mutual fund. Focus on funds that have low minimums and low expenses.

I think individual stocks are probably better for youngsters than funds because stocks are more interesting teaching tools. What you are trying to do by starting a youngster investing is to instill discipline and teach about the capitalistic system. Those lessons will probably hit home more if they feature a company to which the child can relate rather than a truly "faceless" mutual fund.

If you decide to establish an investment account for a youngster, consider carefully how you want the account registered. If you choose to have the account in your own name, you will be responsible for taxes on the account. The good thing is that you also retain complete control over the account for as long as you want.

An alternative is to set up the account as a Uniform Gift to Minors Account (UGMA). Funds in the account are in the minor's name and Social Security number and are considered to be owned by the minor. Dividends paid on the account are taxable, most likely at a preferred tax rate. The adult custodian is responsible for the account until the minor reaches the age of majority. Any withdrawals from the account are payable to the custodian on the minor's behalf until that time. However, once the youth has reached the age of majority, which is eighteen in most states, control of the account re-verts to the child to do with as he or she sees fit. This is the down-side of setting up a UGMA. Parental control is lost at the age of majority. Another consideration is that college financial aid deci-sions could be impacted if a child has sizable assets in a UGMA. It is important to understand the pluses and minuses of UGMAs be-fore registering investments in that form.

One way to draw a youngster's interest to an investment pro-gram is by offering "matching" funds. Make a deal with your kids: For every dollar they save or invest, you'll match it with another dol-lar. Consider it your child's "401(k) plan" for taking out the garbage, cleaning around the house, doing the dishes, walking the dog, mow-ing the lawn, etc.

The last point I want to make is that while certificates of deposit and savings bonds are okay investments, kids should own stocks or stock mutual funds. Risk is the last thing your child needs to worry about in an investing program. He or she needs to capitalize fully on the power of time in their investment program. That's done with stocks.

Many of our millionaire investors started investing as children or young adults. Sandra Pfister, seventy-three, whom we'll meet later in this chapter, started putting money away at age eleven. "When I was a child, I trapped gophers, sold the tails, and put the money in a savings account at the bank."

EXCUSE #6: I'M TOO OLD

Shelley Weaver didn't start investing until age sixty-two. Today, at age seventy-five, she has a portfolio worth $1.8 million.

Saul Shimone didn't start investing until age sixty-two. Today, at age seventy-six, Saul has an investment portfolio worth $2 million.

Pat Kingston didn't start investing until age forty-one. Today, at age fifty-nine, Pat has a portfolio worth $1.2 million.

These and many other everyday millionaire investors didn't start investing in their teens and twenties. Many started in their forties, fifties, and even sixties. Yet, all were able to reach seven figures.

You *do* have time to build a decent financial future.

You have more time than you think. We are living longer. Many people live into their seventies and eighties, and the number of individuals reaching ninety and even the century mark continues to swell. Look at the numbers:

- A male who is currently thirty-five years old is expected to live another forty years.
- A forty-five-year-old male should live at least another thirty-one years.
- A fifty-five-year-old male is expected to live another twenty-three years.
- A sixty-five-year-old male's life expectancy is fifteen years.
- A seventy-five-year-old male is expected to live at least another ten years.

The life expectancy is even better for women:

- A thirty-five-year-old female is expected to live to age eighty-one.
- A forty-five-year-old female has a life expectancy of thirty-six more years.
- A fifty-five-year-old female should live to at least age eighty-two.
- A sixty-five-year-old female has a life expectancy of nineteen years.
- A seventy-five-year-old female is expected to live to age eighty-seven.

As you can see, even at age sixty-five you probably will live at least another fifteen to twenty years, and maybe even longer. Also notice that the longer you live, the longer you're expected to live. This seemingly obvious point may not be fully appreciated by most people. Notice that a thirty-five-year-old male is expected to live to age seventy-five; a fifty-five-year-old male is expected to live to seventy-eight. The reason for the difference in life expectancy is that a certain percentage of males die between the ages of thirty-five and fifty-five. Thus, the farther along you get in age, the longer your life expectancy. This is a relevant point to understand when you determine your investment time horizon.

The average portfolio size of the millionaire investors we surveyed was nearly $2.2 million. It took an average of thirty years to accumulate that amount. Keep in mind that the first million takes much longer than the second and third million. Indeed, if it takes twenty-two years to accumulate the first million, it will take only seven years to accumulate the second million (assuming a 10 percent annual return and no new investments). That means that if you're forty-five years old, you still have a decent shot of building a nest egg of $1 million by the time you're sixty-seven and $2 million by age seventy-four.

But let's say you're forty-five and you don't want to wait until age sixty-seven to have a seven-figure portfolio. You want $1 million by age sixty so you can retire a bit early. What will you need to invest each year for fifteen years? Assuming an average annual return of 11 percent, you'll need to invest roughly $2,200 per month ($26,400 per year) to reach $1 million.

Interestingly, had you started investing just five years earlier, at age forty, you would need to invest about $1,200 per month to have $1 million by age sixty. And that monthly investment amount drops to around $650 if you start at age thirty-five. In other words, you can reach $1 million even if you start in your forties and fifties; it's just much easier if you start a little sooner.

Even if you're at the age and the income level that makes it virtually impossible to achieve a seven-figure portfolio, you should still get started. Suppose you make "only" $500,000. An investment portfolio of $500,000 is still a whole lot better than depending completely on Social Security.

Don't compound your mistake of not starting an investing program earlier by refusing to start now. It can still have a huge impact on your financial future.

Excuse #7: I Don't Have a Broker

This might be the worst reason for not starting an investment program. You don't need a broker. DRIPs, no-load stocks, mutual funds, 401(k) plans—none of these investment vehicles requires a broker. You can get started on your own, with little money in most cases.

BUYandHOLD.com

If you want a broker, it's never been easier to find one, nor cheaper to use one. One company in which I'm involved offers an easy way to buy stocks with very little money. That company, **BUYandHOLD.com**, is a unique online brokerage concept. BUYandHOLD takes the best of the DRIP world—low-cost investing with small amounts of money—and combines it with the best of the online brokerage world—more timely buy and sell execution and consolidated account statements. Individuals may purchase stock through BUYandHOLD.com for just $2.99 in brokerage fees. Minimum investment is just $20. BUYandHOLD.com will buy both full and fractional shares of stock for investors. You'll also receive a consolidated statement showing all of your holdings. No deposit is required to establish an account. You can purchase shares with a check or by having your bank account automatically debited. For more information on BUYandHOLD.com, visit the Web site—**www.buyandhold.com.**

Brokerage Firm	Internet Address http://	Minimum commission to buy one share	Minimum amount to open an account	Telephone
Accutrade	www.accutrade.com	$29.95	$5,000.00	800-882-4887
American Express	www.americanexpress.com	$24.95	$2,000.00	800-658-4677
AmeriTrade	www.ameritrade.com	$8.00	$2,000.00	800-669-3900
Brown & Co.	www.brownco.com	$5.00	$15,000.00	800-822-2829
Charles Schwab	www.schwab.com	$29.95	$5,000.00	800-435-4000
Datek	www.datek.com	$9.99	$2,000.00	888-463-2835
Discover	www.discoverbrokerage.com	$14.95	$2,000.00	800-688-3462
E*Trade Securities	www.etrade.com	$14.95	$1,000.00	800-387-2331
National Discount Brokers	www.ndb.com	$14.75	No Minimum	800-888-3999
Quick & Reilly	www.quickwaynet.com	$14.95	No Minimum	800-672-7220
Sovereign Securities	www.mydiscountbroker.com	$12.00	No Minimum	888-882-5600
SureTrade	www.suretrade.com	$7.95	No Minimum	401-642-6900
Trading Direct	www.tradingdirect.com	$9.95	No Minimum	800-925-8566
Wall Street Access	www.wsaccess.com	$25.00	$10,000.00	800-925-5781
Wall Street Electronica	www.wallstreete.com	$14.95	$2,500.00	888-925-5783
Waterhouse Securities	www.waterhouse.com	$12.00	$1,000.00	800-934-4134
Web Street Securities	www.webstreetsecurities.com	$14.95	No Minimum	800-932-8723

OTHER ONLINE BROKERS

The preceding table provides additional choices among online brokers. I have used Schwab's online brokerage system and have found it to be a quality, though expensive, offering. I've also been pleased over the years with my Waterhouse account.

EXCUSE #8: THE MARKET'S TOO HIGH

It continues to surprise me when someone says the market is too high. Nobody—Alan Greenspan, Peter Lynch, Chuck Carlson—*nobody* knows whether the market is too high at any given time.

Guessing whether the market is too high is a loser's game. You can't do it consistently over time. Investing is an inexact science. Every investment you make comes with uncertainty. Successful investors play the percentages. What you know for sure as an investor is that time is the greatest ally your portfolio has. Delaying an investment program because you think the market is "too high" means keeping money on the sidelines. And keeping money on the sidelines limits the power of time.

So I ask you, which should you do? Keep money on the sidelines because you *guess* the market is too high? Or invest regardless of the market level because you *know* that doing so maximizes the power of time?

Moral of the story: There is *never* a bad time to start an investment program.

CONCLUSION

I spent a lot of time on step 1, for good reason. It's the most important of all. You can't get to the other seven steps without starting.

Oftentimes, it is the most difficult step. You may have to break old habits and start new ones. You may have to sacrifice current consumption. However, you'll never get to seven figures without starting.

The millionaire profiled in this chapter is Sandra Pfister. Sandra, a retired teacher and farmer's wife, is a good example of an individual who is now reaping the benefits of starting an investment program early. Sandra started investing when she was eleven. "Having grown up in the Depression when money was scarce, we hung on to money we got," says Sandra. She had no problem saving for a better future. "We had so little when we were young that we still don't need much to satisfy us. We don't have e-mail or cell phones. We are satisfied with just the necessities."

Today, at age seventy-three, Sandra's investment portfolio is worth $5.3 million. She plans to donate a chunk of her wealth to her college alma mater to build a performing arts center (Sandra was a music major).

"I would like my name on something more than a tombstone," says Sandra.

NAME: Sandra Pfister

AGE: 73

HOME: North Dakota

MARITAL STATUS: Married for 37 years. Never divorced.

CHILDREN: 0

EDUCATION: College (advanced degree) graduate

OCCUPATION: Retired teacher and farmer's wife

HIGHEST INCOME: $125,240

HOW MANY DIFFERENT JOBS SINCE AGE 25? 2

HOW IMPORTANT WERE YOUR PARENTS IN DEVELOPING YOUR DISCIPLINE AND EXPERTISE IN INVESTING? Very important

HOW MANY YEARS HAVE YOU BEEN INVESTING? 62

WHAT IS THE SIZE OF YOUR ENTIRE INVESTMENT PORTFOLIO? $5.3 million

WHAT IS THE BREAKDOWN OF THESE ASSETS? Mutual funds (18 percent), stocks (76 percent), bonds (6 percent)

HOW MANY INDIVIDUAL STOCKS DO YOU OWN? 33

NAME YOUR 5 LARGEST STOCK HOLDINGS: Medtronic, AlliedSignal, GTE, Exxon, SmithKline Beecham

HOW MANY INDIVIDUAL MUTUAL FUNDS DO YOU OWN? 10

NAME YOUR BIGGEST FUND HOLDINGS: American Express High Yield Tax Exempt, American Express Equity Select

HOW MANY INDIVIDUAL BONDS DO YOU HAVE? 38

HAVE YOU EVER PURCHASED STOCK/INDEX OPTIONS? No

HAVE YOU EVER BOUGHT STOCK/INDEX FUTURES? No

DO YOU OWN GOLD OR PRECIOUS METALS? No

HAVE YOU EVER SOLD STOCK SHORT? No

DO YOU RECEIVE ADVICE ON YOUR INVESTMENTS FROM AN OUTSIDE SOURCE? Yes, my broker.

WHAT TYPE OF BROKER DO YOU USE? Full service

HOW DID YOU FIND YOUR BROKER? My brother had used him.

WHERE DID YOU GET THE MONEY TO START INVESTING? When I was a child, I trapped gophers, sold the tails, and put the money in a savings account at the bank. After college, I taught school and bought certificates of deposit.

HAVE YOU INHERITED WHAT YOU THOUGHT WAS A LARGE SUM OF MONEY? Yes, and it was important to my investing program.

DID YOU START INVESTING WITH A SPECIFIC PLAN IN MIND? No

HOW DID YOU EDUCATE YOURSELF ABOUT INVESTING? DID YOU FIND THE EDUCATION PROCESS DIFFICULT? FUN? I was lucky to have a brother who was a businessman and he talked business to me all his life. I enjoyed listening to him and getting his advice. His death nearly shattered my world.

DID YOU HAVE ANY SPECIAL EXPERTISE IN INVESTING WHEN YOU STARTED? Not really. But I was successful in making money, so I got more involved.

HOW MUCH DO YOU SPEND PER YEAR ON INVESTMENT RESEARCH RESOURCES? $250

DO YOU USE A COMPUTER TO KEEP TRACK OF YOUR INVESTMENTS? No

HOW MANY HOURS PER WEEK DO YOU DEVOTE TO YOUR INVESTMENTS AND INVEST-MENT STRATEGIES? 2

WHAT CRITERIA DO YOU USE TO PICK STOCKS/MUTUAL FUNDS? I look at a stock's rate of return during the previous years. I select a company that is expected to be around for years. I find out what kind of managers they have. Sort out the advice the broker gives.

HOW OFTEN DO YOU BUY INVESTMENTS? Monthly

ON AVERAGE, HOW LONG DO YOU HOLD AN INVESTMENT BEFORE SELLING? 10 years

DO YOU "MARKET TIME"? No

WHAT HAVE BEEN YOUR BEST-PERFORMING STOCKS? Medtronic, AlliedSignal

WHAT HAVE BEEN YOUR WORST-PERFORMING STOCKS? Pace Health Management, Digital Biometrics, Coda Music

WHAT WERE SOME OF YOUR BIGGEST INVESTMENT MISTAKES? Letting a broker sell me something that I really didn't want. Getting hooked with a few new things that never got off the ground, like music piped into a funeral home.

HOW WOULD YOU BEST DESCRIBE YOUR INVESTMENT APPROACH? I am getting a little choosier in what I invest. I certainly want some reliable established companies in my portfolio. But I am still willing to buy into new technology and medical stocks if they have good reports. I know farming, have real estate, and can select good renters so I can live from that income. My portfolio is my extra money.

DO YOU BELIEVE IT IS POSSIBLE TO BEAT THE MARKET ON A CONSISTENT BASIS? No

WHAT DO YOU THINK ARE SOME OF THE GREATEST MYTHS OF INVESTING? Thinking that you can time the market. That you are never going to lose.

WHAT IS THE BIGGEST BENEFIT OF A SEVEN-FIGURE PORTFOLIO? The greatest benefit of having a 7-figure portfolio is the feeling that you should always be able to support yourself, be able to take a few vacations (I have been on all seven continents), and still be able to donate to charity and hopefully leave the world a better place in which to live.

IF YOU COULD GIVE JUST ONE PIECE OF ADVICE TO INDIVIDUAL INVESTORS, WHAT WOULD THAT PIECE OF ADVICE BE? Never borrow money to buy stocks.

If you have the money, invest in a good company and hold the stock forever. In 30 years a small amount can turn into a large amount.

IF YOU WOULD, PLEASE SHARE WITH ME YOUR FAVORITE INVESTMENT STORY: My most interesting stock is Medtronic. That stock made me rich. My broker was a medic during World War II so was naturally interested in medical stocks. During the 1980s I bought Bio Medicus stock and as the stock went up, I sold enough to recover my initial cost. In 1990 Bio Medicus was bought by Medtronic, so I received Medtronic stock. That company helps so many people, they publish a good report, and their meetings are fantastic—speakers receive standing ovations. Medtronic split 4 times since 1990, so I accumulated 44,000 shares.

4

ESTABLISH A GOAL

Women kept leaving me because I had no money.

—PETER STRUNK, NEW YORK,
$3 MILLION INVESTMENT PORTFOLIO

STEP 2: ESTABLISH A GOAL—ANY GOAL—
IT REALLY DOESN'T MATTER WHAT IT IS
AS LONG AS IT MATTERS TO YOU.

A million years ago, I raced in triathlons. A triathlon race consists of three legs—swimming, biking, and running. The best known triathlon event is the Ironman Triathlon held in Hawaii every year. When I was racing, I found it extremely easy to get to the gym every day to exercise. I had a goal in mind—to improve my time in the race. I also had a fear factor. I knew that if I wasn't ready for the swim leg, for example, my lack of preparation might have dire consequences.

Now that I've stopped triathlon racing, I find it difficult to drag myself to the gym. I know that exercise is good for me. I know I'll live a longer and healthier life if I exercise regularly. However, without that goal of preparing for the next race, of besting my best time, the day-to-day grind of exercise becomes difficult to sustain.

Without goals, maintaining a regular investing program is a lot like maintaining a regular exercise program—easy to start, difficult to sustain.

When I started this project, I had some preconceived notions about how millionaire investors behave. One of those notions was that all millionaire investors basically have the same goals: Enough money to retire early and fund kids' college plans.

What I found was that everyday millionaires have all sorts of goals:

- Robert Peterson has two long-term goals—maintain purchasing power and leave a good estate to children and grandchildren. With his $1 million portfolio, he's well on his way to achieving both.
- Tim Kellar has the usual financial goals—leave a large sum of money to children and grandchildren and retire early at age fifty-five. He also has another financial goal shared by many millionaire investors—leave a healthy chunk of money to a college. Tim, who is fifty-seven, has a portfolio valued at around $1 million. His five biggest holdings are IBM, AT&T, Procter & Gamble, Johnson Controls, and SBC Communications.
- Felix Rose's financial goals are simple—"Bring in more than I spend." Felix, sixty-one, has been investing for forty years. Felix should have no problem meeting his goal. His investment portfolio is worth more than $29 *million*.
- Donald Spock's long-term goal is very specific—"Amass $3 million by death, living reasonably during life." Donald, who is sixty-four, is halfway there with an investment portfolio worth $1.5 million. He should meet his goal before his seventy-first birthday, assuming a 10 percent annual return in the market.
- Samantha Jones' long-term goal is to be able to generate $100,000 annually from her investments without dipping into the principal. If Samantha earns 5 percent per year on her portfolio, she'll need an investment portfolio worth $2 million to meet her goal. Samantha, age sixty-seven, now has

$1.4 million and should reach $2 million before age seventy-two.

- Gio Mallard has two goals that go hand in hand—build an estate that will exceed $2 million and to provide financial security for my son. "When my son was classified as learning disabled, I was aware that his future potential earnings would be limited. So it was a given that I put off consumption." Now fifty-five, Gio has an investment portfolio worth $1.1 million.

- Tess Gordon expressed a goal common to many millionaire investors—that "our children will not have to worry about us financially." With an investment portfolio of $1 million, Tess is unlikely to be a burden to her children.

- Gil Palmer wants to have residences in three different countries. Failing that, he wants to have one seaside residence and three chefs—"Italian, Chinese, and Indian." Gil, a college teacher, has a portfolio worth $1.5 million.

- A. J. Wright's long-term investment goal is as simple and personal as it gets. "A single-digit golf handicap," says A.J. With an investment portfolio worth $1.7 million, A.J. can afford the greens fees.

What's important to understand is that, despite a diversity of goals, each of these people has a seven-figure portfolio.

The message here? Don't worry so much whether your investing goal is noble or logical. Perhaps you want to invest so you have enough money to move to Italy and paint. Maybe you invest because, like Peter Strunk (whose quote leads off this chapter), you were tired of women leaving you because you had no money. Maybe you invest because you have nothing else to do with your time.

In the end, it really doesn't matter *why* you invest. Just that you have a *why.* The why provides an anchor to your investment program, the *raison d'être.* You'll need this anchor to develop the discipline to invest regularly over a long period of time.

QUEEN OF THE HILL

"I NEVER SET A GOAL OF HAVING $1 MILLION BY THE TIME I was 50," says Mary-Edith Hill, age 50 and a millionaire. "I started out saying I'm not going to consume more than I can use and I'm not going to be frivolous." Mary-Edith, who owns a real estate agency in Boise, Idaho, has an investment portfolio worth more than $1 million as a result of careful spending and prudent investing.

"I hate spending money on cars. If you wash, wax, and vacuum a car regularly and don't let people eat or smoke in it, you can drive it for 20 years. Watching my spending has allowed me to invest as much as half my income some years.

"I don't have a real philosophy about investing, except to stick to companies with which I'm familiar," says Mary-Edith. "I began buying stock in Hewlett-Packard back in the '70s, when it was selling for the equivalent of $2.60 per share. My husband John, who died in 1979, and I had both worked for the company, so we knew it made great products.

"The other recommendation I have about investing is to stay in for the long haul. When the market gets topsy-turvy, the best thing you can do is forget about the daily blitz."

SOURCE: *MONEY* MAGAZINE, JUNE 1997

On average, the millionaire investors I surveyed have been investing for three decades. That's a long time. If you don't have some goal in mind, some target, some finish line, you probably won't complete the race.

DEVELOPING A GOAL

To be sure, if you have specific goals, you will find the road to seven figures easier. Rex T., a software developer, had no special expertise in investing when he started, other than being "pretty good with math." Rex also had a specific goal when he started investing at age twenty-two—"To have $1 million in stocks by age forty."

Rex, now forty years old, has an investment portfolio worth $1.2 million.

As you develop a goal, keep in mind the following:

- *Make sure the goal is something you truly want.* This goal has to matter to you because achieving it will require a great deal of time and some effort. You've got to want it *bad,* so bad that failure is not an option. The goal has to be extremely personal, something *you* care about a great deal. Powerful goals feed off powerful values. What do we value most in life? Family. Freedom. Spirituality. Leisure. Health. Friendship. Self-preservation. Charity. Creativity. Tie goals to important values, and your chances of succeeding skyrocket. Spirituality and charity are important values to Millie S. One of her goals is to have the money to make one mission trip per year. Millie, fifty-eight, has an investment portfolio worth $1.6 million. No doubt the strong personal nature of her goal helped her succeed financially.
- *Goals and plans should be specific.* Rex's goal was very specific—to have $1 million in stocks by age forty. It wasn't "to

have a lot of money some day." Specific goals focus your commitment. Progress is more easily measured and evaluated. That's key, especially given the length of time necessary to stay on the right track.

- *Written goals are better than mental goals.* A goal in your mind is merely a dream. Dreams are fine. But let's face it—dreams are, well, *dreams.* They lack a concrete quality that demands a commitment on your part. Dreams are hopes and wishes. That's why dreams don't come true. A written goal, on the other hand, takes the abstractness of a dream and makes it concrete. The dream is now on paper in black and white. In a way, you've signed a contract. You've made an official record. I know it sounds a bit silly, but try it. You'll feel a much greater level of commitment to pursuing the goal simply by writing it down.

- *Limit your goals.* Limiting your goals focuses your efforts. If you have too many objectives—you want to retire early, endow a chair at the university, travel around the world, pay for the grandkids' tuition—you'll lose the focus necessary to reach your primary goal.

- *Keep the goal to yourself.* The world is full of naysayers. You don't need someone telling you that you'll never reach your goal.

- *Think of reaching your goal as a series of small steps.* When I establish a goal, I don't think of the goal in its entirety. I break the process of attaining the goal into small steps. Doing so makes the ultimate goal much more attainable. Most people look at the goal as one giant leap from here to there. It's easy to see why such people fail. They become impatient. The goal seems beyond their reach. Dissect the goal into a series of "mini" goals. For example, if you want, say, $1 million by age sixty-five, you may want to break that goal into a series of smaller victories—$250,000 by age fifty, $500,000 by age fifty-seven, and so on.

SMART GOALS

Paul J. Meyer, a noted expert and lecturer on goal setting, summarizes the goal-setting process in one acronym—**SMART**. The goal must be:

- **Specific.** To set a specific goal, you must answer the six "W" questions:
  - Who—Who is involved?
  - What—What do I want to accomplish?
  - Where—Identify a location.
  - When—Establish a time frame.
  - Which—Identify requirements and constraints.
  - Why—Specific reasons, purpose, or benefits of accomplishing the goal.
- **Measurable.** Establish concrete criteria for measuring progress toward the attainment of each goal you set. When you measure your progress, you stay on track and post minor victories. It is those minor victories that spur you to reach your final goal.
- **Attainable.** When you identify goals that are most important to you, you figure out ways to make them come true. You see new and previously overlooked ways to attain your goals.
- **Realistic.** To be realistic, a goal must be one toward which you are willing and able to work. Don't be afraid to set your goals high.
- **Tangible.** Goals should be tangible. If you can experience a goal with your senses—what you taste, touch, see, smell, or hear—it becomes much more real and attainable. It also makes it easier to visualize the goal, and visualization is extremely important. The more you can visualize attaining your goal, the better chance you have of actually achieving it.

A GOAL IS MORE IMPORTANT THAN A PLAN

One preconceived notion I had about millionaire investors was that each had a definite plan in mind to achieve his or her goal.

I was wrong.

An overwhelming number of everyday millionaires I surveyed and interviewed had no plan when they started investing. And those that did have a plan had something extremely basic—"To save 5 percent to 10 percent of my income" was a popular plan of attack.

That sounds hard to believe, yet, in retrospect, it makes perfect sense.

When I started investing, I had no real plan. I wanted to accumulate wealth via investing. I felt that the best way for me to do so was in my employer's 401(k) plan and via dividend reinvestment plans. But I didn't have any specific plan in mind. I probably didn't know enough to have a plan. I just started the process.

Over time, as I learned more, I formalized my investing strategies. I began investing every month. I focused on quality stocks. I bought more of a particular stock when it was down. I set aside the maximum amount permitted in my 401(k) plan.

I suppose I now have a plan. But I didn't when I started.

Don't forget that millionaire investors are often just like you. Most of these successful investors were clueless when they started investing. Almost to a person, the millionaire investors I surveyed had no investment experience before starting. The reason they didn't have a plan is because they didn't know enough to have a plan. But not having a plan didn't stop them from starting.

What got them off square one? The goal.

DEVELOPING A PLAN

Now I'm not saying that investing without a plan is necessarily the best approach. In fact, millionaire investors who had a specific plan usually did better than those who did not. Remember our forty-year-old millionaire Rex T.? He not only had a specific goal—$1 million by age forty—but he also had a specific plan—invest 10 percent from his pay each month and 50 percent of any found money.

An investment plan is like a map. You don't always need a map to get from point A to point B. In fact, many men (much to their wives' dismay) *refuse* to use a map to get from point A to point B. And, in most cases, you eventually reach your destination without the map. But you probably would have gotten there a lot sooner if you had used one.

You may get to your financial goals without a plan. But you'll get there a whole lot easier and sooner with one.

What were typical plans of everyday millionaire investors? Bart Hayes, forty-eight, lives with his wife and two children in the Upper Midwest. Bart started investing at age twenty-four. He now has an investment portfolio worth nearly $1.2 million. Bart had one of the more interesting investment plans of all the everyday millionaires I surveyed:

> To understand my investment plan, you first need to understand my personal situation. I am a farmer with a secondary part-time, off-the-farm job. My wife is employed part time out of the home. My farm income is unstable, and farming requires high cash-flow demands in the spring for inputs and for tax payment purposes. Farmers' income tax and Social Security tax are due on March 1. Because of this potential for cash-flow needs, my investment plan was to build a foundation of bonds, which would provide an income stream if necessary. Because taxes are also due in the

spring, I decided to use municipal bonds to cushion the tax consequences of this current income stream. I started with mutual funds until I could get adequate diversification in individual bonds. I now hold only individual bonds in a ladder and hold all until maturity. I reinvest only the principal amount of the bonds when they mature and use the income generated for cash flow if necessary to make additional stock investments. After establishing this foundation of bonds, I began building my stock portfolio with mutual funds at first and then switched to individual stocks when I could properly diversify by industry and growth and value. I now, with few exceptions outside of my retirement plan, use mutual funds only for index and special higher-risk situations. I use DRIP plans for my core holdings and reinvest all dividends in addition to optional investments. I never started with a specific dollar amount in mind but rather with the desired result. We invested as much as we possibly could as fast as we could.

Bart's plan exemplifies several characteristics of winning investment plans:

- *The best investment plans are simple.* Simple plans are easy to implement, which is important for new investors. Simple plans are also easy to maintain.
- *The best investment plans are personalized to meet your goals.* Bart's plan probably doesn't make sense for many investors, but it met his needs and goals.
- *The best investment plans are specific.* "Saving ten percent per paycheck" is a better plan than "saving whatever I can from my weekly pay." Specificity helps focus commitment.

The following are additional investment plans that our millionaire investors used to start investing.

Initial plan was to invest 10 percent and every time we received a raise, we allocated an additional amount. We also paid cash for our purchases. (*$1.4 million investment portfolio*)

I would try to save 25 percent of everything I made. (*$6.1 million investment portfolio*)

My wife and I started with a specific dollar amount as opposed to a percentage. As our income rose, the amount invested grew much more than the percentage increase—virtually all our raises since we started investing have gone to investing, and our expenses have remained pretty constant except for inflation. (*$1.4 million investment portfolio*)

We always saved as much as 50 percent post-tax income. When we both worked, we lived on one income. (*$14 million investment portfolio*)

When I started my regular permanent job, we made enough so that we could live on 53 to 55 percent of my income. That is my gross income minus taxes, IRA purchases, savings, etc. As money accumulated, I bought more stock. (*$3.5 million investment portfolio*)

My plan was to max my contribution to my 401(k) plan. I also committed to putting $2,000 in my IRA every year. (*$1.1 million investment portfolio*)

Upon graduation from the Naval Academy, I set up an allotment of $50 per month. After marriage, we managed about 10 percent of salary. (*$1.3 million investment portfolio*)

Started investing with 3 percent of my income, very soon moved up to 10 percent because I saw the potential. (*$1.2 million investment portfolio*)

What's particularly noteworthy is that many of these investors started with little money and increased their savings once they saw how easy and profitable regular investing can be. This gets back to the addictive nature of the investment process. Once you start, you'll want to do more. That's how $50 per month becomes a seven-figure portfolio.

CONCLUSION

Goals are an integral part of successful investing. If you don't have a goal, get one. If you have a goal, make it more compelling by focusing and simplifying it. If you don't have a plan, our everyday millionaire investors have provided a number of simple approaches to starting an investment program.

The everyday millionaire profiled in this chapter is Rex Trotter. Rex lives on the West Coast with his wife of three years. Rex, a software developer who has been investing since he was twenty-two, started with a specific goal and a detailed plan to meet that goal. Because of his planning and an early start, Rex, who is just forty years old, now has an investment portfolio worth $1.2 million. His largest stock holdings include General Electric, Merck, Intel, Cisco, and Chevron.

Rex is one of the everyday millionaire investors who believes that individual investors have advantages in the investment process. "Large investors have to spread the money around, usually in good, but not great companies. Little guys can put everything in the best five or ten companies."

Rex offers this one piece of advice for individual investors— "Invest regularly, as much as you can comfortably for as long as you can," says Rex. "One hundred dollars a month for twenty years turns into a lot of money. Don't wait."

NAME: Rex Trotter

AGE: 40

MARITAL STATUS: Married for 3 years. I have been divorced.

CHILDREN: 0

EDUCATION: College (advanced degree) graduate

OCCUPATION: Software developer

FIVE-YEAR AVERAGE INCOME: $180,000

HOW MANY DIFFERENT JOBS SINCE AGE 25? 7 (including mergers)

HOW LONG HAVE YOU WORKED FOR YOUR CURRENT EMPLOYER? 5 years

HOW MANY YEARS HAVE YOU BEEN INVESTING? 18

WHAT IS THE SIZE OF YOUR ENTIRE INVESTMENT PORTFOLIO? $1.2 million

WHAT IS THE BREAKDOWN OF THESE ASSETS? 401(k) (10 percent), mutual funds (10 percent), IRA (30 percent), individual stocks (45 percent), cash (5 percent)

HOW MANY INDIVIDUAL STOCKS DO YOU OWN? 20

WHAT ARE YOUR 5 BIGGEST STOCK HOLDINGS? General Electric, Merck, Intel, Cisco, Chevron

HOW MANY INDIVIDUAL FUNDS DO YOU OWN? 5

WHAT ARE YOUR BIGGEST FUND HOLDINGS? Janus Worldwide, Janus Mercury, AIM Aggressive Growth, AIM Constellation, Seligman Communications and Information

HOW MANY INDIVIDUAL BONDS DO YOU OWN? 0

HAVE YOU EVER PURCHASED STOCK/INDEX OPTIONS? Yes

HAVE YOU EVER PURCHASED STOCK/INDEX FUTURES? No

DO YOU OWN GOLD OR PRECIOUS METALS? Yes

HAVE YOU EVER SOLD STOCK SHORT? No

DO YOU RECEIVE ADVICE ON YOUR INVESTMENTS FROM AN OUTSIDE SOURCE? Yes, from my broker and accountant. But not much.

WHAT TYPE OF BROKER DO YOU USE? Full service

HOW DID YOU FIND YOUR BROKER? He cold-called about 15 years ago.

DID YOU HAVE ANY SPECIFIC INVESTMENT GOALS WHEN YOU STARTED INVESTING? Yes. Pay off the house and have $1 million in stocks by 40. Then get a fun job, which probably won't pay much.

WHAT ARE YOUR SHORT-TERM GOALS? Pay off/pay down new house, land-scape, decorate.

WHAT ARE YOUR LONG-TERM GOALS? Get enough of a dividend stream to pay regular monthly expenses so we can retire if/when we want.

WHAT HURDLES, IF ANY, DID YOU OVERCOME TO BEGIN INVESTING? The obvious—money. Then where to invest. Then how.

HOW, PSYCHOLOGICALLY SPEAKING, DID YOU DEAL WITH THE NOTION OF PUTTING OFF CONSUMPTION TO SAVE FOR A BETTER FINANCIAL FUTURE? I treated it just like any other bill.

WHERE DID YOU GET THE MONEY TO START INVESTING? A little bit at a time, every month, out of my regular paycheck.

WAS THERE ANY SPECIFIC EVENT THAT LED YOU TO BEGIN INVESTING? Not really. The fear of living on the streets and eating cat food maybe.

HAVE YOU INHERITED WHAT YOU THOUGHT WAS A LARGE AMOUNT OF MONEY? No

DID YOU START INVESTING WITH A SPECIFIC PLAN IN MIND? Yes. I would invest 10 percent or more of my pay, 50 percent or more of any "found" money, e.g., the stray bonus or tax refund. Usually the found money is allocated for 10 percent fun stuff and 90 percent for investments/house.

DID YOU HAVE ANY SPECIAL EXPERTISE IN INVESTING WHEN YOU STARTED? None. Being pretty good with math didn't hurt, but that's not exactly a special investment expertise.

WHAT MAGAZINES, NEWSLETTERS, TELEVISION, RADIO SHOWS, ETC., DO YOU FIND THE MOST USEFUL FOR INVESTMENT RESEARCH? *Forbes, Individual Investor* magazine, *CNBC, DRIP Investor* newsletter.

HOW MUCH DO YOU SPEND PER YEAR ON INVESTMENT RESEARCH RESOURCES? Less than $250 per year

HOW MANY HOURS PER WEEK DO YOU DEVOTE TO YOUR INVESTMENTS AND INVEST-MENT STRATEGIES? 10

WHAT CRITERIA DO YOU USE TO PICK STOCKS/FUNDS? For stocks, companies/prod-ucts I know and understand. Products I use, see other people use/talk about. Established companies, usually with dividend rein-vestment plans (DRIPs). I work in high tech and have a degree in chemistry. Most of our stocks are high tech, pharmaceutical, or based in California. Mutual funds are in areas I can't/don't buy individual stocks, such as international and small-cap stocks. I focus on funds with low expenses and respectable returns.

HOW OFTEN DO YOU BUY INVESTMENTS? Monthly

ON AVERAGE, HOW LONG DO YOU HOLD AN INVESTMENT BEFORE SELLING? 10 years or longer

DO YOU "MARKET TIME"? No

WHAT WERE SOME OF YOUR BIGGEST INVESTING MISTAKES? Experimenting too much and too long with mutual funds. Listening to a boiler room cold-caller with a can't-miss idea. Should have started more DRIPs earlier.

DO YOU INVEST IN WHAT YOU KNOW? Yes

HAVE YOU EVER FOLLOWED A HOT TIP? Yes. It did not pay off for me.

HOW WOULD YOU BEST DESCRIBE YOUR INVESTMENT APPROACH? Invest a little bit, regularly, for a long time. Invest in things you know and trust. Don't be greedy. Invest in things you use or see used.

DO YOU THINK IT IS POSSIBLE TO BEAT THE MARKET ON A CONSISTENT BASIS? Yes

WHAT MADE YOU THINK YOU COULD BE A SUCCESSFUL INVESTOR? I didn't. I'm a reasonably bright person. I knew I wouldn't screw up.

WHAT DO YOU THINK ARE SOME OF THE GREATEST MYTHS ABOUT INVESTING? It's quick, easy, and painless. You need expert help. You can catch up. The Internet is filled with good, sound ideas.

WHAT IS YOUR GREATEST FEAR AS AN INVESTOR? The market will correct and not come back for a long, long time.

WHAT IS THE BIGGEST BENEFIT OF HAVING A 7-FIGURE PORTFOLIO? Credit is not a problem. Buying a house, refinancing a loan . . . all as easy as possible.

DOES YOUR EMPLOYER OFFER A 401(K) PLAN? Yes. I invest the maximum.

DO YOU HAVE ANY FINAL THOUGHTS? Be smart, be patient, don't be greedy. If it sounds too good to be true, it probably is. Stay away from things you don't know. Don't listen to people you don't know, especially if they have something you have to buy right now for a quick huge profit.

5

BUY ONLY STOCKS AND
STOCK MUTUAL FUNDS

*Being in bonds and certificates of deposit is risky because
one's money loses value over time.*

—SANDRA BALLY, VIRGINIA,
$4.6 MILLION INVESTMENT PORTFOLIO

STEP 3: BUY ONLY STOCKS AND STOCK MUTUAL FUNDS.
FORGET ABOUT ASSET ALLOCATION.

You *get* rich buying stocks. You *stay* rich buying bonds.

It's as simple as that.

If you want to grow your money over time, stocks are the only
game in town. Don't waste your time on gold or options or futures
or hog bellies or corporate bonds or certificates of deposit or passbook savings accounts or money-market accounts or rare coins or
stamps or Picassos or baseball cards or ostrich farms or collectibles.

Buy stocks.

LONG-TERM PERFORMANCE OF STOCKS

Stocks, given enough time to grow, provide huge returns for investors. Jeremy Siegel, in his fine book, *Stocks for the Long Run*

(McGraw-Hill), provides the following example of the long-term potential of stock investing:

> $1 invested in stocks in 1802 would have been worth nearly **$7.5 million** at the end of 1997.

Granted, none of us has a 195-year holding period. You don't have to hold stocks for that long to get a nice bang for your buck. For example, for the ten-year period ended December 1998, $1,000 invested in large-company stocks became $5,780, a 478 percent gain.

Since 1926, stocks have returned, on average, 11.2 percent per year. During that same time, government bonds have returned an average of 5.3 percent per year.

That performance gap of nearly six percentage points per year (11.2 percent per year for stocks versus 5.3 percent for bonds) may not seem like much.

In fact, however, it's huge.

For example, $1.00 invested in the S&P 500 index at the end of 1925 grew to $2,350 by the end of 1998. That's what 11 percent per year does to your money over seventy-three years—$1,000 into $2.35 *million.*

If you had your money in bonds for that seventy-three-year period, $1.00 would have become $44. In other words, 5 percent per year for seventy-three years turns $1,000 into $44,000 in 1998.

Hmmm. $2.35 million (stocks) versus $44,000 (long-term government bonds).

Which would you rather have?

11 PERCENT WILL DO NICELY

Keep in mind that 11 percent is the market's long-run average annual return since 1926. Stocks periodically do better than 11 percent. A lot better. From 1996 through 1998, for example, stocks (as measured by the S&P 500) rose roughly 30 percent per year. To show you how powerful 30 percent per year returns are, consider this: If you entered 1996 with $200,000 in stocks, you finished 1998 with $439,000. In three years, you would have more than doubled your money, without putting another penny into the market.

Obviously, you cannot rely on such brief market periods to extrapolate the future. Clearly the last three years have been an aberration. Do I hope they continue? You bet. But I'm not banking on it. You shouldn't either. Run from any broker or financial adviser who promises 20 percent annual returns going forward. You will be assuming a huge level of risk to try to capture such high expected returns.

Fortunately, you don't need 20 percent or 30 percent annual returns in stocks to build a seven-figure portfolio. Even if stocks return to more traditional annual returns of 11 percent, that 11 percent annual return will be adequate for you to achieve seven figures.

RULE OF 72

I find the Rule of 72 useful when comparing expected returns between stocks and other investments. The Rule of 72 says that in order to find out how many years it takes your money to double in a particular investment, choose a rate of return and divide it into 72.

For example, if the long-run average annual return of stocks is 11 percent, the Rule of 72 means that, on average, stock returns double every 6.54 years (72 divided by 11). If the long-run average return on bonds is 5 percent per year, then bonds double every 14.4 years (72 divided by 5).

Let's see what happens to a $10,000 investment, over 26 years, earning 11 percent per year. That $10,000 will double nearly four times (26 divided by 6.54). Thus, $10,000 becomes $20,000 becomes $40,000 becomes $80,000 becomes approximately $151,000.

Now let's look at bonds. Since bonds return, on average, 5 percent per year, the value of the bond doubles nearly twice in 28 years. That means $10,000 becomes $36,000 at the end of 26 years.

Which would you rather own—stocks or bonds?

Moral of the story: Your money grows best by investing heavily in stocks.

WHAT ABOUT RISK?

But, some of you might ask, aren't stocks riskier than bonds?

I'll answer that question with a question: What do you mean by risk?

Do you mean the risk associated with the volatility of investment returns?

Do you mean the risk that your money won't grow enough to offset the rising cost of living?

Do you mean the risk that the market and your individual investments will tank?

Do you mean the risk that the "safe" investments you buy will kill you because of opportunity costs?

Risk means different things to different people. I asked our everyday millionaires what risk means to them. Here are some responses:

- *Buying bonds where return is so small that inflation and taxes eat up all return.*
- *Future is unknown—but more risk in not investing.*
- *Risk means a stock with a high price/earnings ratio that is being bid up on a purely speculative basis.*

- *Risk means you can lose your money.*
- *Can you afford to lose everything if the investment turns sour?*
- *Being a trader is risky, but buying and holding is not.*
- *There is risk the sun won't rise tomorrow, but I don't refuse to buy groceries on that basis. If your time frame is thirty or forty years, history indicates you will not suffer from a depreciation in capital in the long term.*
- *Risk is playing for big profits in a short time. Risk at my age equals greed.* (This millionaire investor is sixty-four years old.)
- *Risk is not investing at all and losing ground to inflation.*
- *Risk is not achieving my goals.*

Perhaps the most interesting response came from Bud Teller. Bud, sixty-two, has an investment portfolio worth $2.2 million. What is risk to Bud? One word.

Opportunity.

I like Bud's definition because he understands a key principle of investing. Risk is not necessarily a four-letter word. In fact, you won't achieve a seven-figure portfolio without taking risks. Why? Because risk and return are joined at the hip. You cannot have higher expected returns without assuming a higher level of risk.

I'm going to repeat that statement since it is a concept lost on most investors.

You cannot have higher expected returns without assuming a higher level of risk.

What that means is that if you invest strictly in risk-free investments, such as passbook savings accounts or CDs at your local bank, you'll never achieve the expected returns of stocks. It cannot be done. Period.

Likewise, if your broker promises an annual return of, say, 20 percent on your investment, rest assured that you are going to be assuming an extremely high level of risk to try to capture that 20 percent.

VOLATILITY OF RETURNS

In investment circles, risk means volatility of returns. In other words, riskier investments experience larger swings in annual returns.

If you define risk in terms of volatility, then yes—stocks are riskier than bonds.

So what?

To build your seven-figure portfolio, you'll likely be investing for at least the next twenty to thirty years. Volatility is a measure of short-term risk. Who knows how investments will behave today, tomorrow, a week from now, a month from now, a year from now. The shorter the time frame, the more random the likely returns. Buying and holding stocks for one year is risky. Who knows how the market will behave in a one-year time frame?

According to Siegel, stocks have risen as much as 66.6 percent and fallen nearly 39 percent over any given year. That's a huge spread in potential returns. That's *risk*.

When you lengthen holding periods, however, that spread reduces. For ten-year holding periods, stocks have risen nearly 17 percent and fallen 4 percent. For twenty-year holding periods, stocks have risen nearly 13 percent on the high end and 1 percent on the low end. These numbers mean that for any twenty-year holding period since 1802, the worst stocks have performed is a positive 1 percent. If you look at thirty-year holding periods, stocks have risen roughly 11 percent at the peak and nearly 3 percent at the bottom. In other words, there has never been a twenty- or thirty-year period in the market since 1802 when stocks did not provide a positive return.

The longer your holding period, the less volatile your returns. Said another way, the longer your holding period, the less risky it is to own stocks.

Interestingly, while bonds are usually considered "safer" investments because of their lower volatility of returns, a funny thing happens when you extend holding periods. Indeed, while there has never been a thirty-year period where stocks produced negative returns, the same cannot be said for bonds or Treasury bills.

This brings up an interesting, and increasingly controversial, question: For long holding periods, are bonds less risky than stocks?

James Glassman and Kevin Hassett, in their book *Dow 36,000* (Times Books), take the stance that over long periods of time, stocks are actually *safer* than bonds.

Siegel, a professor at the Wharton School of the University of Pennsylvania, makes a compelling case for owning stocks rather than bonds if you hold stocks for a long period of time. Siegel writes that "for 10-year horizons, stocks beat bonds and bills about 80 percent of the time; for 20-year horizons, it is over 90 percent of the time; and over 30-year horizons, it is virtually 100 percent of the time. The last 30-year period in which bonds beat stocks ended in 1861, at the onset of the U.S. Civil War."

If your investment time horizon is twenty years or more—and it will have to be if you want to achieve a seven-figure portfolio—there's only one investment vehicle.

Stocks.

INFLATION RISK

What is the value of money? Interesting question, isn't it. Actually, the only value of money is what it buys. Money provides purchasing power.

Inflation is an erosion of purchasing power. Inflation means a dollar buys less tomorrow than it does today.

Investors often equate risk with loss of principal. You buy a stock at $45 per share. It drops to $41. You've just lost (at least on paper) $4.00 per share.

Inflation is much sneakier, but no less lethal to investors. You

IRWIN UNDERSTANDS THE POWER OF STOCKS

IRWIN WAYNE URAN, 71, DOESN'T OWN A BIG HOME. IN FACT, he doesn't own any home at all. He lives in a Best Western motel in Leesburg, Virginia. And he doesn't wear Armani. Denim is his fabric of choice. And he doesn't own a Jaguar or Rolls-Royce. He doesn't own any car. He prefers the bus. That's why Leesburg residents were surprised when Irwin gave the town a check for $1 million.

Was Irwin giving away his life savings? Hardly. According to Irwin, he's worth about *$400 million*. This everyday millionaire investor, who has given away more than $30 million since 1991, made his money in the stock market by investing in small corporations and reaping benefits as the companies grew. For example, when Guardsman Products, Inc., a maker of furniture polish, was bought out in 1996, Irwin came away with $70 million.

Few people in town even realized there was a multimillionaire in their midst. "He always said he was wealthy, but I had no idea he had that kind of money," said Ken Meyer, owner of a bagel shop next to the Best Western where Uran has lived with his dog. "He always asked for a senior citizen discount on his sandwich."

SOURCE: ANNE GEARAN,
ASSOCIATED PRESS/*AKRON BEACON JOURNAL*, MAY 22, 1997

buy a stock at $45. It rises to $46 over a four-year period. Congratulations, you have a gain of $1 per share. But wait. Inflation has eroded the purchasing power of that dollar. Your "real" gain is more like $0.85 per share. Where did the other 15 cents go? It disappeared in "lost" purchasing power.

The stealth nature of inflation makes it especially dangerous. You don't see the losses. You may be thinking you're doing okay since your portfolio is increasing each year. But unless your investments are outpacing inflation, you are losing.

The following example shows just how mean an animal inflation is. Assuming inflation of just 3 percent per year, what you can buy today for $80,000 will cost you $200,000 30 years from now.

A lot of investors have forgotten about the evils of inflation in recent years because it has been rather benign. That hasn't always been the case. There have been plenty of periods in our nation's economic history when inflation exceeded 3 percent per year. At 5 percent per year, inflation doubles your cost of living every 14.5 years. Said another way, an inflation rate of 5 percent per year means that $41,000 in today's dollars is equal to nearly $180,000 thirty years from now.

That's what makes inflation so dangerous. You have a nice chunk of money in your portfolio. You eliminate "risky" investments (i.e., stocks) by moving into "safe" (i.e., bonds) investments. You've decided, in effect, to tread water with your investments. The problem is that you don't tread water. You actually sink little by little each year.

As an investor, inflation has big implications on how you run your portfolio. Just because you have, say, $200,000 today, you can't rest on your laurels. You have to keep growing your money each year.

What's the best way to combat inflation risk?

Once again, the answer is stocks.

"In the long run, stocks are extremely good hedges against inflation, while bonds are not," says Professor Siegel.

One reason stocks are better at outpacing inflation is that common stock dividends are not fixed, unlike bond coupon rates. You buy a 7 percent yielding bond, you receive $70 per year for every $1,000 bond. If inflation jumps from 3 percent to 5 percent, you'll still receive only $70 in interest for every bond you own. And if it is a twenty- or thirty-year bond, you'll receive that same $70 for twenty or thirty years. With stocks, the annual dividend can increase. Since dividend yield is an important component of a stock's annual return, rising dividends provide some hedge against inflation over the long term.

For example, let's say you pick a stock with an annual dividend of 50 cents per share. If you own 100 shares of the stock, your annual dividend income is $50. If the company grows that dividend at 5 percent per year over thirty years, that 50-cent dividend becomes a $2.16 per share dividend.

Keep in mind that we're talking about stocks as a long-term inflation hedge—twenty or thirty years. In the short term, say a year or two, stocks are a lousy inflation hedge. So are bonds and Treasury bills.

THE PERILS OF ASSET ALLOCATION

Should you own any investment other than stocks? If you invest for the long term, in most cases, I'd answer that with a "no."

Even if an individual is forty or fifty?

Again, "no" and "no."

I know that conventional wisdom says that investors should allocate their assets across a variety of securities—stocks, bonds, money-market investments, etc. You allocate across assets, says conventional wisdom, in order to diversify. You diversify because you don't know which asset class (stocks, bonds, etc.) will be doing well at any particular point in time.

Diversification is a noble and valid concept. The aim of diversification is to reduce risk. Remember, however, that a reduction in risk also reduces expected returns.

I'm not a big fan of asset allocation to reduce risk. I would rather reduce risk by lengthening my investment time horizon. *Time* diversification, if you will. In that way, I remain invested in securities (i.e., stocks) that have the probability of highest returns over the long term.

My position on asset allocation is not exactly textbook. Your financial planner would probably say I'm nuts. If that's the case, then many of the millionaire investors I surveyed are nuts, too. Few own a significant amount of bonds or bond mutual funds. And the ones who do have big bond positions are in their sixties and seventies and own bonds to *preserve* the wealth created by owning stocks.

Millionaire investors' attitudes toward bond investments are best capsulated by Sandra Bally, an attorney whose quote graces the beginning of this chapter. Sandra, who is fifty-nine years old, began investing at age thirteen. Today, after forty-six years of investing, Sandra has more than $4.6 million in her investment portfolio.

In Sandra's portfolio you'll find such stocks as Berkshire Hathaway, American Home Products, Exxon, IBM. You'll find such growth mutual funds as Fidelity Magellan, Janus Twenty, and Neuberger & Berman Partners.

You'll find no bonds.

Sandra and other everyday millionaires understand another type of investment risk—opportunity risk. Investing in bonds means you are forgoing better expected returns elsewhere.

The esteemed economist and market watcher James Lorie was a professor of mine at the University of Chicago. Professor Lorie said something during one of our classes that has always stuck with me. I was in the last class Professor Lorie taught at University of Chicago's business school before he retired. He must have been in his late sixties or early seventies at the time. He mentioned that he was just starting to shift money out of stocks and into bonds. In fact, prior to this shift, he had always owned stocks *on margin*. Buying stocks on margin means he bought stocks with borrowed money in hopes that the stock returns would exceed the interest on the borrowed funds.

Now here is a man, at an age when most people are afraid to own any stocks, who not only bought stocks exclusively, but also bought them *on margin*. Crazy, right?

Actually, his logic made perfect sense. He believed that, since stock prices trend higher over time, you are better off playing the percentages and owning stocks and even leveraging the upside probabilities via margin.

Professor Siegel concurs with Professor Lorie. In his book, *Stocks for the Long Run,* Siegel provides a series of portfolio allocations based on two factors: holding period and risk tolerance. For moderate-risk investors who are willing to hold investments for thirty years, Siegel advises a portfolio allocation of *112.9 percent* of stocks. (Any percentage above 100 percent means using borrowed funds to buy stocks.) For risk-taking investors with thirty-year holding periods, Siegel advises a portfolio allocation of *131.5 percent* stocks.

Now I'm not saying that investors should buy stocks on margin. I am saying that if you have a long investment time horizon, you should play the percentages and buy stocks and only stocks.

ALLOCATE ACROSS STOCK INVESTMENTS

One allocation strategy that makes sense for building wealth is to allocate investments across different *stock* groups. Large stocks. Small stocks. Mid-sized stocks. International stocks. Speculative stocks. Value stocks. Growth stocks. Income stocks.

I'll give you an example of allocating investments across different stock groups. In my 401(k) program, I have roughly 50 percent invested in large-company stocks. These are stocks that have market capitalizations (market capitalization is stock price times the number of shares outstanding) of more than $10 billion. I have about 25 percent in international stocks. I have the remainder split between small- and mid-sized caps.

Why don't I have all of my money in a fund that mimics the S&P 500? Actually, some professionals make a case that is exactly what I should do. I take a slightly different approach. While I anchor my portfolio with large stocks, I try to add value at the margin with investments in other stock sectors. I do this because, historically, long holding periods have shown that small-company and international stocks can post big gains.

According to Ibbotson Associates, a Chicago-based research company, $1,000 invested in large-company stocks at the end of 1925 grew to $2.35 million at the end of 1998. Pretty impressive, right? Now check out these numbers for small-company stocks: $1,000 at the end of 1925 became *$5.12 million* at the end of 1998.

What is interesting about these two results is that small-company stocks had an average annual return of 12.4 percent. That's only 1.2 percentage points greater than large-company stocks. Yet, that 1.2 percent, over seventy-three years, accounted for more than doubling in the investment.

Moral of the story: Small improvements in annual portfolio performance have huge repercussions for long-term performance.

INTERNATIONAL STOCKS

Non-U.S. companies account for over 60 percent of the world's stock-market size. That share is likely to exceed 70 percent within the next ten years. To exclude overseas investment is to exclude a lot of the world's potential growth.

To exclude overseas investments is also to exclude an investment group that has produced stellar returns for nearly three decades. According to Professor Siegel, the average annual compound capitalization-weighted dollar return on all foreign markets has been almost 13 percent per year from January 1970 through June 1997. Granted, this return has been accompanied by high volatility. As is the case with U.S. equities, investors can limit the impact of short-term volatility in global markets by lengthening their holding periods. At a minimum, all investors should have at least 10 percent of their assets in overseas equities.

BUYING STOCKS VIA DRIPS

If you should own stocks and nothing but stocks in a portfolio, how should you go about buying them? Of course, stockbrokers provide one way to buy stocks. With the advent of online brokers (see Chapter 3), it's never been cheaper to buy stock with a broker. There's an even cheaper way to buy stocks, however, and it requires no broker.

Some of you are probably familiar with my work in the field of dividend reinvestment plans (DRIPs). Indeed, I have spent a large part of the last eight years of my working life singing the praises of these investment programs. Why? Because DRIPs are the best investment vehicle ever for bringing Wall Street to Main Street. DRIPs allow *any* investor to buy quality stocks in amounts compatible with his or her pocketbook.

What are DRIPs? These are programs, offered by approximately 1,100 publicly traded companies, that allow investors to buy stock directly from the company, *without a broker.* Investors buy stock from companies in two ways. First, instead of receiving dividend checks, investors have the company reinvest dividends on their behalf to purchase additional shares. Second, most DRIPs permit investors to send money directly to the company to buy additional shares. In many cases, these "optional cash payments" may be as little as $10 or $50. If you have deeper pockets, most DRIPs permit investments of up to $100,000 or more per year.

DRIPs are an extremely friendly way for investors with just a little money to buy blue-chip stocks. Indeed, the minimum investment in Coca-Cola's DRIP, for example, is just $10. For nearly all DRIP programs, the minimums are rarely above $100 per investment.

DRIPs offer four main benefits for investors:

- Many DRIPs charge no fees to purchase shares in their plans, and DRIPs that do charge fees usually have fees that are much lower than even the lowest online brokerage firm.
- In more than 8 percent of all DRIP plans, you can buy stock at a *discount* to the market price. These discounts are usually in the 3 percent to 5 percent range. I don't know of any other investment that allows investors to buy stock at 95 cents or 97 cents on the dollar. It's instant profit. You're probably wondering why companies sell shares at a discount. Companies use DRIP discounts to lure investors to their plans. Firms can sell shares at a discount to individual investors and still raise money more cheaply than if they had to hire an investment bank to sell its stock.
- DRIPs allow investors to buy both full and fractional shares of stock. If, for example, your $10 investment isn't enough to buy a full share of stock, you buy a fractional share, and that fractional share is entitled to a fractional part of the dividend. In short, DRIPs allow you to buy high-priced stocks on the installment plan, a little bit at a time.
- DRIPs offer a lot of flexibility for any investor to mold an investment program in high-quality stocks based on his or her financial situation. If you have a lot of money, you can invest a lot. If you have a little money, you can invest a little. If you don't have any money in a given month, you are not obligated to invest.

There are two types of DRIPs. The first type is the traditional DRIP, which requires investors to already be a shareholder of the company in order to participate in the plan. The share requirement in most traditional DRIPs is just one share. Coca-Cola, for example, requires that you own at least one share of Coca-Cola stock in order to enroll in the plan, and that share must be registered in your own name, not the broker name (also known as "street" name).

Obviously, DRIPs that require prior share ownership present the problem of how to get that first share. Brokerage firms offer one avenue for getting the first share. However, newcomers to investing may not have a broker or may feel uncomfortable choosing one.

Fortunately, a number of companies are taking their DRIPs to the next level by allowing individuals to buy even their *initial* shares directly. These "DRIPs on steroids" are often referred to as "direct-purchase plans." I call them "No-Load Stocks" because you buy directly, without a broker, much the same way you buy a no-load mutual fund. To participate in a direct-purchase plan, you'll need to obtain the enrollment information and a plan prospectus (the prospectus provides all of the details of the plan). This material is available by calling the company or downloading the information off the company's Web site. The minimum initial investment in more than half of the approximately 600 direct-purchase plans now available is $250 or less. Once you've made the initial investment, subsequent investments can be made with as little as $50 or $100 in most plans.

In addition to buying your initial shares directly, direct-purchase plans provide a number of other features common with no-load mutual funds. For example, most direct-purchase plans permit investors to invest via automatic monthly debit of their bank account. These plans are excellent for helping to maintain a regular investment program. Many direct-purchase plans have IRA (Individual Retirement Account) options built directly into the plans. For example, **Exxon Mobil** (800-252-1800) allows investors to buy even initial shares directly from the company. Minimum initial investment is just $250, and subsequent investments may be as little as $50. Exxon Mobil permits investment via automatic electronic debit of your bank account. Furthermore, Exxon Mobil has an IRA option built into its plan. In other words, you can invest directly with Exxon Mobil, without a broker and without any purchase fees, and earmark those investments for an IRA that Exxon Mobil administers for you. Exxon Mobil charges a small annual fee to administer the IRA, but some direct-purchase plans, such as **Philadelphia Suburban** (800-774-4117), have *no-fee* IRAs as part of their direct-purchase plans. A growing number of direct-purchase plans allow you to sell your shares over the phone. Telephone redemption is a big departure from traditional DRIPs, which require you to submit your sell instructions in writing.

Many quality, blue-chip stocks offer direct-purchase plans. Indeed, thirteen of the thirty stocks that make up the Dow Jones Industrial Average offer direct-purchase plans for first-time buyers:

American Express
Caterpillar
Disney (Walt)
Eastman Kodak
Exxon Mobil
General Electric
Home Depot
International Business Machines
McDonald's
Merck
Procter & Gamble
SBC Communications
Wal-Mart Stores

Other well-known companies with No-Load Stock programs include **Pfizer, Walgreen, Equifax, BellSouth, McGraw-Hill, Duke Energy, Lucent Technologies,** and **Quaker Oats.**

One of the more interesting developments in the direct-purchase world is the advent of foreign companies that permit U.S. investors to buy stock directly from the company. These foreign companies trade on U.S. stock exchanges. Familiar names of foreign companies that allow direct investment include **Sony, BP Amoco, DaimlerChrysler,** and **British Airways.**

Before you invest in DRIPs, it's important to know the plans' shortcomings:

- You won't have the precision over the buy and sell price that you have through a broker. Most DRIPs buy stock either once a week or once a month. If you like a stock's price today, it could be higher or lower by the time the shares are purchased for you in the plan. I don't consider this that big of a deal since I hold DRIPs for a long time. However, if you want exact control over the buy and sell price, these plans may not be for you.
- If you invest in, say, five different DRIPs, you will receive account statements from each company. These statements provide all the information you need for tracking your shares for tax purposes. However, there is no such thing as a single consolidated statement in the DRIP world.
- Some DRIPs have been implementing fees in recent years. These fees may include a one-time enrollment fee of $5.00 to $15 and per-transaction fees of $1.00 to $10. Make sure you know all of the details of the plan, including fees, before investing. The plan prospectus provides information on fees.

For many of our millionaire investors, DRIPs and direct-purchase plans were their passport to a seven-figure portfolio. "I could have never owned so many great companies or so many shares without the help of DRIP investing," says Shelley Weaver. Shelley, seventy-five, lives with her husband of fifty years in South Carolina. Among the biggest holdings in Shelley's $1.8 million portfolio are General Electric, Merck, SBC Communications, and Lucent

Technologies. All of these stocks allow investors to buy even their initial shares directly.

DRIPs and direct-purchase plans have had a big impact on my investment program. I currently participate in the DRIP/Direct-Purchase Plans of the following companies:

AT&T
Block (H&R)
Bristol-Myers Squibb
CNH Global NV
Equifax
Exxon Mobil
Lucent Technologies
McDonald's
Motorola
New Holland NV
Paychex
PepsiCo
Popular
Procter & Gamble
Regions Financial
Reuters
Tricon Global
Walgreen

The Appendix in the back of the book provides a complete list of all U.S. and foreign direct-purchase plans. Each company listing includes the minimum initial investment and toll-free number to obtain the necessary enrollment information. Be sure you read the plan brochure before investing so you understand all the details of the plan.

A WORD OF WARNING

The approach laid out in this chapter—invest in stocks and only stocks (or stock mutual funds)—works only if you obey the following rules:

- You must stay invested in stocks continuously for a long time, preferably twenty years or more. Long holding periods reduce the risk of owning stocks. If you plan on owning stocks for only a few months or even a few years—perhaps you are saving for a down payment on a house that you'd like to purchase in the next two years—an all-stock approach could be disastrous.

- You must buy during market declines. Over the next twenty or thirty years, stocks will get murdered periodically. Indeed, stocks could track downward for one year. They could stagnate for five years. Although unlikely, they could lose value over a ten-year stretch. To maximize the power of an all-stock strategy, you must buy during down markets as well as good markets. That's how you accumulate enough shares to win big when the market's uptrend returns.

- Remember—you buy stocks to *get* rich. Let's take an investor who is fifty and has $3 million in stocks. Should this person's portfolio be exclusively stocks? Probably not. He or she is *already* rich. This person should be thinking as much about *staying* rich as becoming richer. Only you know how much money will make you "rich." Once you reach that point, however, you'll want to protect your wealth, regardless of your age. You do this by expanding the types of assets you hold to include bonds and cash. If you're someone who wants to protect his or her wealth (or merely someone who doesn't have the stomach for an all-stock portfolio), a fairly conservative rule of thumb for asset allocation is the following: Subtract your age from 110, and that is the percentage of assets that you should have in stocks. The remainder should be in bonds and cash. According to this rule, if you're fifty-eight years old, you should have 52 percent of your investments in stock and 48 percent in bonds and cash.

CONCLUSION

You will not build a seven-figure investment portfolio without owning stocks for a long time. Fortunately, you don't need anything else but stocks and time to get rich. So why doesn't everyone buy and hold stocks? Because most people don't have the patience to buy and hold stocks for twenty or thirty years. They panic and sell at every little market blip. Or they sell because they made a little profit. Or they pull money out of stocks to buy a bigger house or a fancier car.

It really is that simple—buy nothing but stocks and hold for twenty or thirty years. Of course, it's one thing to say invest solely in stocks; it's another to know *what* stocks to buy. We'll discuss stock selection in the next chapter and examine the stocks most responsible for creating our everyday millionaires. For now, just remember what I said at the beginning of this chapter:

You get rich buying stocks. You stay rich buying bonds.

The everyday millionaire profiled in this chapter is Sandra Bally. I introduced Sandra earlier in this chapter. She's the attorney with an investment portfolio of $4.6 million—all stocks and no bonds. Sandra's sizable income has been a big help in building a seven-figure portfolio. But there are plenty of people with big incomes who fail to create seven-figure portfolios.

Sandra offers a good example for would-be millionaires in many respects:

- She started investing early (age thirteen). "I saw my father and two aunts investing as I was growing up, so I was encouraged to save," says Sandra. "I saved aggressively up to ninety percent of my salary at times. I taught school in 1965–66 and earned $6,000. I saved $3,000. In the Peace Corps, I earned $50 per month. I saved $20. Peace Corps found out and cut my salary to $30 a month. I still saved. Nothing could stop me. Once I saw the savings grow, there was no stopping me."
- Sandra invested in quality stocks, Exxon, Unilever, IBM.
- She maximized her employer's 401(k) plan.

Given her saving habits and great head start, Sandra is well on her way to a $10 million portfolio before her seventieth birthday.

"It feels incredible to walk down the street and know you can buy anything you want," says Sandra when asked what she likes about having a seven-figure portfolio. "To go to Rome for a week and not have to watch the price of every meal is a joy. To provide money for a scholarship at my old college, to help a young person in the Philippines go to school, to pay for medical treatment without depending on insurance, to be free to work or not to work, those are some of the benefits."

NAME: Sandra Bally
AGE: 59
HOME: Virginia
MARITAL STATUS: Married. Never divorced.
CHILDREN: 0
EDUCATION: College (advanced degree) graduate
OCCUPATION: Lawyer
CURRENT INCOME: $228,000
HOW MANY DIFFERENT JOBS SINCE AGE 25? 10
HOW LONG HAVE YOU WORKED AT YOUR CURRENT EMPLOYER? 21 years
HOW IMPORTANT WERE YOUR PARENTS IN DEVELOPING YOUR DISCIPLINE AND EXPERTISE IN INVESTING? Very important

HOW MANY YEARS HAVE YOU BEEN INVESTING? 46

WHAT IS THE SIZE OF YOUR ENTIRE INVESTMENT PORTFOLIO? $4.6 million

WHAT IS THE BREAKDOWN OF THESE ASSETS? Pension plan (43 percent), mutual funds (13 percent), stocks (30 percent), IRA/Keogh (14 percent)

HOW MANY INDIVIDUAL STOCKS DO YOU OWN? 35

NAME YOUR FIVE LARGEST HOLDINGS: Berkshire Hathaway, American Home Products, Exxon, Unilever NV, IBM

HOW MANY INDIVIDUAL MUTUAL FUNDS DO YOU HAVE? 16

WHAT ARE YOUR LARGEST FUND HOLDINGS? Fidelity Magellan, Janus Twenty, CGM Capital Development, Neuberger Berman Partners, Templeton World

HOW MANY INDIVIDUAL BONDS DO YOU OWN? 0

HAVE YOU EVER BOUGHT STOCK/INDEX OPTIONS? Yes

HAVE YOU EVER BOUGHT STOCK/INDEX FUTURES? No

DO YOU OWN GOLD OR PRECIOUS METALS? Yes

HAVE YOU EVER SOLD STOCK SHORT? No

DO YOU RECEIVE ADVICE ON YOUR INVESTMENTS FROM AN OUTSIDE SOURCE? No

DID YOU HAVE SPECIFIC INVESTMENT GOALS WHEN YOU STARTED INVESTING? Yes. I wanted to save as much as possible. I saw my father buying stocks and saving, and he set an example for me.

WHAT ARE THE PLANS FOR YOUR ESTATE? My trust is to be divided among my 4 sisters and brothers. My pension plan and IRAs go to my husband. I plan to leave/give some to charity, but it is not in my will and trust presently. Or I may give it away and spend it during my lifetime so I can see where it goes and enjoy the fruits of my labor. I have no children so I have no specific responsibility to anyone other than to my husband.

WHERE DID YOU GET THE MONEY TO START INVESTING? I began working when I was 13. My father bought me some shares of IBM when I was young and some shares of Selected American Shares. He also bought me shares of a bank he started. I held on, bought more, and eventually the bank was bought by the Bank of Montreal.

HAVE YOU INHERITED WHAT YOU THOUGHT WAS A LARGE AMOUNT OF MONEY? Yes.

WAS THIS INHERITANCE INSTRUMENTAL IN PROVIDING THE CAPITAL TO START AN IN-
VESTMENT PROGRAM? No.

HOW DID YOU EDUCATE YOURSELF ABOUT INVESTING? I have always found it fascinating and fun. I have gone to seminars and conferences sponsored by the American Association of Individual Investors (AAII). I read several newspapers daily, books, go to lectures, listen and learn. I know about stocks. I do not bother with bonds, futures, insurance, annuities, and some other investment vehicles. I do not use a broker because I want to do it myself. Then I have only myself to congratulate or to blame.

DID YOU HAVE ANY SPECIAL EXPERTISE IN INVESTING WHEN YOU STARTED? I learned from my father about stocks. I have seen stocks grow over my lifetime, and I believe very strongly in the market. I am optimistic. If the market drops, I say that all the stocks are on sale.

HOW MUCH DO YOU SPEND PER YEAR ON INVESTMENT RESEARCH RESOURCES? $501 to $1,000

HOW MANY HOURS PER WEEK DO YOU DEVOTE TO YOUR INVESTMENTS AND INVESTMENT STRATEGIES? 5

WHAT CRITERIA DO YOU USE TO PICK STOCKS/FUNDS? Each stock was bought for a different reason. When British Air, Telephone, Steel, Gas, etc., went public, I bought them because I had lived several years in England and knew the companies there. I drink Pepsi; I bought the stock. I bought Boeing because I travel a lot. If a stock is doing well, I buy much more. I reinvest almost all the dividends and capital gains.

ON AVERAGE, HOW LONG DO YOU HOLD AN INVESTMENT BEFORE SELLING? 10 years or longer

DO YOU "MARKET TIME"? IN OTHER WORDS, DO YOU TRY TO TIME PURCHASE/SALE OF INVESTMENTS BASED ON YOUR EXPECTATIONS FOR MARKET MOVEMENTS AND/OR MOVEMENTS IN THE INDIVIDUAL STOCKS? No

WHAT HAVE BEEN YOUR 3 BEST-PERFORMING STOCKS? Berkshire Hathaway, American Home Products, Exxon

WHAT HAVE BEEN YOUR 3 WORST-PERFORMING STOCKS? Mobil Unicom, Continental Bank, and Trafalgar Group

HAVE YOU EVER FOLLOWED A HOT TIP? Yes. It did not pay off.

HOW WOULD YOU BEST DESCRIBE YOUR INVESTMENT APPROACH? Conservative, blue chip, buy and hold, don't sell when the market goes down. On October 1, 1987, I became a millionaire when my stocks were worth $1,023,150. On December 21, 1987, my stocks were worth $839,000. I stayed in the market and by November 1994, my stocks were worth $2 million. Even if the market makes a correction, it will eventually go back up. One should save enough so that a 20 percent correction makes no difference in one's lifestyle.

DO YOU FEEL INDIVIDUAL INVESTORS HAVE ANY ADVANTAGES IN THE INVESTMENT PROCESS? Yes. I can control what I buy and sell. I am not pressured to show results each quarter. I can keep a stock for many years.

WHAT MADE YOU THINK YOU COULD BE A SUCCESSFUL INVESTOR? I have a lot of discipline. If I lose, I don't panic. I am willing to do any kind of work such as waitress, farm work, law practice. I have worked since I was 13 years old and always saved.

WHAT DO YOU THINK ARE SOME OF THE GREATEST INVESTMENT MYTHS? Some people say that the market is too high and they will not buy. To me, the market is never too high to buy stocks.

IF YOU COULD GIVE ONE PIECE OF ADVICE TO INDIVIDUAL INVESTORS, WHAT WOULD THAT PIECE OF ADVICE BE? If you inherit money, do not spend it. Resolve to invest it, make it grow, and pass it on to the next generation, encouraging them to make it grow and pass it on. I think we are stewards of money that is inherited. It is ours to pass on. We did not earn it as we earned a salary so it is our duty to pass it on. Also, it is necessary to educate the next generation about investing. Few parents teach their children, it is not learned in school. It is up to us who have invested well to teach the next generation that they can also save and invest and be wealthy.

DO YOU INVEST IN A 401(K) PLAN? Yes, I invest the maximum.

IF YOU WOULD, PLEASE SHARE WITH US YOUR FAVORITE INVESTMENT STORY: In

1959, when my sister was 16 years old, she started working as a Bell telephone operator. She got her first paycheck and asked my father what she should do with it. His advice was to use 50 percent to buy stock in the company you work for and the rest is for you. She took his advice, Illinois Bell became AT&T, which split into 7 companies, and you know the rest. She is sitting pretty with all her dividend checks from the Bell companies.

ANY FINAL THOUGHTS? Pay off your house and car as soon as possible or pay cash from the beginning. Pay off credit cards each month. Avoid paying the interest. It is a tremendous waste of good money. Put $2,000 in your IRA on the first day of each year. Reinvest all dividends and capital gains. Buy stocks directly. Buy mutual funds that are no-load. Invest aggressively, much more than 10 percent of monthly gross income. Invest over 50 percent of your income and you will see it grow quickly. Instead of buying more things, enjoy the things you already have. If both husband and wife work, save the entire salary of one or the other. Make the decision to be very wealthy. It is a conscious decision you must make. Marry someone who thinks of money and saving the same as you do.

6

SWING FOR SINGLES

Forget hitting the home run. Concentrate on building a quality portfolio and adding to those positions on a regular basis.

—JACKSON FOGLE, MISSOURI,
$1.2 MILLION INVESTMENT PORTFOLIO

STEP 4: SWING FOR SINGLES. YOU'LL STRIKE OUT FEWER TIMES AND HIT SOME HOME RUNS IN THE PROCESS.

Selecting stocks is scary stuff. There are about 10,000 publicly traded stocks and thousands of mutual funds. A lot of junk is out there just waiting to snatch your hard-earned dollars.

How do you separate the good from the bad?

I'll tell you shortly. But before we discuss how millionaire investors pick stocks and mutual funds, let me underscore the following:

That you invest is much more important than in *what* you invest.

Stated another way, you become a seven-figure investor not because of the stocks you choose, but because you choose to invest in stocks.

Approaching stock picking with this concept in mind frames the stock-selection process in a less intimidating way. You don't need to hit a home run in order to get to seven figures. Singles will do just fine. Singles and time.

In fact, I would argue that hitting a quick home run may do you more harm than good over the long term. Indeed, I would rather have a stock that rises 15 percent per year than a stock that jumps 80 percent after three months. I'm crazy, right? I don't think so. The stock that jumps 80 percent in three months forces you to make a decision, and that decision is usually to sell. After all, who wants to lose an 80 percent profit in three months. That's a home run, right? The problem is that you may be selling a stock that ultimately rises 500 percent or 1,000 percent. Oh sure, you can try to play the trading game and buy back the stock at a lower price. But what if the stock never declines? Or when it declines, you don't buy because you think it will decline even more?

Give me a stock that rises 15 percent per year, year after year after year. A stock that rises 15 percent per year doesn't force me to make a bad decision. It's an easy hold. A stock rising 15 percent per year doubles every five years or so. Over twenty-five years, a stock that rises 15 percent per year doubles roughly five times. That means a $10,000 investment becomes $330,000.

That's how you get rich hitting singles.

HIT FOR AVERAGE

You might find comfort in knowing that many millionaire investors are not great stock or fund pickers. Most have their share of clunkers in their portfolios. Yet, each of them hit enough singles to get to seven figures.

How do our millionaire investors hit for average?

- Paul Fuller has a five-point system for picking stocks: "1) I need to be able to understand what the company does. 2) The company increased earnings for the last two years. 3) Friends work at the company. 4) Good information on the company is in the magazines I read. 5) Either it is a large company or located in the Northwest." Paul, who lives in the Northwest, has an investment portfolio worth $3 million. Only thirty years old, Paul has been investing since age sixteen and owns such blue chips as General Electric, Merck, BellSouth, Pfizer, and Johnson & Johnson.

- Gil Palmer has a very detailed approach to stock selection: "A consistent growth rate of greater than fifteen percent per year. A price-earnings ratio at one-to-three-year low. Rising dividend." At age fifty, Gil has an investment portfolio worth $1.5 million. His three best-performing stocks are Lucent Technologies, Computer Associates, and Automatic Data Processing.

- Tim Campbell likes consistent growers, companies that "increase sales every year, increase earnings every year." He also likes "high pretax profit margins, high return on equity, and low debt levels." Tim, fifty-two, has nearly $2 million in his investment portfolio. His largest holdings include Merck, Hewlett-Packard, and Abbott Laboratories.

- Trent Sorenson likes leading companies in their businesses "that have good long-term growth prospects and look favorable in terms of global and demographic trends." Trent, forty-nine, has an investment portfolio worth $1.2 million. His big stock positions include Microsoft, Merck, and Merrill Lynch.

- Sonya Reich likes to buy companies whose products are "useful to society." She also likes companies with rising earnings and good dividend growth. Sonya's $1.1 million portfolio holds such blue chips as AT&T, BP Amoco, Microsoft, GE, and Intel.

- Alex Vick likes companies with a competitive advantage, such as patents. He also likes to buy companies with 15 percent to 20 percent growth, little or no debt, where management owns

shares. Alex, sixty-seven, has a $2 million investment portfo-
lio. Among his largest holdings are IBM, GE, and Intel.

- Cal Stevens is a member of the National Association of
Investors Corp. The NAIC is the umbrella organization for investment clubs in the United States. The NAIC has a very detailed system of stock selection that instills quite a bit of
discipline into the process. Cal picks stocks the NAIC way:
"Companies should have ten years of prior history, a consistent success with increasing sales and earnings, prospects to
grow 15 percent per year, good management based on pretax
profit margins and return on equity, a reasonable price-earnings ratio." Cal, fifty-seven, has been successful using the
NAIC system, as his portfolio totals $1 million. His largest
holdings include Intel and Home Depot.

- For Kendall Farmer to invest in a stock, "I must understand
the company's products and business." Kendall, fifty-two, has
an investment portfolio worth $1.6 million. "The company
must be established and have a proven record. The company
must be the best in its business or command a market segment. There must be a compelling reason for the investment—new product, double-digit earnings growth. I must
also receive confirmation on my idea from at least two of my
information sources." Two of Kendall's best-performing stocks
are Citigroup, the banking concern, and AFLAC, the insurance company.

QUALITY, QUALITY, QUALITY

One common denominator among our millionaire investors is a
focus on quality. A quality company shows its spots in several ways:

- *Quality companies dominate their industries.* The global mar-
ketplace is becoming an increasingly competitive place to do

business. Foreign competition. The Internet. The technological revolution. All of these factors make it doubly difficult for small, undercapitalized companies to compete on a global scale. Size matters, probably more than ever. I know the Internet is helping many smaller companies compete in certain markets, such as retailing. My guess is, however, that the eventual giants of the Internet are not those now dominating it. It will be the big elephants, Wal-Mart, IBM, GE, Disney—companies with the size, scale, financial firepower, and brand power to overtake smaller players in these markets. If you bet on a third- or fourth-tier player in a particular industry making a run at the leaders, you are making a bet with long odds. *Buy the industry leader.* It may not be the sexiest approach, but it's probably going to be the most profitable.

- *Quality companies play in growing markets.* To reach seven figures, you'll invest for at least twenty years. You want your money in industries that will grow consistently during that twenty-year period. Your money won't grow consistently if it's invested in cyclical stocks. Cyclical industries are heavily dependent on the economy for growth. Autos, chemicals, paper, steel—these are all cyclical industries. You can make money in cyclical industries. But it's more of a trading game. That's a much tougher game to play for individual investors. I prefer putting my money into companies in growth industries, where I'm not forced to buy and sell frequently to make money. I can let my stock positions grow in line with the growth of the industry.

- *Quality companies have consistent profit records.* Stock prices follow earnings. Let me repeat that statement. *Stock prices follow earnings.* The relationship between stock prices and earnings can get out of whack in the short term. Over the long haul, however, a rising earnings stream leads to higher stock profits. If you buy that statement—and you should—you should buy stocks with consistently rising earnings streams.

How do you find stocks with rising earnings? It's helpful to look at a company's track record. Past performance is not always indicative of future results. But it's probably the best tool an investor has to gauge the likelihood of future profit increases. If a company has boosted profits every year for the last ten, chances are high that growth will continue.

- *Quality companies have sound financial positions.* You want to own companies that will be around for twenty years or more. One way to assure that a company won't be around is poor finances. You want companies to have strong cash flow and manageable debt. Long-term debt should not be more than 60 percent of total capital. (Total capital is a company's long-term debt plus shareholder equity.) These numbers are available in the firm's financial statement. I'll make an exception to this rule occasionally. Still, a company with strong finances can stay in the game even when business turns south.

- *Quality companies have above-average dividend growth.* Dividends are the cash flows stocks throw off to their owners. Dividends are paid out of a company's earnings. I own stocks that pay dividends. I own stocks that don't pay dividends. All things equal, a stock that pays a dividend is probably a better way to go for long-term investors. Dividends compound over time to provide nice returns. Dividends also provide a hedge against market declines. Actually, what truly matters is not so much the absolute dividend but the ability for the dividend to grow over time. If I'm choosing between a company with a big dividend but little dividend-growth prospects or a company with a small dividend and great dividend-growth prospects I'll choose the faster dividend-grower every time. Over twenty or thirty years, a fast-growing dividend has huge implications for a stock's total return. Many of the stocks I and our millionaire investors own—Lucent Technologies, Intel, and Walgreen— have very small dividend yields. (A stock's yield is the dividend divided by the stock price.) However, these companies will probably increase dividends at least 5 percent to 10 percent annually over the next two decades. That kind of rapid dividend growth will provide a nice boost to total return.

- *Quality companies are companies that you would want to own, lock, stock, and barrel.* "I want to invest in companies that are good enough that I would want to own myself, not just as a stockholder," says Kelvin Moroney. Kelvin's portfolio is worth about $1 million. I know what Kelvin means. I like to pick stocks by asking myself the following question: Is this a company that I would like to own? In other words, if I had Bill Gates–type money and could buy the entire company outright, is this a company that I would like to buy? I think if investors approached stock picking with an owner's mentality, they would make wiser investment decisions. They wouldn't fixate on stock charts or market gossip or hot tips or quarter-to-quarter results. They would look at the big picture. They would ask themselves better questions—Is this company involved in an industry that has good long-term prospects? How big a role does the government play in this industry? Is the workforce unionized? How long will it take me to earn back my investment? How strong are my competitors? Does this company have a defensible market niche? These are questions that smart investors ask when considering a stock purchase. You should do the same.

PLAY TO YOUR STRENGTHS

Millionaire investors find quality stocks in a variety of ways. One way is by investing in what they know.

You know more than you think about investing. You may not realize it, but you do.

You're a consumer, gaining market intelligence every day about a host of consumer products.

You're a laborer in your respective field, a position that affords certain advantages in assessing your industry, company, and competitors.

You have associates, family, friends, relatives, and confidantes doing fieldwork every day in their respective areas of expertise.

Most people have quite an array of investment intelligence at their fingertips. They just don't think of it as such.

Millionaire investors, on the other hand, understand the leverage in using what they know in the investment process.

Take Thomas Pall. Thomas, fifty-four, is an oil refinery worker living on the West Coast with his wife of twenty-three years. Tom's investment portfolio is worth about $1.4 million. One of Tom's best-performing stocks is America Online. Listen to how Tom came across this big winner. "Six or seven of us from work would play poker about once every six weeks," says Tom. "One of the people was our computer technician. We started talking about stocks and the Internet. The computer technician thought that the Internet was for real and an investor should have at least one Internet stock. This was before the 'dot.com' stock craze. A week later I bought America Online."

Michael Walker, another of our millionaire investors, picked his best stock because he did business with the company. "I was a screen printer in years past. My best customer's stock, Tellabs, is the one I followed before I had any money. It was the first stock I bought when I had some money to invest. I still own a bunch of it." Despite being in his mid-forties, with only a high school diploma, Michael, a salesman making about $60,000 per year, has an investment portfolio worth $1.2 million.

Sometimes our best stock ideas are right under our noses. Take Matt T., a retired executive living in the Upper Midwest. Matt has an investment portfolio worth more than $2.1 million. For much of his working life, Matt was employed by a publicly traded electronics and electrical equipment company. "My first three shares were given to me for Christmas in 1946 by my wife, the year I got out of the Army and joined the company," says Matt. "I received my first stock options in 1955. For many years this was the only stock I owned."

How did Matt do with his company stock? Pretty well. The company was eventually purchased for $88 per share.

"The cost basis for this company stock [that was given to him by his wife] was about $1.00 per share as nearly as I can recall," says Matt.

Admittedly, not all of us work for corporations with publicly traded stock. But that doesn't mean you don't have certain valuable insight into other investment opportunities.

Take the "Dellionaires" created over the years by the huge gains posted by Dell Computer stock. Did everyone who made money off Dell Computer work for the company? Of course not. But you didn't have to work for the company to know about the company. Chances are these Dellionaires had friends or relatives working for the company who could provide insight into the company's prospects.

A year ago I spoke to an investment group in Austin, Texas, home to Dell Computer. Judging from conversations, I would venture to say that many people in the room had a healthy chunk of Dell Computer, even though most of them never worked for the company. One guy told me his cost basis on his Dell stock was less than $1.00 per share.

While you may not have a Dell in your backyard, you might have some other fast-growing company that offers an interesting investment opportunity.

More than three quarters of our everyday millionaire investors, when asked whether they invest in "what they know," answered in the affirmative. One of those millionaires was Paula Cass. Paula has been an extremely successful investor. At age fifty-two, Paula has an investment portfolio worth more than $6 million. One reason Paula has been successful is that she played to her strengths. Paula is a retired bank president. Not coincidentally, the vast majority of her holdings are bank stocks. Two of her largest holdings are banking concerns National City and Bank One. (For more on Paula and her investing strategies, see her profile at the end of Chapter 7.)

But remember that Paula truly *knows* the banking industry. To know a company or an industry means more than just using the company's products.

Consider bacon. I like bacon. I know how to cook bacon. I know that bacon works well in club sandwiches.

On the other hand, I know nothing about investing in pigs. I know nothing about investing in pork bellies. I couldn't tell you the first thing about the fundamentals driving the hog market.

Now, if I were a pig farmer, I might have a different view. I would know about bacon, the breakfast item, *and* bacon, the investment opportunity. A pig farmer has advantages he or she brings to the investment table because he or she understands all aspects of bacon.

A pig farmer truly knows bacon.

There's a big difference between truly knowing the company and the industry and believing you know the company because you like its products. Liking a company's products is a step in the right direction, but you need to do further homework:

How are the company's net profit margins?

Is its bottom line growing?

Is the company's financial position in good shape?

What kind of dividend growth can you expect?

Is its market position defensible?

How strong are its brands?

Does corporate management own a sizable stake in the company?

That's how you get to know a company. You start with an idea and dig deeper to see if the firm's underlying fundamentals are sound.

THIS INVESTOR BOUGHT WHAT HE KNEW— AND RETIRED AT AGE FORTY-ONE

WHEN LONNIE FOGEL BEGAN WORKING FOR ATLANTA-based Home Depot, he never expected things to work out quite the way they have. Because of his position with the company and his knowledge of the industry, Lonnie knew that Home Depot would be a good stock to own. And when he could buy Home Depot stock at cents on the dollar via the company's stock ownership program, he took full advantage of the opportunity. Because of the strength of Home Depot stock, the shares Lonnie was accumulating through the company's stock ownership plan were rapidly growing in value. They rose in value so much, in fact, that Lonnie retired at age forty-one. He now spends his days bicycling, doing volunteer work, and writing a screenplay. Says Lonnie, "This sense of freedom is a gift."

SOURCE: ANITA SHARPE,
THE WALL STREET JOURNAL/CONTRA COSTA TIMES AUGUST 25, 1996

STAY AWAY FROM WHAT YOU DON'T KNOW

A major part of investment success is keeping your money in play. When money is in play, the power of compounding can work its magic. You keep money in play by avoiding huge mistakes. One way to avoid big mistakes is by refusing to venture into the investment unknown.

I asked the 170 millionaires surveyed for this book to list their worst-performing stocks. Here were some names they mentioned:

ACX Technologies
Aileen
American Industrial Properties
Applied Magnetics
Audiovox
Bethlehem Steel
Biogenetic Technology
Calgene
Chyron
Columbia/HCA Healthcare
Corel
Diageo
Digital Biometrics
Golden Bear Books
H&Q Health Care Investors
Hopewell Holdings
Keldon Oil
Meditrust
Mohawk Data
Morrison Knudsen
Nabors Industries
Navistar
New Asia Fund
Noble Drilling
Pace Health Management
Pharmacopeia
Presstek
Prudential Government Income
Quantum
Somatogen
Synthetech
United Records & Tapes
The Villager
Zoltek

To be fair, our millionaire investors also listed some well-known companies, such as Philip Morris, Eastman Kodak, Waste Management, Caterpillar, McDonald's, among their clunkers. However, the vast majority of the "millionaire losers" were names I'm guessing would not be familiar to most investors. Heck, I've never heard of many of the companies. Probably the millionaires who bought them really didn't know much about them.

That's precisely my point. When you invest in small, speculative, high-risk companies, you venture into the investment unknown. Sometimes the payoffs can be huge. More often than not, however, the stocks end up taking your money out of play.

You have a much greater chance having a small, unknown stock blow up on you than a stock like General Electric or Bristol-Myers Squibb. And if GE or Bristol-Myers declines sharply, your chances of a rebound are much greater than high-risk situations rebounding following a crash.

"Buying stocks under $5.00 almost never works," says Arlene Ciardo, one of the everyday millionaire investors I surveyed. Arlene, fifty-eight, has an investment portfolio worth $14 million. Her biggest stock holdings include several utilities (DTE Energy, Atmos Energy, and DQE) as well as IBM.

Another way investors take their money out of play is by buying futures and options. Futures and options are forms of derivative securities. Derivatives are financial instruments whose prices are derived from other prices of underlying securities, assets, or indexes. For example, a "call" option gives an investor the right to buy a stock at a set price. A "put" option gives an investor the right to sell a stock at a set price. Options and futures can register quick and substantial gains if an investor is correct about the movement of the underlying stocks or indexes. But options and futures are not investments. They are *speculations*. Speculations have no place in building a seven-figure portfolio.

I know that some people buy futures and options for "portfolio insurance" purposes. For example, let's say you own 300 shares of

McDonald's. You can hedge against a drop in McDonald's stock by buying a "put" option on McDonald's. One "put" option gives you the right to sell 100 shares of McDonald's stock. Thus, you buy three "put" options to hedge your McDonald's position. Should McDonald's drop, the value of the "put" option rises, offsetting the loss on the stock.

While using options to hedge your portfolio is not a foolish strategy, I would argue that, for long-term investors, there is no need to "insure" your portfolio against market declines. For one thing, I guarantee that you won't be able to call turns in stocks or the market with any consistency. I can't, either. Nobody can, so it's not worth incurring the costs of insurance. (The costs of insurance in the above example are the costs to purchase the "put" option.) Furthermore, since you're investing for a long time, who cares what the market is doing this week, this month, or even this year. That's the mentality you have to assume. That's how millionaire investors think.

I learned my lesson the hard way about options. Early in my investing career, I followed a company called American President Companies. (The company has since been acquired.) American President was one of the few pure shipping plays in the market. There was always takeover speculation swirling around the company. What made me buy "call" options on the stock (speculators buy "call" options on stocks they believe will move higher) were comments made in *The Wall Street Journal* by one prominent corporate raider who was lining up his next target. What triggered my interest in American President was what the corporate raider said to journalists, when asked why he refused to name his next target: "I feel like Oliver North."

Being a brilliant stock analyst, I took that small statement as a sign that this raider, who had been snooping around the shipping industry, was going after American President. After all, who was Oliver North protecting? Ronald Reagan. And what was Ronald Reagan? An *American President!*

Well, you can guess what happened. I bought options in American President. The corporate raider went after some other company. I was left holding the bag.

You would think that fiasco would have been enough to turn me off on options. It actually took a profitable option purchase to bring me to my senses. Several years ago, when I was still dumb and buying options, I purchased a few call options on an airline stock. A few days after I purchased the options, the airline received a takeover offer. Look out, Warren Buffett, I thought. The value of my options doubled on the takeover announcement. But a funny thing happened. After I figured my commissions to buy and sell the options (commissions on options are notoriously high) and the taxes on my short-term capital gains, I was left with hardly any profit.

I haven't bought an option since.

Bottom line: When you invest in speculative stocks or options or futures, you are swinging for the fences. Unfortunately, you'll likely strike out nearly every time. Remember: You don't have to hit home runs to have a seven-figure portfolio. You just need to keep your money in play. Time and compounding will do the rest.

DOESN'T PRICE MATTER?

Up to this point, I've focused primarily on buying quality companies. I've said little about buying the company's stock at the right price.

Of course, everyone would love to "buy low and sell high." The problem lies in determining whether you're buying low or high. You can use traditional gauges of a stock's value. Many investors use a stock's "price-earnings ratio" as a gauge of value.

A stock's price-earnings ratio is determined by dividing the stock price per share by the company's twelve-month earnings per share. A company whose stock price is $20 and whose per-share profits over the last twelve months are $2.00 would have a price-earnings ratio of 10. Value investors generally don't like to buy stocks with price-earnings ratios greater than the price-earnings ratio of the overall market or greater than one times the company's per-share earnings growth rate. That means a company whose earnings per share are growing at 15 percent should not be bought unless the price-earnings ratio is 15 or less.

The problem with using value measures such as price-earnings ratios is that you may miss big opportunities when growth investing is in vogue. That has been the story in the last few years. Low inflation and low interest rates have provided the perfect environment for growth stocks. Investors who bought stocks only when the price-earnings ratio was equal to or less than the earnings-growth rate missed out on huge profits.

Who knows if the growth style of investing will remain in vogue or "value" investing will return. Quite frankly, it's a *guess* whether a stock offers a good "value." Successful investors play the percentages. They invest based on what they *know*, not on what they *guess*. You *know* quality. You know that General Electric or Lucent Technologies or Microsoft or Intel is a quality company with quality products and quality management. You *know* that. You *guess* value. For that reason, I invest in quality and don't pay much attention to a stock's price in the short term.

Now don't get me wrong. It's one thing to invest in a seasoned, quality, industry-leading stock that may be a bit overpriced. It's another to invest in some speculative, high-risk situation that has no seasoning, no track record, but a sky-high valuation. Price ultimately will matter. But the price you pay to purchase a solid, quality, blue chip that you plan to hold for twenty years matters much less than the price you pay to buy some garbage, low-priced stock that you plan to trade.

If you wait to buy great stocks at "cheap" prices, you'll wait forever. Quality is never "cheap." You're never going to buy Merck at a price/earnings ratio of eight. You're never going to see Microsoft trade at twelve times earnings. If you wait to buy Lucent

Technologies at a market price-earnings ratio, you're going to wait a long time.

Theodore Fortsmann is an extremely successful professional investor. His specialty is leveraged buyouts. This quote, which was published in *Money* magazine, should be required reading for all investors:

> You buy the wrong business at 25 percent less than you should, and you take a little longer to go broke. You buy the right business at 25 percent more than you should, and you make five times your money instead of six.

Too many investors focus too much time on buying "value"—stocks that seem cheap based on all the value criteria—and not enough time focusing on quality. These investors often get caught in "value traps." They buy stocks that are "cheap" that get cheaper and cheaper and cheaper.

I cannot think of a time when I made a mistake paying up to buy a quality stock. As an investor, it is much better to err on the side of overpaying for quality. Time can ultimately bail you out.

BUY QUALITY STOCKS ON DECLINES

What do you do if you overpay for a quality stock and it declines sharply? Buy more and wait. Individual investors can afford to be patient with their investments. The clock is not running on your performance. You can buy quality stocks that have been beaten up and wait for the inevitable turnaround. The rebound may take six months. It could take two years. Eventually, however, quality companies usually show their true colors.

Whether you know it or not, being able to buy quality stocks on declines is a huge advantage you have over most professional investors. Most professional investors are reluctant to buy stocks that may be dead money. Dead money hurts short-term performance. Short-term performance garners assets. Fees on assets pay the bills.

This focus on short-term performance actually enhances the advantage you have as a patient investor. Long-term buying opportunities are being created almost daily. A quality stock misses its earnings estimate by a penny and loses 10 percent of its value in a day. Missing earnings estimates is not taken lightly by professional investors and usually signals the company may have some trouble over the next few quarters. Professionals can't afford to own stocks having trouble.

You can, however, if it is a quality company and you're willing to wait out the rebound.

Many millionaire investors I surveyed made money buying quality stocks that had fallen. Let me emphasize the word, *quality*. I would not necessarily recommend investors buy a speculative, small-company stock that declines. Buying an industry leader that stumbles is a different story. In fact, if your investment focus is on buying quality, you *must* be willing to buy quality stocks when they're down. That's how you maximize the power of a long-term growth strategy.

MILLIONAIRE MAKERS

I asked our millionaire investors to name their best-performing stocks. The following "Millionaire Makers" are the top twenty stocks mentioned most by our millionaire investors (the companies are ranked in order of number of mentions). The return numbers come from Standard & Poor's and MSN MoneyCentral (www.moneycentral.msn.com/home.asp):

MILLIONAIRE MAKERS

Company	What $10,000 invested in the stock 12/31/88 was worth 12/31/98
Lucent Technologies	Lucent has been publicly traded only since 1996.
General Electric	$114,590
Merck	$93,650
Intel	$406,340
Microsoft	$931,049
Cisco Systems	Cisco has been publicly traded only since 1990.
Dell Computer	$3,469,630
Exxon Mobil	$48,980
Eli Lilly	$105,390
IBM	$41,180
America Online	America Online has been publicly traded only since 1992.
Pfizer	$208,550
AT&T	$34,380
Home Depot	$403,640
Walgreen	$175,270
Amgen	$392,109
BellSouth	$74,350
Wal-Mart Stores	$109,740
AFLAC	$135,150
American Express	$50,510

These are hardly undiscovered stocks. I'm sure you are familiar with most of these names. These stocks are some of the most heavily covered and analyzed stocks on Wall Street.

For the most part, these stocks represent the "singles" of the investment world.

Solid. Consistent. Sound. Bankable.

These are the types of stocks that make you rich over time.

These stocks do not always produce the biggest gains in a given year. There are years when the tried and the true lag the overall market.

For twenty- and thirty-year time frames, however, you can't beat these stocks. They will be around twenty or thirty years from now. Their earnings will be a lot higher twenty or thirty years from now (and stock prices ultimately follow earnings). They will provide a return that is likely at least to keep pace with the market.

Best of all, as you can see by their performance numbers, several of these singles turned into home runs.

Take Microsoft, the software giant. Buying Microsoft a few years ago didn't require the mind of Einstein. Few companies dominate their industry like Microsoft. How smart do you have to be to buy Microsoft, right?

Microsoft has increased more than *tenfold* since 1995. That's a single that turned into a home run.

In fact, many of the "millionaire makers" turned into home runs. Indeed, a $10,000 investment at the end of 1988 in each of the 17 millionaire makers (a total investment of $170,000) that have been trading since the end of 1988 would have grown to more than $6.7 *million* by the end of 1998. And if you had been lucky enough to own the best-performing stock among the millionaire makers over the last decade—**Dell Computer**—a $10,000 investment would have grown to more than $3.4 *million.*

To say that these stocks have had pretty good runs over the last decade would be an understatement. None of them would be considered "cheap." And my guess is that many of these stocks, going forward, will not match their outstanding gains of the last ten years. Still, I would put my money (and I do own several of these stocks— Intel, Microsoft, Cisco, Lucent, Exxon Mobil, AT&T, and Walgreen) on many of them continuing to do at least as well as the overall market and probably a lot better.

If you're looking for buy candidates to start a stock portfolio, you could do a lot worse than these "Millionaire Makers."

BY THE NUMBERS

If you want to conduct your own search for future millionaire makers, the Internet makes it easier than ever to do so. A variety of Web sites exist that allow investors to screen thousands of stocks based on a variety of criteria—size, earnings growth, stock price, price-earnings ratio, financial strength, etc. Two sites that are particularly useful for screening stocks are **www.stockscreener.com** and **www.irnet.com** (for the latter site, click on "Investing Tools" on the left-hand side of the home page).

When using these or other stock-screening tools, make sure you include the following criteria:

- **Return on equity.** Return on equity measures how productive a company is in generating profits from the money contributed by shareholders. Ideally, you want to own companies with stable or rising return on equity. Focus on companies with return on equity consistently above 20 percent.
- **Net profit margins.** Net profit margins show how efficient a company is in squeezing profits from revenues. Again, you want stable or rising net profit margins. I like to see net profit margins of at least 8 percent to 10 percent. Admittedly, these levels are fairly high, especially for companies in cyclical industries. However, you want growth investments. Screening for high net profit margins assures you'll be investing in high-growth industries.
- **Per-share earnings growth.** Stock prices follow earnings, so you want to own companies with rising profitability. Ideally, you want to own companies where profits are rising every year

for at least the last five years. Focus on companies with five-year earnings growth of at least 12 percent.

- **Revenue growth.** It's not enough for a company to have rising earnings. Those earnings could be generated by cost cutting and not increased demand for its products. You need to own companies with rising sales. Rising sales sustain rising profitability. A company can boost profits via cost cutting for only so long. Focus on companies with ten years of rising revenues. Also, look for companies in which revenues are rising at least 8 percent per year.

- **Debt levels.** You want companies that will be around for the twenty or thirty years you plan to hold them. Strong finances are essential to corporate survival. To measure a company's fiscal health, one useful ratio is the firm's long-term debt as a percentage of total capital (total capital is long-term debt plus shareholder equity). Ideally, you don't want companies with debt-to-capital levels greater than 60 percent and preferably below 30 percent.

- **Market capitalization.** A company's market capitalization is the stock price times the number of shares outstanding. A company with a stock price of $50 per share and 2 million common shares outstanding has a market capitalization of $100 million. You can think of market capitalization as the price tag Wall Street assigns the company at any point in time. You should focus your attention on companies with market capitalizations of at least $3.5 billion.

- **Company ownership.** Ideally, you want to invest with companies whose management are also shareholders. When interests are closely aligned between management and shareholders, you know the company is likely to make decisions that benefit shareholders. A useful Web site for tracking the buying and selling of corporate executives and other company insiders is **www.insidertrader.com.**

Of course, once you run the screen, your work isn't done. You'll need to research particular companies of interest. A good Internet tool for general research on companies is **www.dailystocks.com.** This "aggregator" Web site provides links to many research tools and information you can use to analyze a stock of interest.

An excellent research tool for noncomputer users is **Value Line Investment Survey.** This publication is found in most libraries. Value Line provides research reports on some 1,700 companies. What's particularly useful about Value Line is that the publication provides "safety" ratings on stocks. Focus your attention on stocks with safety ratings of 1. (the highest rating) or 2. A screen of all 1- and 2-rated stocks for safety appears in the front of the publication. Once you've focused on stocks with high Value Line safety ratings, focus on companies in growing industries. A list of "highest growth stocks" is also provided in the front of the publication.

As you might guess, I have some specific ideas on stocks that I believe are millionaire makers. I give my stock recommendations in Chapter 11.

SELECTING MUTUAL FUNDS

You probably own a mutual fund. The rapid growth of 401(k) plans has made most Americans mutual-fund holders. Unfortunately, many Americans have no clue how to choose mutual funds.

With a stock, you have a variety of criteria to evaluate. With a fund, the information is much more limited. That's why most investors chase the hottest-performing funds. Performance is all they have to judge. Sadly, chasing hot funds usually winds up being a losing proposition.

What are useful strategies for choosing mutual funds? Our millionaire investors provide some sound tips:

- Mark Hogan likes no-load mutual funds—funds sold without sales fees. He focuses on funds with low expenses and low turnover. He looks for a good long-term track record and a strong fund family name. Mark's portfolio, which is worth $2 million, includes such mutual funds as **Vanguard International Growth** (800-662-7447), **Vanguard U.S. Growth** (800-662-7447), **Janus Worldwide** (800-525-8983), and **T. Rowe Price Science and Technology** (800-638-5660).

- Paul Fritzker evaluates funds partly on the fund's top holdings. "Are the top ten holdings in companies I would like to buy?" Paul asks himself. You can get some idea about a fund's largest holdings by looking at the fund's quarterly report. Also, most mutual-fund families have Web sites that provide information on their funds, including major holdings. Paul's $1.4 million investment portfolio includes **Legg Mason Value Trust** (800-577-8589), **Vanguard Tax Managed Growth and Income** (800-662-7447), and **Transamerica Small Cap** fund (800-892-7587).

- A. J. Wright likes to buy funds that have solid three-year performance, low expenses, and stable management. A.J.'s fund holdings include **Vanguard 500 Index** (800-662-7447) and **Vanguard Growth and Income** (800-662-7447).

FAVORITE MILLIONAIRE FUNDS

The following are the five most widely held mutual funds among our everyday millionaire investors:

Janus Fund (800-525-8983)
Vanguard 500 Index (800-662-7447)
Janus Worldwide (800-525-8983)
Janus 20 (800-525-8983)
Fidelity Magellan (800-544-8888)

When considering your fund choices, follow these rules:

- Buy only no-load funds. (No-load funds have no sales fees.) While there are good load funds, no research has ever shown that load funds outperform no-load funds. Stick with no-load funds.
- All funds charge annual expenses to manage their funds. These expenses are expressed as a percent of fund assets. Don't buy a fund whose annual expense ratio is greater than 1.4 percent. In other words, avoid funds in which you'll lose $1.40 to fees for every $100 you invest. One of the strongest predictors of fund performance is expenses. Yes, a number of good funds have done well despite having high annual expenses. Still, the percentages say invest in low-expense funds.
- Buy funds whose annual turnover is less than 100 percent and preferably less than 50 percent. Turnover measures how quickly a fund manager turns over the holdings in his or her portfolio. A turnover ratio of 100 percent means a fund manager turns his or her entire portfolio over one time during the year. High turnover means the fund manager sells frequently. Frequent selling means the fund manager may be realizing capital gains that eventually are passed along to shareholders and added to their tax returns. High-turnover funds generally are less tax friendly. High-turnover funds also reflect a more active investment approach by the fund manager. Few investors, professional or otherwise, are good traders. Don't expect your fund manager to be the exception.
- Avoid fast-growing funds that invest in small-company stocks. Large inflows into a small-company fund make the fund manager's job more difficult. He or she may not be able to buy the same types of stocks when the fund is much larger since small stocks don't afford the needed liquidity.
- Focus on funds that have at least a three-year track record with the same fund manager.

Index Funds—the Ultimate "Singles" Play

An efficient fund investment strategy is to choose index funds. Index funds mimic the performance of a market index. The most popular index funds mimic the Standard & Poor's 500. You can purchase index funds that mimic other indexes, such as the Dow Jones Industrial Average, Wilshire 5000, Russell 2000, or an index of international stocks, as well.

Index funds are the ultimate "singles" play for fund investors. If you invest in an index fund that mimics the S&P 500, you're assured of getting a return that roughly matches the index's return. Matching the market may not sound very sexy. It is. In any given year, half to three quarters of all funds don't match the market. That percentage has been even higher in recent years.

One reason index funds do so well is that they have extremely low expenses. **Vanguard's 500 Index** fund (800-662-7447), for example, has annual expenses of just 0.18 percent. That means that you lose just $90 per year in expenses for every $50,000 you have in the fund. Compare that to a fund with annual expenses of 1.5% (or $750 in annual expenses for every $50,000), and you can see why index funds beat most actively managed funds. Index funds are also extremely tax friendly since they are not actively managed. Thus, turnover is extremely low. **Vanguard** mutual fund family (800-662-7447) is the king of index funds, although most fund families now offer index funds. The mutual fund I comanage—the **Strong Dow 30 Value Fund** (800-368-6010)—is an enhanced index fund. The fund invests only in the thirty stocks that comprise the Dow, although I and the coportfolio manager, Rich Moroney, have latitude in how much we invest in each Dow stock. Strong also offers an index fund based on the S&P 500. When investing in any mutual fund, make sure you obtain and read the prospectus.

MORNINGSTAR MUTUAL FUNDS

Morningstar Mutual Funds is the bible of fund research. Morningstar's Star Rating system is followed by everyone in the industry. It's estimated that funds ranked four or five stars by Morningstar (five stars is Morningstar's highest rating) capture roughly all mutual-fund inflows. Morningstar Mutual Funds is available in most libraries. You can also check out Morningstar on the Web at **www.morningstar.com.** The site provides tools for screening mutual funds based on a variety of criteria—fund objective, Morningstar rating, expense ratios, etc.

CONCLUSION

When buying individual stocks, the best approach is to focus on quality. That is the pond in which everyday millionaire investors fish. That's the pond in which you should fish, too. Remember: You don't need your stocks to generate 50 percent annual returns in order to get rich. You don't need to find that one cheap stock among the 10,000 publicly traded stocks. You don't have to take huge risks in speculative stocks to grow your portfolio. You can do just fine keeping your money in play, buying the tried and true, and taking your 10 percent or 15 percent annual gains.

The millionaire profiled in this chapter is Humberto Cruz (that's his real name). You may have seen Humberto's name in your local business section. Humberto is a financial journalist who writes for the *Sun-Sentinel* newspaper in Fort Lauderdale, Florida. His columns are syndicated throughout the country. Given Humberto's position as both an investor and a commentator on the markets, I think his comments and experiences are especially valuable for readers.

Humberto's path to a $1 million investment portfolio is especially interesting. He came with his family to the United States from Cuba in 1960. His parents had a grand total of $300. Humberto's investment education got off to a relatively slow start. He didn't start investing in stocks until age thirty-nine. However, in the next fifteen years, Humberto made up for lost time. His portfolio grew rapidly, benefiting from positions in such top performers as Tribune Company.

I asked Humberto if he thinks individual investors can compete with big investors. "Yes. They don't have to worry about short-term performance to satisfy bosses or fund shareholders," says Humberto. "They can think for themselves."

NAME: Humberto Cruz

AGE: 54

HOME: Florida

MARITAL STATUS: Married for 28 years. Never divorced.

CHILDREN: 1

EDUCATION: College (undergraduate) graduate

OCCUPATION: Journalist

CURRENT INCOME: Low end of 31 percent tax bracket

HOW MANY DIFFERENT JOBS SINCE AGE 25? 4

DO YOU HAVE AN ANNUAL HOUSEHOLD BUDGET THAT YOU FOLLOW? Yes

WOULD YOU CONSIDER YOUR PARENTS TO BE FRUGAL? Yes

AT WHAT AGE DID YOU START INVESTING? 39

HOW MANY YEARS HAVE YOU BEEN INVESTING? 15

WHAT IS THE SIZE OF YOUR ENTIRE INVESTMENT PORTFOLIO? $1.4 million

WHAT IS THE BREAKDOWN OF THESE ASSETS? Mutual funds (45 percent), stocks (25 percent), bonds (30 percent)

HOW MANY INDIVIDUAL STOCKS DO YOU OWN? 8

NAME YOUR LARGEST STOCK HOLDING: Tribune Company

HOW MANY INDIVIDUAL MUTUAL FUNDS DO YOU OWN? 8

NAME YOUR BIGGEST FUND HOLDINGS: Bridgeway Ultra Large 35 Index,

Vanguard Health Care, Vanguard Total Bond Market Index, Guinness Flight Wired Index, Citizens Index

HOW MANY INDIVIDUAL BONDS DO YOU HAVE? 0

HAVE YOU EVER PURCHASED STOCK/INDEX OPTIONS? No

HAVE YOU EVER BOUGHT STOCK/INDEX FUTURES? No

DO YOU OWN GOLD OR PRECIOUS METALS? No

HAVE YOU EVER SOLD STOCK SHORT? No

WHAT ARE THE PLANS FOR YOUR ESTATE? Come as close as possible to die broke but have life insurance in place for heirs.

WHAT ARE YOUR LONG-TERM GOALS? To have enough to be able to stop work full time if I so choose.

WHAT HURDLES, IF ANY, DID YOU OVERCOME TO BEGIN INVESTING? Total lack of investment knowledge from parents.

HOW, PSYCHOLOGICALLY SPEAKING, DID YOU DEAL WITH THE NOTION OF PUTTING OFF CONSUMPTION TO SAVE FOR A BETTER FINANCIAL FUTURE? I always kept the goal in mind. Also, after my parents lost everything in Cuba, I wanted to work toward a secure financial future.

WHERE DID YOU GET THE MONEY TO START INVESTING? By paying ourselves first, and paying off the mortgage. The money that would have gone to the mortgage every month was used—it is still being used—for investing.

WERE THERE ANY SPECIFIC EVENTS, LIFE-CHANGING MOMENTS, ETC., THAT SPURRED YOU TO BEGIN INVESTING? A coworker showed me a copy of *Changing Times* (now called *Kiplinger's Personal Finance* magazine). I saw that returns beyond those offered by banks were not only possible but quite common at the time.

HAVE YOU INHERITED WHAT YOU THOUGHT WAS A LARGE SUM OF MONEY? No

DID YOU START INVESTING WITH A SPECIFIC PLAN IN MIND? My wife and I started with a specific dollar amount as opposed to a percentage. As our income rose, the amount invested grew much more than the percentage salary increase—virtually all our raises since we started investing have gone to investing, and our expenses have remained pretty constant except for inflation.

HOW DID YOU EDUCATE YOURSELF ABOUT INVESTING? DID YOU FIND THE EDUCATION PROCESS DIFFICULT? FUN? Reading, reading, reading. It was not difficult. It is mostly fun, although I can think of much more fun things to do than reading about the stock market.

DID YOU HAVE ANY SPECIAL EXPERTISE IN INVESTING WHEN YOU STARTED? None, other than I am good at math and think analytically.

WHAT INVESTMENT RESEARCH TOOLS DO YOU USE? *quote.yahoo.com, www.morningstar.com, The Outlook* newsletter, *Dow Theory Forecasts* newsletter, *Mutual Funds* magazine

HOW MUCH DO YOU SPEND PER YEAR ON INVESTMENT RESEARCH RESOURCES? Less than $250 per year

DO YOU USE A COMPUTER TO KEEP TRACK OF YOUR INVESTMENTS? Yes

HOW MANY HOURS PER WEEK DO YOU DEVOTE TO YOUR INVESTMENTS AND INVESTMENT STRATEGIES? Two hours at the most

WHAT CRITERIA DO YOU USE TO PICK STOCKS/MUTUAL FUNDS? Socially responsible. I will not invest in certain companies and will not invest in mutual funds that own tobacco stocks (thus no S&P 500 Index funds for me). Consistent performer. I must feel comfortable that if I were sent away to a deserted island for ten years or more, I could hold this investment until I return. Capable management with a stake in the company (or in the case of a mutual fund, the manager has his or her own money in it). For mutual funds, low expenses. Tax efficiency.

HOW OFTEN DO YOU BUY INVESTMENTS? Monthly

ON AVERAGE, HOW LONG DO YOU HOLD AN INVESTMENT BEFORE SELLING? 5 years or more

DO YOU "MARKET TIME"? No

WHAT HAVE BEEN YOUR BEST-PERFORMING STOCKS? Tribune

WHAT HAVE BEEN YOUR WORST-PERFORMING STOCKS? The old NCR

WHAT WERE SOME OF YOUR BIGGEST INVESTMENT MISTAKES? Waiting too long to get started. When I started out, switching too much between investments based on something I read.

DO YOU INVEST IN WHAT YOU KNOW? For many years now I have not invested in anything I do not fully understand.

HAVE YOU EVER FOLLOWED A HOT TIP? No

HOW WOULD YOU BEST DESCRIBE YOUR INVESTMENT APPROACH? Systematic and methodical

DO YOU THINK INDIVIDUAL INVESTORS ARE DISADVANTAGED IN THE FINANCIAL MARKETS RELATIVE TO LARGE INVESTORS? Not any more, with the tremendous amount of available information.

DO YOU BELIEVE IT IS POSSIBLE TO BEAT THE MARKET ON A CONSISTENT BASIS? Yes, but not by much.

WHAT MADE YOU THINK YOU COULD BE A SUCCESSFUL INVESTOR? I am very disciplined.

WHAT DO YOU THINK ARE SOME OF THE GREATEST MYTHS OF INVESTING? That it is too difficult. That you have to spend hours on it. That there are "experts" who know what is going to happen.

WHAT IS THE BIGGEST BENEFIT OF A 7-FIGURE PORTFOLIO? I don't have to work at anything I do not like.

IF YOU COULD GIVE JUST ONE PIECE OF ADVICE TO INDIVIDUAL INVESTORS, WHAT WOULD THAT PIECE OF ADVICE BE? Stop watching CNBC.

IF YOU WOULD, PLEASE SHARE WITH ME YOUR FAVORITE INVESTMENT STORY. I became an investor by accident. A coworker showed me a copy of the financial magazine because it had a feature on her brother-in-law, a home remodeler. I thought the story about her brother-in-law was not nearly as interesting as the stories about investments and they, in turn, not nearly as interesting as the ads.

7

INVEST EVERY MONTH

*Keep investing on a regular basis in great companies, no
matter what the market, Wall Street, or the clowns on TV are
saying.*

—PATRICK JOHNSON, CALIFORNIA,
$2.5 MILLION INVESTMENT PORTFOLIO

STEP 5: INVEST EVERY MONTH,
NO MATTER HOW SMALL THE INVESTMENT

Being a successful investor is all about keeping your money in play.
That's why successful investors invest on a regular basis. Among our
everyday millionaire investors, well over half invest at least once a
month. Another 28 percent invest at least quarterly (every three
months).

INVESTING MEANS YOU'RE NOT SPENDING

When you don't invest regularly, you're not keeping your money in
play. Money that's not in the market doesn't reap the benefits of
time and compounding. In fact, money that's not in the stock market is eventually money that's spent. And money that's spent creates
a *negative* return.

Huh?

Think about it. The stuff you buy usually costs you more than the initial price tag. Homes require insurance, maintenance, utilities, and furniture. Autos require gasoline, insurance, and maintenance. Clothing requires cleaning and mending, not to mention new clothes to go with the clothes you just bought. Computers require Internet connections, printers, toner cartridges, software, and computer paper. Stereo systems require speakers and compact discs.

It's Carlson's Rule of Stuff—Stuff begets stuff begets more stuff.

If you spend instead of invest, you're not just losing returns on the money you spend. The money you spend generates a *negative* return because you spend more money to support the stuff you buy. That's why spending is so dangerous. It has a negative multiplier effect. Spending is really *negative compounding*.

If you invest every month, even if it is only a few bucks, you rid yourself of money that, if spent, will cost you even more money in the long run. That's why it pays to invest even a little amount each month—$10, $50, $100, whatever you can afford. Don't wait until you save a larger amount to invest. This is a common mistake investors make. The problem with waiting until you accumulate funds is that the money is readily available and tempts you to spend on some foolish toy. Get the money into the stock market as soon as possible. You'll be much better off in the long run.

ONE AND DONE IS NOT ENOUGH

A big reason to invest regularly is that, without doing so, you'll never get to seven figures. It's doubtful your initial investment will grow enough to reach seven figures. You need to put more money into the market over time. Run the numbers:

- Let's say you invest $10,000 and never make another contribution again. Over twenty years at 11 percent per year, that $10,000 grows to $80,623.

- Now, let's say you make that $10,000 investment and add just $50 per month. Instead of $80,623 at the end of twenty years, you'll have $133,029. What makes this example so powerful is that, in order to achieve an additional $52,406 ($133,029 minus $80,623), you had to invest only an additional $12,000 ($50 per month for 20 years).
- Now, let's say that instead of $50 per month, you invest $100 per month. The amount at the end of twenty years (assuming 11 percent annual return) grows to $176,707. Remember that you invested just $34,000 ($10,000 plus $100 per month for twenty years) to create a portfolio worth $176,707.

These examples drive home two important points. First, in order to make big money, *seven-figure* money, you need to invest regularly. Second, small changes in monthly investments have huge impacts on your portfolio over a long time frame. That's why it is so important to invest every month, regardless of the amount. Even small amounts of money can add up to big dollars over twenty or thirty years.

TIME DIVERSIFICATION

Investing every month lowers your investment risk. Diversification usually refers to investing in a variety of assets—stocks, bonds, real estate, etc.—in order to lower portfolio risk. You can also diversify across *time*. How? By spreading investments over a period of time. Investing every month is a form of *time diversification*. When you invest monthly, you limit your risks of buying at market peaks. You also assure yourself of periodically buying near market low points.

DOLLAR-COST AVERAGING

An easy way to implement time diversification in an investment program is by using "dollar-cost averaging." Dollar-cost averaging (DCA) takes emotion out of the investment process. Dollar-cost averaging requires you to make regular contributions to your investments, regardless of market levels.

For example, let's say you own the fund I comanage, the Strong Dow 30 Value Fund. A dollar-cost-averaging strategy dictates that you contribute the same amount of money to the fund over some regular time interval, usually monthly. That means every month, you buy $100 (or $500 or $1,000 or whatever you can afford) of the fund. If the market is high, your $100 investment buys fewer fund shares; if the market is down, your $100 buys more fund shares.

Using a dollar-cost-averaging strategy, your average cost of an investment will always be less than the average of the prices at the time the purchases were made. This is significant for it means that dollar-cost averaging can make you money even if your investments, over time, show no net positive change.

Let's look at a series of twelve monthly investments made in a stock using a DCA strategy:

Month	Amount Invested	Cost Per Share	Shares Bought
January	$1,000	$50	20.00
February	$1,000	$55	18.18
March	$1,000	$51	19.61
April	$1,000	$49	20.41
May	$1,000	$45	22.22
June	$1,000	$46	21.74
July	$1,000	$44	22.73
August	$1,000	$46	21.74

Month	Amount Invested	Cost Per Share	Shares Bought
September	$1,000	$49	20.41
October	$1,000	$49	20.41
November	$1,000	$51	19.61
December	$1,000	$50	20.00

Total Investment: $12,000
Number of shares purchased: 247.06
Average cost per share: $48.75
Profit per share (at current $50 price): $1.43 (3 percent gain)

Notice that even though the stock price started and ended the period at $50 per share, you now sit with a profit. You have this profit because dollar-cost averaging forced you to buy when the stock dipped below $50. That's one strength of DCA. Everyone wants to buy low. Few have the guts to do so. DCA forces you to buy on declines.

What this example also shows is that market declines are a long-term investor's friend if that investor uses DCA.

To be sure, DCA doesn't assure that you'll buy at the exact bottom every time. No investment strategy can guarantee that. Fortunately, you don't have to invest at the lows to make big money. Standard & Poor's looked at a dollar-cost-averaging approach versus buying at the exact market lows. According to S&P, if you had invested $10,000 at the exact bottom of the eighteen corrections of 5 percent or more in the market that have occurred since 1991, your $180,000 investment would be worth $429,000 (before dividends). If you had invested $10,000 at six-month intervals from December 31, 1990, through June 30, 1999 (in other words, dollar-cost averaged every six months beginning December 31, 1990), you would have done even better. Your $180,000 investment would have grown to $439,000 (before dividends).

If you plan to dollar-cost average, be aware of the following:

- Make your investments at the beginning of the month rather than the end. This distinction may not sound like much. Over time, the difference can add up. For example, if you invest $500 per month—and you invest at the *end* of the month— and earn 11 percent per year, you'll have $788,067 at the end of twenty-five years. If you invest the $500 at the beginning of the month, over twenty-five years you would have earned an additional $7,200.
- Dollar-cost averaging can be disastrous if you DCA in a stock that goes from $50 to $5.00 and never recovers. Choose your DCA investments wisely. Don't dollar-cost average in small, speculative stocks or second- and third-tier technology companies. These stocks rarely come back after being crippled. Do dollar-cost average in blue-chip stocks that are leaders in their industries and have solid finances.
- Don't be afraid to modify your dollar-cost-averaging program to take advantage of big sell-offs in favored stocks. I do this occasionally with my investments. However, don't tweak your DCA plan too much based on your perceptions of value. After all, that defeats the whole purpose of dollar-cost averaging.
- Dollar-cost averaging works best with low-cost/no-cost investment vehicles. If you use a full-service broker and pay $75 or more per transaction, dollar-cost averaging gets very expensive. Focus on no-load mutual funds with low expenses. Buy stock using low-cost discount brokers. I like to use dividend reinvestment plans (DRIPs) to dollar-cost average. DRIPs have little or no fees. Most DRIPs also permit investments with as little as $10 to $100.

DOLLAR-COST AVERAGING VERSUS LUMP-SUM INVESTING

One question that invariably is asked relative to dollar-cost averaging is the following: Is it better to dollar-cost average or invest a lump sum all at once?

Oftentimes, the choice between investing via dollar-cost averaging and lump-sum investing doesn't arise because we don't have lump sums to invest. Occasionally, however, we may have a lump sum to invest. A pension rollover. An inheritance. Proceeds from the sale of property. In those cases when you have a big chunk of money, what should you do?

When considering this question, remember that the market has an upward bias over time. Also remember that time is the greatest ally your money has. When you consider these two items, it's not surprising that academic studies show that lump-sum investing usually beats dollar-cost averaging. You want to put your money in play as soon as possible to maximize the power of time and compounding. Lump-sum investing puts your money in play quickly; dollar-cost averaging spreads out investments and thus keeps some money on the sidelines.

From a practical standpoint, however, I find most investors just can't bring themselves to lump-sum invest. The fear of investing a lot of money at what may turn out to be the top of the market makes it extremely difficult to sleep at night. In these situations, dollar-cost averaging provides a more palatable approach than lump-sum investing. It becomes a less stressful way to invest a large amount of money. If you have a lump sum and feel uncomfortable putting all of it into the market at one time, try dollar-cost averaging the money into the market over some relatively short period of time, perhaps twelve to eighteen months.

For example, let's say you retire and receive $200,000 in a pension rollover. You could put the money into the market all at once and maximize the power of time and compounding. A more conservative approach would be to invest the money over a twelve-month period, investing $16,666 per month. In that way, you assure yourself of not investing the entire amount at a market peak.

INVESTING ON AUTOPILOT

Investing on a monthly basis instills discipline to an investment program. This is crucial since you need to invest during good times and bad. In fact, you cannot build a seven-figure investment portfolio *without* buying during crummy market periods. That's when stocks are on sale. That's when you get the best buys. That's when your investment dollars offer the most leverage. If you fail to routinize your investment program by investing every month, you may not have the courage to invest during down markets.

How do everyday millionaires develop such discipline in their investment programs? They put their investments on autopilot. Investments are done automatically, oftentimes without having to write a check. In many cases, they never see the money going to their investments.

Felix Peters understands the value of putting an investment program on autopilot. Felix started investing early, at age eighteen. He invested on a regular basis, at least every three months. His early investments included mutual funds that automatically took $50 a month from his checking account. Felix also took full advantage of his employer's retirement program by investing the maximum amount each year. The beauty of investing in employer retirement plans is that you never see the money.

Today, at age forty-three, Felix has a $1 million portfolio.

Many years ago, I bought a whole life insurance policy. I paid the monthly premium via electronic debit of my bank account.

Was the investment a smart one? Yes and no. On the one hand, whole life insurance is a dumb way to invest. At the time, my thoughts were, "You mean I can have life insurance *and* an investment account? Where do I sign up!" Unfortunately, I later learned that a whole life policy is a lousy way to invest and a lousy way to buy insurance. If you want to invest, buy stocks. If you want insurance, buy term insurance. Don't combine the two in a whole life policy. (I've since cashed out the policy and bought term insurance.)

On the other hand, having money every month taken from my bank account showed me the merits of investing on autopilot. The investing process becomes painless. I don't see the money, so I don't miss it. No checks to cut. No muss, no fuss investing. I liked that.

A few years later I applied this "no muss, no fuss" investing approach to a much more productive investment—my employer's 401(k) plan. I began putting the maximum amount of money in my 401(k) plan. Since the funds are taken automatically, I never miss the money.

Thanks, in part, to the lessons learned investing in that lousy whole life insurance policy, I now have a six-figure sum in my 401(k) plan.

REINVESTING DIVIDENDS

One way to invest on autopilot is by reinvesting dividends on your investments.

An investment has two ways to make money. The investment can rise in price. This is called price appreciation. The investment can also throw off cash flows in the form of dividends. An investment's total return is the sum of the return generated from price appreciation plus the return generated by dividends.

For example, let's say you buy a stock that yields 3 percent. (Dividend yield is the annual dividend per share divided by the stock price per share. A $20 stock that pays an annual dividend of $0.50 per share has a yield of 2.5 percent.) For the year, the stock rises 15 percent. What is your total return of the investment? The total return is approximately 17.5 percent (15 percent appreciation plus the 2.5 percent dividend yield).

Let's say you own 100 shares of IBM. IBM currently pays 48 cents per share in dividends each year. Your 100 shares entitle you to $48 in annual dividends. If you want, you could receive a check for the dividends. Millionaire investors, however, choose to put dividends back into their investments via dividend reinvestment. You can invest that $48 in dividends to buy additional share or shares of IBM. You can reinvest dividends on mutual funds, too.

Reinvesting dividends offers a variety of wealth-building benefits. First, since dividends are paid every three months, reinvesting dividends assures that you will invest regularly, at least once a quarter. Second, reinvesting dividends amplifies the power of compounding in your investment since you are leaving more money in your investments to grow.

Reinvested dividends, over time, can make up a huge portion of an investment's total return. For example, if you had invested $10,000 in the Standard & Poor's 500 index at the end of 1988—but did not reinvest your dividends—your money would have grown to around $44,200 as of April 30, 1999. Had you reinvested your dividends, the amount of money would jump more than 30 percent to nearly $58,000.

It seems investors are catching on to the importance of reinvesting dividends. According to Investment Company Institute, nearly 80 percent of dividends in mutual funds are reinvested. That's up from less than 60 percent in 1993.

You can set up dividend reinvestment with most mutual funds and brokerage firms. You can also reinvest dividends automatically by enrolling in a company's dividend reinvestment plan.

AUTOMATIC ELECTRONIC INVESTMENT PROGRAMS

One way to put your investment program on autopilot is to establish automatic electronic investment services with your funds and DRIPs. Automatic debit services allow you to have your bank account electronically debited each month to invest regularly. Virtually all mutual-fund families allow investors to set up automatic monthly debit services for their funds. If you prefer individual stocks, you can also set up automatic monthly investment services in many dividend reinvestment plans. The following blue-chip direct-purchase plans permit initial purchases directly and allow investors to make automatic monthly investments of $100 or less:

AFLAC
Air Products & Chemicals
Allstate
American Express
Bard (C. R.)
Becton, Dickinson and Company
BellSouth
Campbell Soup
Compaq Computer
CSX
Dayton Hudson
Disney (Walt)
Duke Energy
Eastman Kodak
Enron
Equitable Companies
Exxon Mobil
Fannie Mae
Finova Group
Ford Motor
General Electric
Gillette
Guidant
Home Depot
International Business Machines
Johnson Controls

Lilly (Eli)
Lucent Technologies
McDonald's
Merck
Pfizer
Philadelphia Suburban
Procter & Gamble
Quaker Oats
Regions Financial
SBC Communications
Texaco
Wal-Mart Stores
Walgreen

To obtain enrollment information for these companies, call the toll-free numbers provided for these firms in the Appendix.

PAYROLL DEDUCTION

Another way to put your investment on autopilot is payroll deduction, especially to fund a 401(k) plan. The beauty of payroll deduction is that you don't have to do anything once you've chosen your investments. You don't have to remember to cut a check. It's truly no muss, no fuss investing. That's what you want as an investor—an investment so simple that you never see the money, so you never spend it. Your employer's 401(k) plan is perfect for dollar-cost averaging.

FIFTY DOLLARS BECOMES $1 MILLION

It's a lot easier investing every month if you are willing to invest as little as $25 or $50 at a time. One problem I see with many new investors is they never start nor maintain a regular investment program because they think they need a lot of money to buy investments. That's simply not the case, and millionaire investors know this.

Did you know that in many plans you can invest as little as 1 percent of your income in your employer's 401(k) plan? That means if you make $300 per week, you can invest as little as $3.00 in your 401(k) plan.

Three bucks.

Many mutual-fund families, including Strong, T. Rowe Price, and Invesco, allow individuals to invest as little as $50 per month via automatic monthly investment services.

Many companies, including such blue chips as Disney, IBM, McDonald's, Walgreen, and Wal-Mart, allow any investor to buy stock directly from the company—without a broker and for little fees—*with just $50 or $100.*

Bottom line: Regardless of your income, quality investments exist that will allow you to make monthly contributions with little money.

Now some of you may be saying, "What's the point investing $3.00 or $50 or even $100 per month? That kind of money won't ever amount to anything."

Don't tell that to Ben Jackson, a college professor living in the Midwest. Ben has an investment portfolio worth nearly $1.4 million. But Ben didn't get to a seven-figure portfolio in big chunks.

"My start was modest—$100 per pay period," says Ben. Now read closely what Ben is about to say. It truly is one of the secrets to accumulating wealth via investing.

"It was so easy that I just kept increasing the amount until I was at the maximum allowed for the account."

That last statement is how $100 becomes $1 million. Millionaire investors understand how infectious the investment process becomes. Once you see the fruits of your efforts, you'll want to invest more—$50 per month becomes $100 per month becomes $150 per month.

Even investing $50 per month, and never increasing the amount, can give you a seven-figure portfolio. You just have to start early. A fifteen-year-old who invests $50 per month until age sixty-five, or a total of $30,000, will have an investment portfolio of more than $1.3 million (assuming an average annual return of 11 percent). While that may not be much help to you given your age, I'm sure you know a teenager who would benefit from this knowledge.

THE POWER OF BABY STEPS

Ben Jackson understands the power of "baby steps." As an investor, you can create a seven-figure portfolio merely by taking a series of small steps over many years.

I came across an amazing little article on the Internet entitled "The Slight Edge Philosophy" (**www.topachievement.com/slight-edge.html**). The article, written by Jeff Olson, talks about the power of baby steps and how small incremental changes can have huge impacts.

"In the process of learning how to walk," writes Mr. Olson, "you probably spent more time failing than you did succeeding. But did you ever have the thought of quitting? Did you ever tell yourself, 'I'm not cut out for walking—guess I'll crawl for the rest of my life?' No, of course you didn't. So why do you do that now?" Mr. Olson believes we fail to achieve our goals because we become unwilling to take baby steps. "You put your trust in achieving breakthroughs, making quantum leaps, instant this, instant that, hitting the lottery. You began a habit of settling for less, just because more was so far out of your reach. You forgot about the most proven powerful success philosophy on earth—The Slight Edge."

Mr. Olson uses the following example to show the power of the

"Slight Edge" philosophy. If you were to improve just .003 each day—that's only three tenths of 1 percent, a very slight edge—and you kept that up for the next five years, here's what would happen to you:

- The first year you would improve 100 percent.
- The second year you would improve 200 percent.
- The third year you would improve 400 percent.
- The fourth year you would be a better person by 800 percent.
- By the end of year five—simply by improving three tenths of 1 percent per day—you will have magnified your value, your skills, and the results you accomplished *1,600 percent*.

The "Slight Edge" philosophy works the same way with investing. The table below shows the power of the "Slight Edge" philosophy as it applies to investing regular amounts each month:

Investment Amount	Annual Return	Holding Period	Total
$50 per month	11.0 percent	10 years	$10,949
$60 per month	11.0 percent	12 years	$17,973
$75 per month	11.2 percent	15 years	$35,070
$80 per month	11.3 percent	18 years	$56,360
$95 per month	11.4 percent	20 years	$87,544
$100 per month	11.5 percent	25 years	$173,659

Check out the payoff of squeezing out $50 more each month ($100 versus just $50), earning just 0.5 percent more per year (11.5 percent versus 11.0 percent), and holding for twenty-five years instead of ten. Your reward is more than $162,700 ($173,659 minus $10,949). What is especially telling is the jump in return by adding just $5.00 to your monthly investment ($100 versus $95), earning 0.1 percent more per year (11.5 percent versus 11.4 percent) and lengthening your holding period five years (twenty-five years versus twenty years). The reward for these baby steps? *$86,115.*

That's how you get rich in the market. Not in quantum leaps. But in baby steps.

KEEP INVESTING, EVEN DURING BEAR MARKETS

Too many people allow their investing habits to be influenced by whether the market is a "bear market" or a "bull market." During "bear markets," when stock prices are undergoing a general decline (the typical bear market since 1899 has lasted about fifteen months), many investors refuse to invest. Admittedly, it's difficult to invest when stock prices fall almost daily. Nevertheless, the only way you make a long-term investment strategy work is to buy stocks during bear markets. That's how you build positions to take advantage of bull markets.

Smart investors buy during bull and bear markets. Indeed, when I asked our millionaire investors if their investment style differed from bull markets to bear markets, 70 percent said that they invested no differently. In other words, to these investors, bull or bear markets are just labels for the same thing—a place to invest and grow your money over time.

CONCLUSION

This step may be the most difficult of the eight to follow. Let's return to the analogy about sit-ups I used earlier in the book. Doing one sit-up is simple; it's the subsequent sit-ups that are difficult to do day in, day out. So it is with investing. Investing on a monthly basis—heck, doing *anything* on a monthly basis—requires disciplines that few of us possess.

Yet, investing every month is essential to a successful investment program. Investing every month means you're spending less and not incurring spending's negative compounding. Investing every

"TEDDY BEAR" MILLIONAIRE
BENEFITS FROM REGULAR INVESTMENTS

GLADYS HOLM MAY NOT HAVE BEEN THE BEST STOCK PICKER on her own. But she knew how to ride the right horse. That horse was her boss. She also knew that investing regularly would pay off over time.

Gladys worked for forty-one years as a secretary at Hospital Supply Company in Evanston, Illinois. She was the secretary to the company founder, Foster C. McGaw. Gladys retired in 1969. When she died in 1996, this former secretary left money to Children's Memorial Hospital in Chicago. A lot of money—$18 million, to be precise.

"We were all stunned and surprised by the magnitude of her generosity," a hospital spokesperson said.

Known as the "Teddy Bear Lady" for handing out stuffed toys to children in the hospital, Ms. Holm made her money by investing wisely in the stock market.

How did Gladys become such a successful investor? She followed the investing strategies used by her boss, Mr. McGaw. "If McGaw made an investment and purchased 1,000 shares of some company, Gladys would buy 10 shares of the same thing," said Marjorie Pochter, who worked at the company with Ms. Holm. "Nobody gave her that money. She didn't inherit it, she earned it."

Not bad for a woman who, at the time she retired, was making a career-high $15,000 per year.

SOURCE: ASSOCIATED PRESS/PHILADELPHIA INQUIRER, AUGUST 1, 1997

month lowers investment risk because of time diversification. Investing monthly puts more money into play, something you'll need to do if you want a seven-figure portfolio.

Moral of the story: Invest something every month, regardless of the amount. Trust me—it will make a big difference over time.

The millionaire profiled in this chapter is Paula Cass. Ms. Cass is a retired bank president and CEO. Ms. Cass' current income is $1.2 million. However, that income level is a bit deceiving given that, as recently as 1982, Ms. Cass was making $36,000 per year. Ms. Cass has an investment portfolio of $6.1 million. That sizable portfolio is as much the result of Ms. Cass' disciplined investing style as it is her sizable income.

Ms. Cass is especially appropriate for this chapter given that she started small to build her portfolio. Her first foray into saving and investing consisted of saving half of her 10-cent allowance each week when she was a child. When she started working, she set aside money from her $2.00-per-hour paycheck to invest. Over time, as her income grew, she set aside more and more money to invest. Her plan was to try to save 25 percent of everything that she made. "I have equaled or exceeded the plan every year," says Paula.

Paula's experience shatters a number of investment myths— "That you have to have a lot of money before you can begin. That you have to know everything there is to know. That you have to take a lot of risk in order to make a good return." Says Paula, "I'm living proof that you don't have to have up-to-the-second knowledge and tips to be a successful investor."

And what does Paula like most about having a seven-figure portfolio?

"The ability to devote time to my heart's desire rather than being employed."

NAME: Paula Cass

AGE: 52

HOME: Midwest

MARITAL STATUS: Single (never divorced)

CHILDREN: 0

EDUCATION: College (undergraduate) graduate

CURRENT INCOME: $1,200,000

FIVE-YEAR AVERAGE INCOME: $590,000

HOW MANY DIFFERENT JOBS SINCE AGE 25? 3

DO YOU HAVE AN ANNUAL HOUSEHOLD BUDGET THAT YOU FOLLOW? Yes

AT WHAT AGE DID YOU START INVESTING? 15

WHAT IS THE SIZE OF YOUR ENTIRE INVESTMENT PORTFOLIO? $6.1 million

WHAT IS THE BREAKDOWN OF THESE ASSETS? 401(k) (5 percent), individual stocks (61 percent), bonds (10 percent), IRAs/Keoghs (5 percent), certificates of deposit (18 percent), other (1 percent)

HOW MANY INDIVIDUAL STOCKS DO YOU OWN? 10

NAME YOUR 5 LARGEST HOLDINGS: National City Corporation, Bank One Corporation, ConAgra, IBM, Lucent Technologies

HOW MANY INDIVIDUAL MUTUAL FUNDS DO YOU OWN? 6

NAME YOUR BIGGEST FUND HOLDINGS: Fidelity Magellan, Armada U.S. Government, Armada Mid Cap, Armada Small Cap, Armada Balanced Allocation

HOW MANY INDIVIDUAL BONDS DO YOU HAVE? 30

DO YOU RECEIVE ADVICE ON YOUR INVESTMENTS FROM AN OUTSIDE SOURCE? Yes

WHAT TYPE OF BROKER DO YOU USE? Traditional discount broker

WHAT ARE YOUR SHORT-TERM GOALS? I have just retired from my job and am devoting my time to charitable organizations, helping small businesses grow profitably, and providing financial counseling to individuals and families who are having financial problems. So obviously, my goal is to provide sufficient income to be able to do those things and still enjoy my hobbies.

WHAT HURDLES, IF ANY, DID YOU OVERCOME TO BEGIN INVESTING? Low-paying jobs in the banking industry.

HOW, PSYCHOLOGICALLY SPEAKING, DID YOU DEAL WITH THE NOTION OF PUTTING OFF

CONSUMPTION TO SAVE FOR A BETTER FINANCIAL FUTURE? I grew up in a rather poor family, economically, and saw how my father spent every dime we had and then some. He was always in debt. I vowed that I would not do that.

WERE THERE ANY SPECIFIC EVENTS, LIFE-CHANGING MOMENTS, ETC., THAT SPURRED YOU TO BEGIN INVESTING? We received a 10-cent allowance each week, but had to save half of it in a savings account. When I turned 15 and had my first bank job, my father asked for the money back that had been saved thus far. It wasn't much—only about $72. But it was all the money I had ever had, and I had saved hard for it. I vowed I would create my own savings and investing program.

HAVE YOU INHERITED WHAT YOU THOUGHT WAS A LARGE SUM OF MONEY? No

HOW DID YOU EDUCATE YOURSELF ABOUT INVESTING? DID YOU FIND THE EDUCATION PROCESS DIFFICULT? FUN? I had lots of good bank training along the way that educated me about investing in general, and specific investments. I also read nearly everything I could get my hands on, including *The Wall Street Journal* and numerous regular and banking publications.

DID YOU HAVE ANY SPECIAL EXPERTISE IN INVESTING WHEN YOU STARTED? No

HOW MUCH DO YOU SPEND PER YEAR ON INVESTMENT RESEARCH RESOURCES? $251 to $500 per year

DO YOU USE A COMPUTER TO KEEP TRACK OF YOUR INVESTMENTS? Yes

HOW MANY HOURS PER WEEK DO YOU DEVOTE TO YOUR INVESTMENTS AND INVESTMENT STRATEGIES? 15

WHAT CRITERIA DO YOU USE TO PICK STOCKS/MUTUAL FUNDS?

- In an industry that is growing and has opportunities in the years ahead.
- Strong earnings history.
- Somewhat below its industry peers on price/earnings ratio.
- Pattern of increasing dividends.

HOW OFTEN DO YOU BUY INVESTMENTS? Monthly

ON AVERAGE, HOW LONG DO YOU HOLD AN INVESTMENT BEFORE SELLING? 5 years

DO YOU "MARKET TIME"? No

WHAT WERE SOME OF YOUR BIGGEST INVESTMENT MISTAKES? I invested in one start-up company that later went bankrupt. I also bought stock on a friend's tip that it was a company about to be acquired. It turned out to be a big loser. Fortunately, neither investment was very big.

DO YOU INVEST IN WHAT YOU KNOW? Yes, the vast majority of my holdings are in bank stocks.

HOW WOULD YOU BEST DESCRIBE YOUR INVESTMENT APPROACH? Conservative. I want to sleep at night. Buy and hold, sell when you need to re-balance the portfolio or when one certain stock has performed so well that it is now too large a percentage of the overall port-folio or has performed too poorly to be considered a "good asset." Don't try to "time" the market.

DO YOU BELIEVE IT IS POSSIBLE TO BEAT THE MARKET ON A CONSISTENT BASIS? No

HOW MANY INVESTMENTS DO YOU BELIEVE ARE NECESSARY TO BE PROPERLY DIVERSI-FIED? 20 to 30

WHAT IS YOUR GREATEST FEAR AS AN INVESTOR? That I will get too greedy and try to make a big killing and abandon my own rules.

IF YOU COULD GIVE JUST ONE PIECE OF ADVICE TO INDIVIDUAL INVESTORS, WHAT WOULD THAT PIECE OF ADVICE BE? Formulate your investment strategy based upon your life goals and stick to it.

8

BUY AND HOLD . . .
AND HOLD . . . AND HOLD

The key to stock market success is time, not timing.

—CHUCK REDER, MISSOURI,
$3.2 MILLION INVESTMENT PORTFOLIO

STEP 6: BUY AND HOLD . . . AND HOLD . . .
AND HOLD . . . AND HOLD . . . AND HOLD

Millionaire investors never sell.

Okay, I exaggerate. But only a little.

Approximately 75 percent of the millionaire investors I surveyed hold stocks for more than five years.

Nearly 40 percent of them hold stocks for ten years or more.

Holding investments for five or ten years or longer seems out of step with today's fast-paced, high-octane, "trade-till-you-drop" markets. After all, why hold stocks for ten years if you can buy and sell stocks in nanoseconds on the Internet and pay low, low, low commissions?

Why? Because trading stocks makes only your broker rich.

On the other hand, buying and holding stocks makes *you* rich.

THE DANGERS OF TRADING

I'm appalled at what I see some individual investors doing these days on Wall Street. Buying and selling stocks by the day, the hour, even the minute. Trading because it's as easy as punching a key on the computer and as cheap as a deli sandwich.

Trading because they *can,* not because they *should.*

One of the things I find most offensive about day trading—or weekly or monthly trading—is its arrogance. Day trading implies that an investor has many, many, many good investment ideas. After all, if you're trading 50 or 100 or, in some trader's cases, 1,000 times in a single year, doesn't it imply that you feel each trade is a good idea, a potential winner?

Let's face it—most of us probably won't have thirty good ideas about *anything* in our lifetimes.

Warren Buffett, arguably the greatest investor of our time, owns fewer than two dozen stocks, many of which he has held for several years. If Warren Buffett has only a relatively few good ideas, why should any investor believe that he or she has fifty or more good investment ideas per year?

A famous college football coach once said, "When you throw a forward pass, three things can happen, and two of them are bad."

It's the same with selling investments. Selling an investment is the most dangerous part of the investment process. When you sell, a bunch of stuff can happen, and most of it is bad.

TRANSACTION COSTS

One bad thing that happens when you sell stocks is you generate transaction costs. Even if you pay only $10 or $15 or $20 per trade, those commissions add up if you trade three or four times a day or even three or four times a week.

Here's an example of how "cheap" commission rates add up to big dollars over time. Merrill Lynch made big news when it began offering online trades for "just" $29.95 per trade—a rate much lower than its standard full-service commissions. Still, even at $29.95, traders can kill themselves by buying and selling frequently. Let's say you have a portfolio of $100,000. If you make just two trades per week at $29.95 per trade, your annual trading costs are $3,114.80—more than 3 percent of your portfolio value.

Losing 3 percent per year to transaction costs has a huge impact on your portfolio over time. Do the math. A $100,000 portfolio that earns 11 percent per year for twenty-five years grows to about $1.4 million. If that portfolio loses 3 percent per year to commissions and fees (thus earning an after-fee return of 8 percent per year), that same $100,000 investment grows to nearly $700,000. That's the cost of those "cheap" commissions over twenty-five years—*more than $660,000.*

And even if you cut Merrill Lynch's online commission rate in half—to $15 per trade—you're still paying more than 1.5 percent per year in transaction fees on a $100,000 portfolio if you make just two trades per week.

And commissions are only part of your transaction fees. A huge hidden cost of trading is the spread between the "bid" and "ask" prices that all investors pay when they purchase stocks. Investors buy stock at the higher "ask" price and sell at the lower "bid" price. For highly liquid, large-company stocks, this spread is extremely narrow (which is yet another reason to focus on large-company stocks when purchasing individual securities). For small-company stocks, however, this spread can be huge, as much as one-half point or more. If you frequently buy and sell small-company stocks— which many traders do—the "low" brokerage commissions you pay often mask the big spreads you also pay.

TAXES

By definition, traders rarely hold investments for twelve months or more. Unfortunately, constantly churning investments means paying taxes on gains at your full tax rate. If you're in the top tax bracket, you'll lose roughly 40 percent of your gains to Uncle Sam versus a maximum 20 percent if you hold the investment for twelve months or more. In other words, the tax penalty for trading stocks runs as high as *100 percent*.

I talk a lot about taxes in Chapter 9. For our purposes here, understand the following—*taxes matter*. What you pay Uncle Sam is money that will never earn you a dime in return.

It's gone forever.

Millionaire investors know the impact taxes have on a portfolio and behave accordingly. Millionaires defer paying Uncle Sam as long as possible. They know every year they defer paying taxes they earn money on Uncle Sam's *tax-free loan*. And if millionaire investors sell, they make sure they sell at the lowest possible tax rates. That means holding investments for at least twelve months.

If you constantly buy and sell stocks, taxes will eat you up over time. Accounting for these trades at tax time will also eat you up. I guarantee you that many of these electronic day traders got a real banjo lesson when they prepared their taxes. Uncle Sam requires you to account for *every* trade you make during the year. If you trade three or four times a day, think of the paperwork you generate come tax time. Think of the time spent tracking down the information for all those trades. Think of the dirty looks, not to mention hefty bill, your tax accountant gives you.

Bottom line: Trading equals taxes equals headaches. *Big* headaches. Of course, you can avoid these headaches by not selling your investments. That's what everyday millionaire investors do. That's what you should do.

REINVESTMENT RISK

As bad as they are, transaction fees and taxes may not even be the worst things that happen when you sell investments. The biggest downside of trading investments is "reinvestment risk."

When you sell any investment, you have to do something with the money. Reinvestment risk is the risk that what you do with the money makes you worse off than if you had done nothing at all.

What happens when you sell investments?

- If you sell because you're concerned about the market, you might keep the money on the sidelines until you feel more comfortable investing. Selling and moving money to the sidelines takes your money out of play. The risk you run keeping money out of the market is that you are not maximizing the power of time in your investment program.

- If you sell because you think you've found a better investment, the risk you run is that the new investment may be worse than the one you sold. An academic study conducted a few years ago by Terrance Odean, a professor at the University of California at Davis, showed that individual investors, on average, buy stocks they should sell and sell stocks they should buy. One reason for this phenomenon is that investors (remember, investors are humans) hate to admit mistakes. So investors sell their winners and keep their losers. In the process, they sell stocks they probably should buy.

- If you sell to buy another stock, the risk you run is that the new stock is only as good or only slightly better than the one you sold. It's not enough that the stock you buy does as well as the one you sold or even a little bit better. It has to do a lot better. When you sell, you incur taxes and transaction fees. The new investment has to make up, at a minimum, the money lost to taxes and commissions. These costs provide a huge hurdle, especially if you generated big gains on the stock you sold. You're asking a lot from your new investment if it has to outperform your old investment by 20 percent or 30 percent just to compensate for taxes and transaction fees.

TRADING AND EFFICIENT MARKETS

The stock market is reasonably efficient. A company's stock price, over time, is a fair reflection of the underlying value of the company. This efficiency is driven by the millions of professional and amateur investors, all seeking undervalued stocks, who push prices to their true value. Stock prices may diverge from a company's real value periodically. Over time, however, finding mispriced stocks is a difficult chore.

I don't think investors should give up on stock picking because markets are efficient. Buying and holding a basket of quality stocks is a tax- and transaction-friendly way of enjoying the overall growth in the economy. Besides, stock picking is fun. I buy individual stocks because I like the thrill and challenge of finding quality stocks.

Nevertheless, at the end of the day, I do believe markets are fairly efficient. That's one reason I own index funds in addition to actively managed funds in my 401(k) plan.

If you buy that markets are reasonably efficient—and boat loads of academic research say you should—then you should also buy the notion that trading stocks is a costly waste of time.

Professor Terrance Odean, mentioned earlier in this chapter, looked at trading patterns of customers at an unidentified discount broker from the period 1991 to 1996. What Professor Odean found was that these stock buyers had an average annual return of 17.1 percent, before costs, during the period. This average annual return roughly matched the market during the period.

Once you accounted for trading costs, however, the average annual return fell to 15.6 percent.

Professor Odean's example demonstrates two key points:

- *The market is reasonably efficient.* Investors were not particularly skillful in picking stocks that beat the market. Nor were they necessarily dreadful stock pickers. Their stock picks neither added nor subtracted value. That's what an efficient market means—that investors, on average, over time cannot add or subtract value with stock picking. Stocks are efficiently priced, and the overall rise in the general level of stock prices accounts for portfolio performance.
- *Trading costs kill performance.* The fact that individual investors, as well as professional investors, don't beat the market has less to do with stock picking and almost everything to do with the costs of trading.

I said it before but it bears repeating—*transaction costs and taxes matter.* If you're losing one or two percentage points in return every year due to trading costs and taxes, your climb to seven figures becomes that much more difficult.

TRADING MEANS NO HOME RUNS

In Chapter 6, I said that smart investors swing for singles. The beauty of swinging for singles, as any major leaguer will tell you, is that you hit some home runs, too. If you trade stocks, however, you pretty well guarantee yourself not hitting any home runs.

By definition, traders *trade* stocks. They don't hold them for many years. They dart in and out, taking a quick profit (hopefully) on each trade.

The problem with taking 25 percent or 50 percent or even 100 percent profits is that you will never—I repeat, *never*—own the stock that rises 500 percent or 5,000 percent. And those are the stocks that give you a huge leg up in building a seven-figure portfolio.

To say Intel has been a pretty good stock over the years is an understatement. If you had invested $10,000 in Intel at the end of 1988, and reinvested all dividends, your $10,000 investment would have grown to $406,340 by the end of 1998. That's a gain of nearly *4,000 percent.* A trader never gets anywhere close to a 4,000 percent return off Intel. Why? Because he or she sold after a 50 percent or 100 percent gain.

Millionaire investors know what can happen when you buy and hold an Intel. They've done it.

Millionaire investors know that great investment ideas have longer shelf lives than six months. That's why they hold them forever.

Millionaire investors appreciate what happens when you combine the power of time with a great investment idea. That's how they got to seven figures.

Chris Master, eighty-six, is one of our millionaire investors. Chris, whose investment portfolio is worth $1.7 million, tells the following story about taking profits prematurely:

> During part of the Depression, I was in my mid-20s, single, and buying 10 to 20 shares of stocks of well-known companies at very low prices of about $1 to $7 per share. As the country was pulling out of the Depression and getting ready for war, stocks moved higher. Soon, I had profits of 100 percent to 300 percent or more in some cases. Since I was expecting to be drafted during 1940–1942, I sold most of my stocks, felt rich for the moment, and volunteered for the Army Air Corps after Pearl Harbor in early 1942. As the war developed, confidence returned to the market, and all of my "sold" stocks advanced substantially. Looking back some 57 years, it was a big mistake to sell all or most of my stocks. They kept on advancing over the years. After WWII ended, I got

back into investments and made adequate money by investing in great companies for the long haul. The lesson—don't panic and sell everything at one time.

YOU DON'T REDUCE RISK BY MARKET TIMING— YOU INCREASE IT

Why do investors sell? One reason is they think they can control risk by timing the market. The thinking goes like this—"If I can sell my investments at the top, I can avoid losing money."

In other words, trying to time the market is a risk-reduction strategy for many investors. The market seems high, so they better pull money out of the market.

Sounds good, right? Unfortunately, the reality is that you're never going to time successfully market tops and bottoms. You might get lucky a few times. But the one time you're wrong, you'll undo all the times you were right.

If you take nothing else away from this chapter, take this:

The biggest risk of investing is not being in the market when it goes down but being out of the market when it goes up.

Markets move in bursts. In 1998, for example, the Dow Jones Industrial Average moved from 7,539 to nearly 9,400—a 24 percent move—in less than three months. Many investors missed this move because they got out of the market when it dropped in August and September.

The following example comes from *Investor's Business Daily:* If you had invested in the S&P 500 at the end of 1981, and reinvested your earnings and dividends until year-end 1998, you would have earned a 21 percent average annual return. If you attempted to time the market and missed just the ten best trading days during that seventeen-year period, your return would have fallen to 16 percent per year.

Losing 5 percent per year doesn't sound like much.

It's huge.

A $10,000 investment earning 21 percent per year (compounded monthly) for 17 years grows to $344,366.

A $10,000 investment earning 16 percent per year for 17 years grows to $149,099.

Your penalty for missing the best ten trading days during that seventeen-year period? *$195,266.*

And if you were really aggressive in timing the market and missed the thirty best market days in that seventeen-year period, your average annual return drops to just 9 percent.

In order to maximize the power of time and compounding, you have to be in the market when these bursts occur. Every time you pull money out of the market, you run the risk of missing those important rallies that create seven-figure portfolios.

Don't worry about reducing risk by market timing. The proper way to reduce risk is by lengthening your holding period and diversifying across various types of stocks.

Besides, the payoff for perfect market timing, when you consider the risks, is rather skimpy.

Let's say you invested $10,000 every year from 1988 to 1997 in the S&P 500 index. And let's assume you are the world's worst market timer. You invested that $10,000 every year at the exact market peak in the S&P 500.

At the end of ten years, how much money would you have? Your $100,000 investment ($10,000 times ten years) would have accumulated to a not-too-shabby value of $246,476. So even with lousy market timing, you more than doubled your money.

What would have been the payoff had you invested the $10,000 at the exact low every year for ten years instead of the exact peak? Surprisingly, you would have added only $60,000 to your take, or an additional 24 percent.

Now $60,000 is not chump change. Still, when you consider the huge risks you incur to attempt perfect market timing for ten years, and the even larger odds you face against being successful, a 24 percent payoff for your efforts seems hardly worth the risks.

And riding through a market downturn isn't the worse thing in the world. For starters, market declines provide opportunities to buy favored stocks at bargain prices. Second, history has shown that markets usually rebound reasonably quickly from major declines. During the twentieth century, the stock market rose in roughly three out of every four years. Furthermore, following every one of the major market declines in the last forty years, the stock market regained its previous peak in an average thirteen months and went on to new highs.

Of course, there have been times when markets declined and didn't recover for years. However, the percentages say that you probably won't have to wait more than a couple of years for markets to regain their lost ground. And if you buy during the down period, you amplify your gains when the markets recover.

The upshot of all this is that you can do just fine riding through market downturns and buying at market peaks. The trick is that you have to be committed to a long-term investment strategy. Conversely, you can get yourself into a world of trouble in the name of risk reduction by trying to time the markets.

More than 70 percent of our everyday millionaires say they don't time the market. In fact, more than 70 percent of our millionaires don't invest any differently whether it's a "bull" or "bear" market. They buy and hold, buy and hold, and leave the timing to the chumps.

I SPEAK OF WHAT I KNOW

Since I suspect I'm no better at trading stocks than the next guy, I don't do it often. In fact, I've sold only one stock since 1992—Browning-Ferris Industries—which I unloaded at the beginning of 1999.

I couldn't even get that one right.

I bought Browning-Ferris several years ago because of my expectations that demand for garbage hauling and landfill space would skyrocket. The growth in this industry, however, never materialized. Pricing pressures hindered Browning-Ferris' ability to post sustained earnings growth.

Needless to say, Browning-Ferris stock didn't keep pace with the overall market. In fact, when I sold the stock, it was trading below 1994 levels and coming off a lousy 1998 in which the shares dropped more than 23 percent.

The stock had no story, no momentum. No reason to hold, I told myself. Time to bail. So I did, somewhere in the $20s.

Big mistake.

Almost immediately after I sold the stock, it began to surge. And then it happened. On March 8—about two months after I had dumped the stock in the $20s—Browning-Ferris received a takeover offer from Allied Waste Industries for $45 per share—$45 *per share.*

Needless to say, selling in January cost me greatly in March when Browning-Ferris popped to over $40 on the takeover news.

In retrospect, I truly was snakebitten by this stock. I held it for years without a whiff of takeover speculation, and the company got a buyout offer less than two months after I sold. Of course, one could argue that my problem wasn't that I sold, but that I sold too late. Browning-Ferris traded for $40 in 1995 and $38 in 1997 and 1998, so I had my chances.

Still, my original point remains irrefutable—trading stocks is tricky business.

WHEN SHOULD YOU SELL?

Does that mean you should never sell an investment? Legitimate reasons exist to sell an investment, but they are few and far between. The primary reason to sell is because the reasons you bought didn't materialize. Perhaps you bought a stock because of an exciting new product only to learn that other companies are coming to market faster with a better mousetrap. That's probably a reason to sell. Perhaps you bought a stock because it pays a hefty dividend only to have the company eliminate the dividend because of poor earnings. That's probably a reason to sell. Perhaps you bought a mutual fund because of the fund manager's strong track record only to see that fund manager jump ship to another fund family. That's probably a reason to sell.

Of course, in order to know when to sell, you have to know why you bought in the first place. I know this may be hard to believe, but it's true—most investors own a few stocks that they have no idea why they own. These may be stocks that are inherited or stocks that were given as gifts or stocks they acquired so long ago that they don't remember the reasons they bought.

Because it's so important to know why you bought a particular investment—especially when deciding whether to sell—I suggest you maintain a journal on your investments. Write down your reasons for buying an investment. Writing your reasons not only provides a record for future reference but also crystallizes your thinking on that particular investment. Indeed, you might find that, after writing down your reasons, your initial excitement for the investment idea wanes.

Another reason to sell is a rapidly rising debt level. A good way to monitor a company's debt level is to watch the ratio between a company's long-term debt and its total capital. (Total capital is long-term debt plus shareholder equity.) If this ratio is rising over time, examine the reasons. Is the company taking on debt to fund acquisitions or stock buybacks? Is the debt level rising at a time when profits are falling? High debt levels are manageable during strong economic periods. But companies that load up on debt during the good times may run into trouble during weak economic climates.

A third reason to sell is the "stupid" acquisition. Admittedly, I don't always follow my own advice here. I own several companies that have been big acquirers in recent years. Again, a strong stock market and healthy economic climates have helped limit the shocks that can come with making bad acquisitions. But know this—on average, mergers provide little, if any, lasting benefits for shareholders. And in many cases, acquisitions lead to major problems.

If you own stock in a company that is buying another firm, try to put the deal in some sort of time context. In other words, companies that buy after takeover activity has heated up in a particular industry sector usually overpay for bad merchandise. The best fruit is picked early in the game. If your company is making a bold move in an industry that has not had much takeover activity, that's a proactive move that probably has been thought out thoroughly. If you own a company that is buying out of what appears to be desperation, that's probably a time to sell.

To Rebalance or Not to Rebalance

A fourth reason to sell is because one of your winning investments now makes up a large part of your portfolio. This type of selling is called "portfolio rebalancing."

Let's say you bought Microsoft several years ago and held the stock through thick and thin. Chances are that Microsoft would now constitute a hefty part of your portfolio, perhaps as much as 30 percent or 40 percent of your portfolio if you had bought a lot of the stock. Many financial advisers believe no single investment should constitute more than 10 percent or 20 percent of your overall portfolio. The thinking is that you don't want the health of your portfolio riding on one or two stocks. To rebalance your portfolio means to sell a portion of your Microsoft and invest the money elsewhere. By selling, you reduce the overall weighting of Microsoft in your portfolio mix.

Obviously, selling to rebalance your portfolio is a risk-reduction strategy. Unfortunately, by definition rebalancing also means selling your winners. That's the problem I have with portfolio rebalancing. I hate to sell winners.

Yes, at some point the prudent thing to do is lower your exposure to an investment whose size overwhelms your other investments. But I believe your investment time horizon should dictate when you rebalance, not so much the weighting of the asset in your portfolio. For that reason, I wouldn't necessarily recommend that a thirty-five-year-old investor should sell Microsoft because it represents 30 percent or 40 percent of his or her portfolio. That thirty-five-year-old has a lot of investing ahead and can handle the risk should Microsoft go through a rough patch. On the other hand, a sixty-year-old has to be a bit more defensive when it comes to holding a few investments that comprise the bulk of his or her portfolio. That sixty-year-old doesn't have as much time to make up for a drop in those investments.

Personally, if I owned a stock that made up 40 percent of my portfolio, I would not be quick to sell the stock as long as I believed the stock's prospects were sound. I would not sell merely to rebalance my portfolio. When would I start to rebalance? That's a tough one and probably would depend, in part, on the nature of the stock. I would feel more comfortable having a big, time-tested, industry-leading blue chip, such as General Electric, make up 40 percent of my portfolio than I would a stock in an extremely competitive, high-technology field, such as America Online, making up 40 percent of my portfolio.

Most investment books provide black-and-white rules for rebalancing—"Rebalance if an asset grows to more than 10 percent of your portfolio," for example. You won't find such rules here. Every investor is different. Every stock is different. I do know that sticking to strict percentage allocations to run a portfolio will cause you to do frequent buying and selling of securities to keep those percentages in line. That's a mistake.

I'm reminded of a typical asset allocation that has been recommended to investors over the years that calls for having 5 percent of

Buy and Hold Never Tasted So Good

You won't confuse Quincy, a town in north Florida, with Beverly Hills, that bastion of glitter and wealth. There's no Rodeo Drive. Movie stars don't hang out in the restaurants. What is in Quincy, however, is money. Coke money, to be precise. No, not money derived from selling the illegal white powder. Money created by the other Coke, that brown liquid with bubbles and fizz.

In 1922, tobacco farmers in this town, after hauling in a bumper crop, decided to do something with their profits. At the urging of Mark Monroe, a local banker, the farmers bought Coca-Cola stock.

Coke had just come public, and "Daddy liked the taste," according to Julia Woodward, Monroe's daughter. "Plus, he figured the stock would be good collateral because folks would always have a nickel to buy a bottle."

Mr. Monroe turned out to be a smart man. A very smart man.

At one time, the town's residents held two thirds of all Coke shares outstanding, says Quincy historian Johnny Blitch. The Coke stock made Quincy one of the wealthiest towns in America. In fact, before World War II Quincy was the richest town in America on a per-capita basis.

Today, money from these Coke millionaires and their heirs still can be readily seen in this city. "The Coke families largely have resisted the temptation to sell," said W. C. Brancon, president of Quincy State Bank.

> Just how much money has Coke created for Quincy over the years? Today, those farmers and their progeny who never sold the stock now own 7.5 million shares valued at more than $400 million.
>
> "Some people have sold shares to buy a car," said Ms. Woodward. "But then a couple years later they realized they sold stock worth half a million dollars for a Cadillac."
>
> SOURCE: ADAM LEVY,
BLOOMBERG BUSINESS NEWS/MIAMI HERALD, JANUARY 5, 1997

a portfolio in gold and precious metals as an "inflation hedge." The problem with maintaining a 5 percent allocation in gold and precious metals is that you would have been investing *a lot* of money in gold and precious metals stocks over the last decade (at the expense of investing in better-performing assets) to maintain that 5 percent allocation. That's because gold and precious metals stocks have fallen dramatically during that period.

In some ways, to rebalance or not to rebalance boils down to what I've said before in this book in one way or another: If you want to *create* wealth, portfolio diversification (i.e., rebalancing) is not necessarily your first concern. If you want to *maintain* wealth, portfolio diversification becomes more important.

BUY WITH THE IDEA THAT YOU *CANNOT* SELL

Millionaire investors put a positive spin on the dangers of selling. Their mind-set is the following: "If I don't sell, I better be right when I buy." The dangers of selling force them to make better and more thoughtful decisions when choosing investments.

This is a critical point to understand. If you could never sell an investment once you bought it, you would make better buy decisions. That's how millionaire investors frame the investment process.

Everyday millionaire Humberto Cruz, who's profiled at the end of Chapter 6, purchases investments based on this credo—"I must feel comfortable that if I were sent away to a deserted island for ten years or more, I could hold this investment until I return."

Trust me. Buy investments as if you could never sell them.

It works.

CONCLUSION

Next time a friend is bragging about all the money he or she is making trading stocks, remember the following: The burgeoning of stock trading in recent years arose from the intersection of the Internet and extraordinary stock market returns from 1995–99. Given the unprecedented returns during that time period, it would have been difficult not to make money regardless of what harebrained investment strategy you used. As the markets return to more traditional returns, my guess is that those friends who crowed about their trading profits will be licking their wounds, or perhaps even be out of the market altogether.

Buying and holding a quality stock for five or ten or twenty years isn't sexy. It won't give you great stories to tell around the water cooler. It certainly won't make your broker happy.

But it will make you rich.

The everyday millionaire profiled in this chapter is Joan Allison. Joan, eighty-six, lives in Ohio. I picked Joan because she understands the power of buying and holding securities. Indeed, her $6 million investment portfolio was built off the backs of buying small amounts of stock over time in quality companies and holding those shares for many years.

"We held onto things and didn't let people talk us into selling them," says Joan.

Joan started investing with her husband, who passed away in 1983. "My husband often would say that we made a wonderful team," says Joan. She and her husband operated a variety of businesses, including a real estate firm and an insurance business. The couple ramped up their investing in the 1950s and '60s as their rising income levels allowed. Joan still holds stocks that were bought in the '60s. One of these stocks is Huntington Bancshares.

"Huntington Bancshares was a big winner for us," says Joan. The couple started buying Huntington in 1967. For the next fifteen years, the couple bought small amounts of Huntington on a regular basis, eventually accumulating 137 shares. "Our cost basis was $1,009," says Joan. Through splits, Joan now owns more than 1,900 shares valued at roughly $57,000.

NAME: Joan Allison

AGE: 86

HOME: Ohio

MARITAL STATUS: Widow

EDUCATION: High school graduate

OCCUPATION: Retired—Insurance and real estate agent

CURRENT INCOME: $150,000

HOW MANY DIFFERENT JOBS SINCE AGE 25? 1

DO YOU HAVE AN ANNUAL HOUSEHOLD BUDGET THAT YOU FOLLOW? No

WOULD YOU CONSIDER YOUR PARENTS TO BE FRUGAL? Yes

HOW IMPORTANT WERE YOUR PARENTS IN DEVELOPING YOUR DISCIPLINE AND EXPERTISE IN INVESTING? Very important. They taught me values, honesty, and consideration for my fellowman.

AT WHAT AGE DID YOU START INVESTING? 38

WHAT IS THE SIZE OF YOUR ENTIRE INVESTMENT PORTFOLIO? $6 million

WHAT IS THE BREAKDOWN OF THESE ASSETS? $5 million common stocks; $1 million tax-exempt and zero-coupon bonds.

HOW MANY INDIVIDUAL STOCKS DO YOU OWN? 30

NAME YOUR 5 LARGEST HOLDINGS: Exxon Mobil, DuPont, Chevron, Lockheed Martin, Burlington Northern Santa Fe, Burlington Resources

HOW MANY INDIVIDUAL MUTUAL FUNDS DO YOU OWN? 0

HOW MANY INDIVIDUAL BONDS DO YOU HAVE? 10

HAVE YOU EVER PURCHASED STOCK/INDEX OPTIONS? No

HAVE YOU EVER BOUGHT STOCK/INDEX FUTURES? No

DO YOU OWN GOLD OR PRECIOUS METALS? Yes

HAVE YOU EVER SOLD STOCK SHORT? No

WHAT ARE THE PLANS FOR YOUR ESTATE? I have built an adult day-care center to honor my husband's memory.

DID YOU HAVE ANY SPECIFIC INVESTMENT GOALS IN MIND WHEN YOU STARTED INVESTING? Yes, to start accumulating common stocks.

WHAT HURDLES, IF ANY, DID YOU OVERCOME TO BEGIN INVESTING? None. We were aggressive and proceeded to live within our means.

HOW, PSYCHOLOGICALLY SPEAKING, DID YOU DEAL WITH THE NOTION OF PUTTING OFF CONSUMPTION TO SAVE FOR A BETTER FINANCIAL FUTURE? Our upbringing gave us a firm foundation.

WHERE DID YOU GET THE MONEY TO START INVESTING? Earnings from business and salaries.

HAVE YOU INHERITED WHAT YOU THOUGHT WAS A LARGE SUM OF MONEY? Yes, from my husband's estate.

DID YOU START INVESTING WITH A SPECIFIC PLAN IN MIND? Yes, to reinvest dividends—not to spend them—and invest all the extra money we could.

HOW DID YOU EDUCATE YOURSELF ABOUT INVESTING? DID YOU FIND THE EDUCATION PROCESS DIFFICULT? FUN? With help of good financial bulletins and *The Wall Street Journal,* and with my husband's keen financial background and business experiences and our discipline. Yes, we enjoyed it.

HOW MUCH DO YOU SPEND PER YEAR ON INVESTMENT RESEARCH RESOURCES? $501 to 1,000 per year

DO YOU USE A COMPUTER TO KEEP TRACK OF YOUR INVESTMENTS? No

WHAT TERM BEST DESCRIBES YOUR INVESTMENT STYLE? Conservative

HOW OFTEN DO YOU BUY INVESTMENTS? Monthly

ON AVERAGE, HOW LONG DO YOU HOLD AN INVESTMENT BEFORE SELLING? 10 years or longer.

DO YOU "MARKET TIME"? No

DOES YOUR INVESTMENT APPROACH DIFFER DEPENDING ON WHETHER THE MARKET IS CLASSIFIED AS A "BEAR" OR "BULL" MARKET? No

HOW IMPORTANT ARE TAXES IN THE INVESTMENT PROCESS? Very important

WHAT HAVE BEEN YOUR BEST-PERFORMING STOCKS? Chevron, DuPont (until recently), Huntington Bancshares

WHAT HAVE BEEN YOUR WORST-PERFORMING STOCKS? PS Group, Occidental Petroleum, Aqua Bottling

WHAT WERE SOME OF YOUR BIGGEST INVESTMENT MISTAKES? Not selling some stocks when reasonable profit was made. Not selling if dividends were cut—I feel that is a good criteria to sell.

DO YOU INVEST IN WHAT YOU KNOW? Yes

HOW WOULD YOU BEST DESCRIBE YOUR INVESTMENT APPROACH? Good common sense. Not being easily swayed by ups and downs of market.

DO YOU THINK INDIVIDUAL INVESTORS ARE DISADVANTAGED IN THE FINANCIAL MARKETS RELATIVE TO LARGE INVESTORS? Yes, they aren't privy to inside information.

DO YOU FEEL INDIVIDUAL INVESTORS HAVE ANY ADVANTAGES IN THE INVESTMENT PROCESS? Yes, if they are astute, are well disciplined, use good horse sense, and are not influenced by the crowds. In other words, do your own thing.

DO YOU BELIEVE IT IS POSSIBLE TO BEAT THE MARKET ON A CONSISTENT BASIS? Yes

WHAT MADE YOU THINK YOU COULD BE A SUCCESSFUL INVESTOR? Why not? I was brought up to believe I could accomplish anything and I set out to do so.

WHAT DOES THE TERM "RISK" MEAN TO YOU? Being careless in making decisions.

HOW MANY INVESTMENTS DO YOU BELIEVE ARE NECESSARY TO BE PROPERLY DIVERSIFIED? 20

WHAT IS YOUR GREATEST FEAR AS AN INVESTOR? Don't know if I have any fear! I'm comfortable. I'm proud. I'm thankful to be a high school graduate. I wouldn't trade my accomplishments and nonacademic commonsense with any Ph.D.

WHAT IS THE BIGGEST BENEFIT OF A 7-FIGURE PORTFOLIO? The pride and sense of accomplishment. The ability to do as occasion might demand.

IF YOU COULD GIVE JUST ONE PIECE OF ADVICE TO INDIVIDUAL INVESTORS, WHAT WOULD THAT PIECE OF ADVICE BE? Don't think you must have everything now! Sacrifice! Enjoy life with moderation but steadfastness in planning for the future. Do that extra thing for others, and many unforeseen things will return to you.

9

TAKE WHAT UNCLE SAM
GIVES YOU

My IRA is a pleasant joy to me.

—NEIL STATLER, FLORIDA,
$1.3 MILLION INVESTMENT PORTFOLIO

STEP 7: TAKE WHAT UNCLE SAM GIVES YOU

Few millionaire investors consider Uncle Sam their friend. In fact, when I asked the everyday millionaires in this book what they fear, many said the government's greedy hand.

"I love my country but distrust my government," says one of our millionaire investors. "The reason is the government raises taxes, re-distributes the wealth, and fiddles with foreign exchange rates and interest rates. The latter two have the greatest effect on the stock market, commodity prices, and real estate values."

Millionaire investors are nothing if not opportunistic, however, especially when investment opportunities are provided by Uncle Sam. And make no mistake—Uncle Sam provides some of the best investment deals around for individual investors.

UNCLE SAM, INVESTMENT PARTNER

You are in a business partnership with a friend. Your friend gives you the following choices for splitting the profits:

- Pay her 40 percent of the profits at the end of every year.
- Pay her just 20 percent of the profits, and you can pay her one year from now, five years from now, twenty years from now, fifty years from now, whenever. You choose when you want to pay.

Which offer would you take? Only a fool would choose the first option, right?

You'd be surprised how many fools there are in this world.

Whether you like it or not, Uncle Sam is your investment partner. The more your investments make, the more he makes.

But like the partner in our example, Uncle Sam gives you some attractive options for paying his share. You can pay Uncle Sam up to 40 percent of your investment gains at the end of every year. Or you can pay a maximum of 20 percent of your investment profits, and defer payment indefinitely.

Actually, Uncle Sam's offer is even better than your friend's deal. If you want, Uncle Sam allows you to leave your investment profits to your heirs, and *they* don't have to pay a dime to Uncle Sam. Better still, Uncle Sam gives *you* a way to avoid paying him *altogether*.

TRIM TAXES BY HOLDING STOCKS FOR A LONG TIME

Uncle Sam gives you a huge tax break if you hold investments for twelve months or more. Indeed, if you are in the top tax bracket (39.6 percent), the tax savings of holding investments for a year or more are *100 percent* (20 percent long-term capital-gains tax versus 39.6 percent tax on short-term gains).

Let's say your investment portfolio has a profit of $5,000 after six months. If you sell (and you are in the top tax bracket), Uncle Sam gets roughly 40 percent of your profit, or $2,000.

By waiting just six more months to sell, Uncle Sam's take gets cut in half ($1,000, or 20 percent of your profit).

Of course, I'm making the assumption that the $5,000 profit will still be around if you wait another six months. Perhaps it will; perhaps it won't. Who knows, it might even grow to $7,000. You don't know for certain. What you do know for certain is this: Even if your profit declines by 20 percent in that six-month interval (from $5,000 to $4,000), you'll still be ahead of the game by holding a stock twelve months before you sell. When you sell with a $5,000 profit after six months, your take, after Uncle Sam's cut, is $3,000. If you wait until 12 months to sell and your $5,000 profit has shrunk to $4,000, your take, after Uncle Sam's cut, is $3,200 ($4,000 times 80 percent).

By waiting six months, you still come out ahead even if your investment profits shrink by 20 percent.

In the first example, the tax savings were 100 percent (paying Uncle Sam $1,000 instead of $2,000). Actually, the savings are *greater* than 100 percent the longer you defer paying Uncle Sam.

Money that you keep from Uncle Sam is money that continues to grow for you. If you don't sell after one year, the $1,000 you would have paid Uncle Sam continues to earn money for you. In effect, Uncle Sam's money makes *you* money.

Do the math. If you earn 10 percent on that $1,000 that you would have paid Uncle Sam, you'll earn an additional $100. True, you'll eventually have to pay Uncle Sam 20 percent of that $100, but you'll be ahead by an additional $80.

It gets better the longer you hold off paying Uncle Sam. Over 20 years, that $1,000 that you would have paid Uncle Sam has turned into roughly $7,000 (assuming a 10 percent annual return). In effect, you just made an additional $5,600 (80 percent of $7,000) off Uncle Sam's *interest-free loan*.

That's the true power of tax deferment. Not only do you pay Uncle Sam a lower percentage of the profits if you hold investments for at least twelve months, but you earn more money the longer you defer paying Uncle Sam his cut.

Let's look at the tax impact from another angle. If you sell an investment before you've held it for twelve months, you need to put your money into an investment that will at least compensate for the money you lost paying the higher capital-gains taxes. If you have a decent gain on the stock you sold, that means your new investment may have to rise 10 percent or more just to cover the taxes.

That 10 percent may not sound like much until you remember that the average annual return for stocks since 1926 is 11 percent. In short, by not holding a stock for twelve months or more, you've effectively lost to taxes one year of expected appreciation. When you're trying to build a seven-figure portfolio, you cannot afford to give back one year of growth in a stock due to taxes.

Of course, investors sell because they think they can do better in another investment. Unfortunately, as I discussed in Chapter 8, studies have shown that individual investors, on average, sell the stocks they should buy and buy the stocks they should sell.

Smart investors play the percentages. What you know for certain when you sell investments prior to holding them for twelve months is that you'll get a big capital-gains tax bill. That's a given. What you don't know is if the new investment will do any better than the one you sold.

Moral of the story: Uncle Sam is making you an offer you shouldn't refuse. Even if you aren't in the top tax bracket, you still save valuable dollars holding investments at least twelve months. In short, you can't afford *not* to hold investments for at least twelve months. The tax break is just too great. Further, you can't afford *not* to defer selling as long as possible. Every day you defer paying taxes to Uncle Sam is one more day Uncle Sam's interest-free loan earns you money.

Millionaire investors clearly understand the importance of exploiting Uncle Sam's largesse. That's why, on average, our millionaire investors hold investments for five years or longer. That's why two out of every three of our millionaire investors say taxes are either "important" or "very important" in the investment process. They understand the power of tax deferment. You need to understand it, too.

401(K) PLANS

I probably should have made 401(k) investing its own step. It's that important.

You won't find a better deal in the investment world than a 401(k) plan.

Every dollar you invest lowers your tax bill.

Every dollar you invest grows tax deferred.

In most cases, your company matches a portion of your contribution.

And all this from Uncle Sam?

As hard as it is to believe, the answer is "yes." But understand that Uncle Sam isn't giving you 401(k) plans out of the goodness of his heart. Uncle Sam is abdicating responsibility for your retirement. Uncle Sam is saying that Social Security is a giant Ponzi scheme. Uncle Sam is saying you had better take advantage of a 401(k) plan. It just might be all there is when you're old and gray.

401(K) NUTS AND BOLTS

The 401(k) plans are so named because they were given birth by Section 401(k) of the Internal Revenue Code. Section 401(k) allows employers to offer a way for their employees to delay payment of taxes while saving for retirement. The counterpart to a 401(k) plan for workers in tax-exempt organizations (schools, hospitals) is the 403(b) plan.

Under a typical 401(k) or 403(b) plan, a portion of your pay (the portion is determined by you) is deposited in an account in your name. Your employer establishes the plan and contracts with a 401(k) provider to administer the plan. Your employer provides a menu of investment choices for 401(k) participants. These choices usually include the employer's stock (if the company is publicly traded) as well as stock, bond, and money-market mutual funds. Participants in the 401(k) choose where their contribution is invested. Participants direct their funds into any or all of the funds based on percentages. For example, a portion of your 401(k) contribution may be deposited in a growth mutual fund, a portion in a bond fund, and a portion in a money-market fund. Most 401(k) plans provide the ability for participants to change their allocations, usually at least quarterly and even daily in some plans.

One huge benefit of 401(k) plans is that your contributions are made with *pretax dollars*. Neither federal nor state income taxes are withheld from this money. Because the amount you contribute to your 401(k) plan is not included on your W-2 form as taxable wages or income, your 401(k) contribution reduces your yearly tax bite.

Another plus is that funds in your 401(k) grow tax deferred. You pay taxes only when you withdraw your money.

And if the tax benefits weren't enough, a 401(k) plan offers one more big advantage—*free money*. Most employer 401(k) plans offer "matching" contributions. My employer, for example, matches 25 percent of my contribution up to the first 6 percent of my salary. In other words, for the first several dollars I contribute to my 401(k) plan, my employer kicks in 25 cents for every dollar.

Let's run some numbers to show the power of 401(k) investing. Let's say you invest $100 per month in your employer's 401(k) plan. (You can invest as little as 1 percent of your salary in many plans. The maximum annual 401(k) contribution in 2000 is $10,500.) Assuming you are in the 28 percent tax bracket, you would have to pay $336 in taxes (28 percent times $1,200) on those earnings if you did not contribute the money to the 401(k) plan. In other words, that $1,200 annual contribution to your 401(k) is only costing you $864 when you consider the tax savings.

Another way to look at a 401(k) contribution is the following: a $1,200 contribution to your 401(k) is the equivalent of investing $1,536 ($1,200 times 1.28) outside your 401(k) since that contribution would be made with after-tax dollars.

To summarize, 401(k) plans offer a bounty of benefits for investors:

- *No muss, no fuss investing.* Since you invest via payroll deduction, you don't have to write any checks. The only decisions you need to make are how much to contribute and where to invest the contributions. Your employer does the rest. Your investment program is truly on autopilot. Investment programs on autopilot are programs that are the most likely to endure.
- *Low minimums, high maximums.* If you make $100 per week, you can invest $1.00 in many 401(k) plans. Anyone can afford to invest $1.00 per week. And if your paycheck is bigger, you can invest as much as $10,500 (the 2000 maximum). That amount is much greater than the $2,000 upper limit in Individual Retirement Accounts.
- *Tax benefits.* Contributions to a 401(k) plan will not incur federal and state taxes and will lower your taxable income.
- *Employer match.* If your employer matches contributions, your money compounds quickly, especially when you include the tax benefits.
- *Flexibility.* Most 401(k) plans allow you to increase or decrease your contribution, usually every three months or so. You can change your allocation among investment options. Some plans permit you to borrow from your 401(k) plan. A number of plans permit after-tax contributions to 401(k) plans. To find out the details of your employer's plan, talk to your benefits department.

GROWTH OF 401(K) PLANS

The total amount of money in 401(k) plans has surged from roughly $92 billion in 1984 to more than $2 *trillion* today. Fueling the growth have been more employers offering plans. *Smart Money* magazine estimates that one out of two American workers is now eligible for a 401(k) or other defined-contribution plan.

Another factor fueling growth is that more employees are participating in plans. According to the Profit Sharing/401(k) Council of America, nearly 90 percent of eligible employees participated in a 401(k) plan. That's up from 71 percent in 1991. The average account balance in 1997 was over $95,000, up from $33,000 in 1991. More investor awareness of the plans, a blazing stock market, and better plans contribute to the increase in popularity.

The latter point is especially important to consider: 401(k) plans are not created equal. Good 401(k) plans share the following attributes:

- *Low costs.* Your employer's 401(k) plan should include low-cost investment options (no-load mutual funds with low fees) as well as low administrative costs. Remember that most, if not all, of the costs of the plan are usually borne by the participants. You wouldn't buy a high-cost load fund outside your 401(k) plan. You shouldn't have to buy one in your 401(k) plan either. Make sure you know the costs that you bear as a plan participant. This information is available from your company and the plan administrator.
- *Flexibility.* You want some level of flexibility to change your investment amounts and allocations. Indeed, your plan should provide more than just one opportunity per year to join the plan. The plan's flexibility should extend to investment options. You don't want a plan that has a limited menu of options. Ideally, your plan should offer large-company, international, and small-company funds; index funds; bond funds; and money-market funds. If your plan offers your company's stock, a few bond funds, and a guaranteed investment contract as its only options, talk to the plan provider to see if you can increase your choices.

THIS WITCH KNOWS THE VALUE
OF A 401(K) PLAN

THE CINEMATIC SURPRISE OF 1999 WAS *THE BLAIR WITCH Project*. The movie—the fictional tale of student film-makers who disappear while making a documentary about the hunt for a witch—was shot for just $35,000. The film went on to gross more than *$120 million* at the box office.

If not for a 401(k) plan, however, the movie may have never been made.

Robin Cowie was one of the producers of the movie. When getting the movie ready to show at the prestigious Sundance Film Festival, Cowie and his colleagues needed more than $300,000 so they could convert the movie from video to a 35-millimeter print.

"I banged on a lot of doors to raise the money," says Cowie. One of those doors belonged to his parents, who took out a loan against their 401(k) plan.

While I don't recommend borrowing against your 401(k) plan, this is one loan that has a happy ending. Indeed, the five *Blair Witch* filmmakers sold their movie to Artisan Entertainment for $1 million. Furthermore, the young filmmakers stand collectively to make up to an additional $40 million from profit clauses.

SOURCES: NICK PACHETTI, *WORTH* MAGAZINE, SEPTEMBER 1999; *THE WALL STREET JOURNAL*, AUGUST 27, 1999

- *A reasonable "vesting period."* All money you contribute to a 401(k) is always your money. All of the matching funds contributed by your employer, however, are usually not yours until you've completed a certain number of years of service. This employment period is referred to as the "vesting period." By law, you must be fully vested after seven years. That is, at the end of seven years, all of your employer's matching dollars are yours. If you leave prior to the completion of seven years of service, you would not be entitled to all of the matching dollars. For that reason, shorter vesting periods are always better. Usually, funds vest on some schedule, such as 25 percent per year for four years or 20 percent per year for five years. Know your firm's vesting schedule. That knowledge may influence your willingness to job jump prior to being fully vested.
- *Quick entry.* Some company 401(k) plans require a year of employment before you can participate. If you've changed jobs, make sure your new employer's plan allows you to enroll no later than after one year of service, and much sooner if possible.

If you find your employer's 401(k) deficient in some way, you're probably not alone. You'd be surprised how much leverage you and other employees have in influencing the structure of 401(k) plans. In order to effect change, make your concerns known at the highest level of your organization.

401(K) DO'S AND DON'TS

The 401(k), if managed properly, is the best investment deal available for individual investors. Don't blow this opportunity by doing goofy stuff:

- *Don't trade your 401(k) plan.* Many 401(k) plans, including my employer's plan, permit participants to buy and sell daily. Having a flexible plan is one thing; abusing that flexibility is quite another. Don't trade your 401(k) investments simply because you can. Trading investments is a bad idea, whether the investments are in a 401(k) plan or not. Granted, you don't incur the tax penalty by frequently trading within a tax-preferenced account such as a 401(k) plan. Still, reinvestment risk—the risk that what you buy doesn't do as well as what you sell—is still great. You'll probably trade 401(k) investments based on fear—these are, after all, retirement funds—and trading on fear is particularly deadly for an investment program. Pick an investment allocation depending on your age (you should have virtually all of your funds in equity investments at least until you are in your fifties) and stay with it through the market's ups and downs.
- *Don't "overinvest" in "safe" investments.* You need to grow your money in a 401(k) plan if these funds are going to take care of you come retirement and beyond. You won't grow your money investing in bond funds or guaranteed investment contracts (GICs). You grow your money investing in equity mutual funds.
- *Contribute as close to the maximum as you possibly can.* The 401(k) plan is simply the best deal you'll likely ever get. You need to maximize this opportunity. In fact, you have no business investing in any other vehicle—including individual stocks—until you max out contributions to your 401(k) plan.
- *Don't fall in love with your company stock.* Some companies make it extremely attractive to buy company stock in their 401(k) plans. I have nothing against an employee owning his or her employer's stock. As an employee, you *should* own your company's stock. There's nothing like having an equity stake in your company to give you a push. And you probably know your

company pretty well. Many employees at certain companies (can you say M-I-C-R-O-S-O-F-T?) have become fabulously rich accumulating company stock. Still, you shouldn't abandon prudent portfolio diversification rules simply because you can buy your company's stock 50 cents on the dollar. Try to limit your employer's stock in your 401(k) plan to no more than 35 percent to 40 percent if you're in your twenties or thirties and no more than 25 percent as you approach retirement.

- *Your 401(k) plan is not a savings account, nor is it a home equity line.* Don't think of your 401(k) plan as a liquid bank account. It is a retirement account. The money is for retirement, not to buy a boat or a house or a car. If you draw on your 401(k) plan before age 59½, you'll likely pay penalties along with taxes. Furthermore, raiding your 401(k) plan impacts the power of time and compounding on these funds. Don't dip into your 401(k). And don't borrow against your 401(k). In 1997, more than 30 percent of participants in plans that permitted loans had loans outstanding. The average loan amount was more than $6,000. That's $6,000 that is not enjoying the benefits of time and compounding.

- *Make sure you roll over 401(k) funds directly.* If you change jobs or retire, you don't want to take possession of 401(k) funds, even if you plan to invest them somewhere. Taking possession of the funds may leave you on the hook for taxes and penalties. The best approach is to direct your old employer to send the funds directly to a new qualified plan (such as an IRA) or your new employer's 401(k) plan.

EVERYDAY MILLIONAIRES LOVE 401(K) PLANS

Our millionaires know a good deal when they see one. An overwhelming percentage of everyday millionaires who are eligible participate in a 401(k) plan. And while less than 50 percent of

Americans participating in 401(k) plans invest the maximum, nearly two thirds of our millionaires max out their 401(k) contributions.

Val Costner is one of those everyday millionaires who invested the maximum in his 401(k) plan. Val, now retired at age sixty-one, worked in the chemical industry. His 401(k) investments account for 75 percent of his $2.5 million investment portfolio. What was an important factor in starting a 401(k) plan? "The incentive from the company to match what I put into the plan," says Val. What advice does Val have for investors? "Start early and invest as much as you possibly can. Leave it alone and let it grow." Val, who started investing at age twenty-five, has built his portfolio through timely stock investments in Lucent Technologies and Merck and fund investments in Fidelity Overseas and Fidelity Value.

Pat Sampson is another of our millionaire investors who took full advantage of a 401(k) plan. Pat, a retired naval officer and aerospace worker, has a portfolio worth $1.3 million. His 401(k) money comprises some 70 percent of the total. Pat's biggest stock holdings include Schering-Plough, BP Amoco, BellSouth, and Colgate-Palmolive. Fund holdings include Vanguard Windsor and Vanguard Life Strategy Moderate Growth.

MY 401(K) INVESTMENTS

I've taken full advantage of my employer's 401(k) plan by investing the maximum each year. Roughly 40 percent of my investment portfolio is in my 401(k) plan. I divide my 401(k) assets in the following manner:

- 25 percent in Strong Dow 30 Value fund (800-368-1030— I'm coportfolio manager of this fund).
- 25 percent in an S&P 500 index fund.
- 25 percent in international funds (Scudder International—800-225-2470—and UMB Scout Worldwide—800-996-2862).

- 10 percent in mid-cap stocks (Sound Shore fund—800-551-1980).
- 15 percent in small-cap stocks (Loomis Sayles Small Cap Value fund—800-633-3330—and Eclipse Small Cap Value fund—800-872-2710)

As you can see, I don't invest in anything except stock funds even though my plan has bond and money-market options. Nor do I trade my investments. I've had the same allocation since these plan options were available.

HELP WITH 401(K) PLANNING

If you're having trouble knowing how to allocate your 401(k) funds, remember that you want a large exposure to stocks. If you don't know which funds to choose, you can't go wrong opting for an index fund if one is available. An S&P 500 index fund or an index fund that mimics the Wilshire 5000 index is an excellent choice. And if your plan offers index funds that mimic small-cap stocks and foreign stocks, those would be acceptable, too.

If you desire further help managing your 401(k), consider some of the Internet Web sites devoted to 401(k) planning. One site in particular—**Financial Engines (www.financialengines.com)**—was cofounded by Nobel Prize–winning economist William Sharpe. The service helps project how much money you'll have in your 401(k) plan down the road based on your current allocation. The service also provides advice and suggestions on constructing a 401(k) portfolio. All you need to do is input basic information—current age, age at which you want to retire, annual retirement income you think you'll need, etc. You'll also need to input the names of your 401(k) plan holdings and the names of investments you hold outside your 401(k). Financial Engines will give you the probability of meeting your retirement income goal based on your current 401(k) allocation and contribution level. For a small fee, Financial Engines will provide more specific advice on asset allocation. Granted, no tool is perfect. However, Financial Engines offers an extremely cost-effective way to generate a second opinion concerning your 401(k) strategy.

401(K) PLANS—THE SUREST ROUTE TO SEVEN FIGURES

I want to close this section on 401(k) plans with this thought. I'm a trustee for my company's 401(k) plan. I talk to all new employees who join the plan. My speech is basically the following:

> A 401(k) plan is the best route available for the little guy to become wealthy.

Indeed, Fidelity Investments reported that at the end of 1998, there were about 10,000 millionaires in 401(k) plans administered by this mutual fund giant.

Bottom line: If you do no investing other than your employer's 401(k) plan, you still have a good chance of creating a seven-figure portfolio. That's how powerful these plans can be.

IRAs—TRADITIONAL AND ROTH

The 401(k) is not the only investment "gimmie" from Uncle Sam. Individual Retirement Accounts provide additional alternatives for retirement investment.

There are two types of IRAs:

Traditional IRA—A traditional IRA lets individuals set aside up to $2,000 per year in an investment or investments of their choice. Money contributed to an IRA grows tax deferred. You pay taxes when money is withdrawn. You must begin to withdraw money from an IRA at age 70½.

Whether your traditional IRA contribution is tax deductible depends on the following:

- If you are not covered by a qualified retirement plan at your place of employment, your contribution to a traditional IRA is deductible, regardless of your income. Thus, if you make $500,000 per year at your job, yet you are not covered by a qualified retirement plan, you can make a deductible contribution to a traditional IRA of up to $2,000 per year.
- If you are covered by a qualified plan, you may still be able to deduct contributions to a traditional IRA. For the year 2000, a full deduction is available to individuals with adjusted gross incomes of $32,000 or less (single filer) or $52,000 or less (married, filing jointly). For incomes between $32,000 and $42,000 (single filer) and $52,000 and $62,000 (married, filing jointly), partial deduction of contributions is permitted. For incomes above $42,000 (single filer) and $62,000 (married, filing jointly), no deductible contributions are permitted. However, you still can make nondeductible contributions to an IRA of up to $2,000. For married couples, the maximum contribution is $2,000 per spouse.

The traditional IRA lost luster several years ago when contributions became nondeductible for millions of Americans. The expansion of 401(k) plans and the emergence of the Roth IRA (see below) have also reduced appeal of the traditional IRA. However, any investment vehicle that allows investors to grow their money tax deferred is a vehicle worth considering.

Since I don't qualify for a Roth IRA, I still fund a traditional IRA. As you would guess, my traditional IRA consists exclusively of the fund I comanage, the **Strong Dow 30 Value** fund.

If you set up a traditional IRA, make sure you focus on stock and stock mutual funds. Also, as is the case with any retirement fund, don't raid the money prematurely. Most withdrawals before age 59½ are subject to taxes and penalties.

Roth IRA—Remember I said earlier in this chapter that Uncle Sam gives you a way to avoid paying him *altogether*. That's, essentially, what the Roth IRA gives you—a way to grow your money tax deferred and withdrawal *tax free*. You pay Uncle Sam not one penny in taxes. *Zero*.

ROTH NUTS AND BOLTS

The Roth IRA is a result of the 1997 Taxpayer Relief Act. Named after Senator William Roth, Jr., the Roth IRA is the best investment deal since the 401(k) plan:

- Money contributed to a Roth IRA grows tax deferred and is withdrawn *tax free*. In other words, if you invest $2,000 per year in a Roth IRA ($2,000 is the maximum per year), and your Roth IRA grows to $1 million, you will never pay a dime in taxes when you start withdrawing that money. This is a big improvement over the traditional IRA in which withdrawals are taxed. In order to withdraw your money tax free, your account has to have been open at least five years and your withdrawal occurs either after you reach age 59½ or due to disability, death, or if the money is used for expenses under the "first-time homebuyer" rule.
- Anyone is eligible to contribute to a Roth IRA as long as you meet certain income requirements. Single individuals with an adjusted gross income of up to $95,000 ($150,000 for couples filing jointly) can make a full $2,000 annual deduction. Partial contributions are allowed for individuals whose adjusted gross income is between $95,000 and $110,000 ($150,000 and $160,000 for couples filing jointly).

- Unlike the traditional IRA, you can make contributions to a Roth IRA after the age of 70½ as long as you have earned income.
- Unlike the traditional IRA, you are not required to make withdrawals beginning at age 70½. In fact, you are never required to withdraw money. If you leave your Roth IRA to your heirs, your beneficiaries do not have to pay taxes on the money either. The ability to leave tax-free income to your heirs makes the Roth an interesting estate-planning tool.
- You can contribute to a Roth IRA as well as a traditional IRA if you have earned income, but the total cumulative contributions cannot exceed $2,000 per person per year.
- You can contribute to a Roth IRA even if you contribute to a 401(k) plan.
- Virtually any stock or mutual fund is eligible to be held in a Roth IRA.

The only major downside to a Roth IRA is that money contributed to the plan is never tax deductible. Also, if you withdraw your money before your account is five years old, your earnings may be subject to federal income taxes plus a 10 percent penalty.

TOUGH CHOICES

Money is finite. In a perfect world, you would have enough money to fund fully your 401(k) plan and an IRA and still have plenty left over to invest outside of retirement plans. The reality is, however, that you may not have enough money to do all the investing you want. So you have to choose. Do I fund a 401(k) plan or an IRA? And which IRA, a traditional or the Roth? And if I already have a traditional IRA, should I convert to a Roth IRA?

Actually, these choices may be rather simple, depending on your income levels. If your income exceeds the limits for a Roth IRA, the decision is pretty easy—contribute the maximum to your 401(k) plan and consider a traditional IRA with the remainder. If you are eligible for the Roth IRA, I still would max out my 401(k) plan first before investing in a Roth. One reason is the "free money" in your 401(k) plan due to employer matching.

And if you have the choice between a Roth IRA and a traditional IRA, take the Roth IRA.

Does that mean you should convert all traditional IRAs into Roth IRAs?

Not necessarily. In fact, you cannot convert a traditional IRA to a Roth IRA unless your adjusted gross income in the year you convert is $100,000 or less. Also keep in mind that when you convert a traditional IRA, you incur a tax liability. The size of the tax liability depends on whether you are converting deductible or nondeductible IRA funds. If you convert IRA funds that were tax deductible upon contributions, the entire amount is considered ordinary income for tax purposes. In other words, if you convert a deductible IRA of $40,000 to a Roth IRA, you'll have to pay taxes on the full $40,000.

If you convert a traditional IRA in which contributions were not tax deductible, only the earnings are subject to tax, not the contributions which were made with after-tax dollars.

It makes sense to convert if:

- You have a lot of time until retirement to make up for the tax hit you'll take upon conversion.
- You expect to be in a higher tax bracket when you retire.
- The amount in your traditional IRA is rather small.
- You can pay the taxes without robbing the account.

Several Web sites provide "Roth conversion calculators." These calculators run scenarios that give you some help on deciding whether conversion makes sense given your situation. Two Web sites with excellent calculators are the Strong Fund Family Web site—www.strongfunds.com—and www.financenter.com.

ROTH IRA INVESTMENT STRATEGIES

A Roth IRA is long-term money. You should invest it for long-term growth. You do that by buying stocks and stock mutual funds. The beauty of both the traditional and Roth IRA is that you can choose any stock or mutual fund you want. If you want to invest in individual stocks, you can set up a self-directed IRA at any brokerage firm. If you prefer mutual funds, any fund family will establish an IRA for you. In fact, many mutual funds reduce the initial investment requirement for investors opening up IRAs. Thus, even if you have limited funds, you may find it possible to get started investing in a traditional or Roth IRA.

CONCLUSION

With Uncle Sam's help, it has never been easier to retire a millionaire—401(k) plans and IRAs, especially the new Roth IRA, are investment vehicles our millionaire investors exploit. Millionaires also exploit the tax benefits Uncle Sam bestows on those who hold investments for at least twelve months.

And Uncle Sam may not be through with his largesse. At the time of this writing, "universal savings" accounts, sweetened tax breaks for IRAs and 401(k) plans, additional cuts in the long-term capital-gains tax rate, even giving individuals control over a portion of their Social Security contributions are all being considered by Congress.

Rest assured if Uncle Sam creates new tax-preferred plans, our millionaire investors will be there to take advantage of them.

You should, too.

The millionaire profiled in this chapter is Bob Thomas. Bob, who lives in the Southwest with his wife of fourteen years and two children, knows the importance of taking what Uncle Sam gives you. Bob holds investments for at least ten years. Such long holding periods reduce the tax impact on his portfolio. Bob also understands the power of investing in tax-preferenced accounts. Bob, an engineer, invests the maximum permitted by law in his 401(k) plan. His 401(k) and IRA investments have paid off nicely. Bob has an investment portfolio worth $1 million. His 401(k) and IRA plans account for a whopping 94 percent of his assets.

What's especially impressive is that Bob has amassed a seven-figure portfolio at the fairly young age of forty-two.

And what's this everyday millionaire investor's ultimate investment goal? "To retire at fifty," says Bob. If Bob maintains his current investment pace, and the market returns 11 percent per year for the next eight years, he'll have well over $2 million at age fifty.

NAME: Bob Thomas

EDUCATION: College (undergraduate) graduate

OCCUPATION: Sales application engineer

CURRENT INCOME: $90,000

FIVE-YEAR AVERAGE INCOME: $75,000

HOW MANY DIFFERENT JOBS SINCE AGE 25? 3

AT WHAT AGE DID YOU START INVESTING? 16

WHAT IS THE SIZE OF YOUR ENTIRE INVESTMENT PORTFOLIO? $1 million

HOW MANY INDIVIDUAL STOCKS DO YOU OWN? 16

NAME YOUR 5 LARGEST HOLDINGS: Philip Morris Companies, Lucent, Microsoft, Citigroup, CMGI

HOW MANY INDIVIDUAL MUTUAL FUNDS DO YOU OWN? 18

NAME YOUR BIGGEST FUND HOLDINGS: Fidelity Dividend Growth, Janus Twenty, Oakmark, IDS New Dimensions, Fidelity Low Priced Stock

HOW MANY INDIVIDUAL BONDS DO YOU HAVE? 0

HAVE YOU EVER PURCHASED STOCK/INDEX OPTIONS? Yes

HAVE YOU EVER BOUGHT STOCK/INDEX FUTURES? No

DO YOU OWN GOLD OR PRECIOUS METALS? No

HAVE YOU EVER SOLD STOCK SHORT? No

WHAT TYPE OF BROKER DO YOU USE? Traditional discount, online

ARE YOU A MEMBER OF AN INVESTMENT CLUB? Yes

DO YOU INVEST ONLINE? Yes

WHAT HURDLES, IF ANY, DID YOU OVERCOME TO BEGIN INVESTING? Education about stock, commodities, and liquid investment vehicles. To do my homework rather than rely on others.

HOW, PSYCHOLOGICALLY SPEAKING, DID YOU DEAL WITH THE NOTION OF PUTTING OFF CONSUMPTION TO SAVE FOR A BETTER FINANCIAL FUTURE? I decided that I could invest my way to a fortune more efficiently than working my way to a fortune.

WHERE DID YOU GET THE MONEY TO START INVESTING? Early, I cut yards and worked at minimum-wage jobs. Later, I maxed out all IRA and 401(k) savings vehicles.

WERE THERE ANY SPECIFIC EVENTS, LIFE-CHANGING MOMENTS, ETC., THAT SPURRED YOU TO BEGIN INVESTING? My father died when I was thirteen and my mother had to teach school. I decided to be prepared for my own death or hopefully a fruitful retirement some day.

HAVE YOU INHERITED WHAT YOU THOUGHT WAS A LARGE SUM OF MONEY? No

DID YOU HAVE ANY SPECIAL EXPERTISE IN INVESTING WHEN YOU STARTED? No

WHAT INVESTMENT RESEARCH TOOLS DO YOU USE? *Barron's, The Wall Street Journal,* and *TheStreet.com*

HOW MUCH DO YOU SPEND PER YEAR ON INVESTMENT RESEARCH RESOURCES? $501 to $1,000 per year

HOW MANY HOURS PER WEEK DO YOU DEVOTE TO YOUR INVESTMENTS AND INVESTMENT STRATEGIES? 3 to 5

WHAT CRITERIA DO YOU USE TO PICK STOCKS/MUTUAL FUNDS? Value with good growth prospects. Growth at a reasonable price. Find good mutual funds that match my investment philosophy and have managers with great track records.

HOW OFTEN DO YOU BUY INVESTMENTS? Monthly

ON AVERAGE, HOW LONG DO YOU HOLD AN INVESTMENT BEFORE SELLING? 10 years or longer

DO YOU "MARKET TIME"? Yes, with very little success.

HOW IMPORTANT ARE TAXES IN THE INVESTMENT PROCESS? Important

WHAT HAVE BEEN YOUR BEST-PERFORMING STOCKS? Dell, Microsoft, CMGI

WHAT HAVE BEEN YOUR WORST-PERFORMING STOCKS? Shanghai Petrochemical, Trans World Airlines

WHAT WERE SOME OF YOUR BIGGEST INVESTMENT MISTAKES? Buying on margin without thorough thought. Expecting hot tips to pay off. Paying high mutual-fund management fees. Attempting to ride momentum investing wave.

HOW WOULD YOU BEST DESCRIBE YOUR INVESTMENT APPROACH? Warren Buffett and Peter Lynch philosophies—find solid companies with great management that will prosper over the next twenty years. Invest in what you know and constantly strive to learn and grow with your investments.

DO YOU FEEL INDIVIDUAL INVESTORS HAVE ANY ADVANTAGES IN THE INVESTMENT PROCESS? Yes, your unique perspective can find opportunities before others (in mass) recognize them.

DO YOU BELIEVE IT IS POSSIBLE TO BEAT THE MARKET ON A CONSISTENT BASIS? No

WHAT MADE YOU THINK YOU COULD BE A SUCCESSFUL INVESTOR? I knew I was smarter than many of my friends and felt that I could read and learn where I was deficient.

WHAT IS YOUR GREATEST FEAR AS AN INVESTOR? A long period of meager stock returns in a deflationary economy.

WHAT IS THE BIGGEST BENEFIT OF A 7-FIGURE PORTFOLIO? Working to teach my children how to begin early and helping them to avoid some of my mistakes. I know I will retire without the fear of uncertainty I see in others.

IF YOU COULD GIVE JUST ONE PIECE OF ADVICE TO INDIVIDUAL INVESTORS, WHAT WOULD THAT PIECE OF ADVICE BE? Start as early as possible and learn what makes the economy run. Technology, services, manufacturing, utilities, transports, etc. Invest in what is now and will be successful over your next twenty years. Don't trade; invest for your future.

10

LIMIT SHOCKS TO YOUR FINANCES

I savor the boredom of watching the grass grow, a little every day.

—KEN CHILTON, OHIO,
$3.2 MILLION INVESTMENT PORTFOLIO

STEP 8: LIMIT SHOCKS TO YOUR FINANCES

Millionaire investors, by society's standards, are boring people.

They don't job hop.

They marry once.

They have two kids, not five or six.

They stay put in the same house for long stretches of time.

They buy and hold the same investments for five years or more.

Boring, right?

Yes, the typical millionaire investor's life may lack a certain variety. But variety, while perhaps the spice of life, is poison to building wealth. Variety breeds change. Change breeds uncertainty. Uncertainty breeds inconsistency. And inconsistency is the bane of investing.

On the other hand, boring breeds stability. Stability breeds consistency.

Consistency creates wealth.

Millionaire investors limit shocks to their finances. They create stable lifestyles. They develop stable and predictable cash flows and expenses. They limit events and activities that inject uncertainty into their financial situations.

Much of this book has discussed the importance of sustaining a long-term investment strategy. Millionaire investors invest consistently for twenty years or more. That's how you get to seven figures—investing consistently, month after month after month after month.

Millionaire investors invest month in, month out because the money is there to invest. Why? Because millionaire investors don't take on greater financial demands as their income levels increase. Millionaire investors don't buy more expensive homes every five years. Millionaire investors don't buy more expensive cars every two years. Millionaire investors don't change jobs—and therefore end up low man or woman on the seniority pole—every three years.

Millionaire investors know what comes in each month and what goes out and what's left for investing.

Most people's financial situations are in constant flux. Much of this uncertainty is self-inflicted. People change jobs frequently and are in a constant state of job insecurity because they're the new guy or girl. People take on debt to buy expensive toys. Most people constantly change how much money is coming in and how much is going out and how much, if there is any, to invest.

If you take nothing else away from this chapter, take the following: *Interruptions kill investment programs.* You don't get to seven figures investing two months and taking five months off because of a job change. You don't get to seven figures taking three years off from your investment program because you bought a house you can't afford. You don't get to seven figures taking eight years off from investing to pay college tuitions.

Interruptions rob your portfolio of time and compounding.

When building a seven-figure portfolio, *every month counts.* You cannot afford to waste time. It's a cliché, but it's true—time is money, especially to your investments.

RECOGNIZE THE SHOCKS

Life is full of surprises. You cannot shield yourself completely from all shocks. In some ways, some shocks, such as children, add to life's richness. Still, I can't think of any of life's major decisions that don't have a big financial component. Recognizing the financial implications of your decisions may help you frame the decision-making process a bit differently.

What are shocks that have the biggest impact on your investments?

Divorce. Divorce is a huge shock to your finances. Forget about being able to maintain an investment program during and usually after divorce. That's the least of your problems. Much bigger issues loom:

- Where can I afford to live?
- What kind of tax hit will I take when we sell the stocks, bonds, house, etc.?
- What will I do about health insurance for the kids?
- Will I have to reenter the job market?

It's an understatement to say that divorce is an extremely costly proposition, emotionally and financially. And the biggest financial hardship of divorce usually falls on women. A 1996 study by the Social Science Research Council in New York City found that one year after a divorce, a woman's standard of living falls about *30 percent* on average.

Divorce is so hard on finances because two households must now be supported instead of one. Divorce reduces the economies of scale that exist in families. In short, divorce injects a huge amount of uncertainty into someone's financial situation. Given that roughly half of all marriages end in divorce, it's not surprising that the vast majority of Americans never reach their financial goals. It's also not surprising that only 21 percent of our everyday millionaire investors have been divorced.

Understand that I'm not making moral judgments about divorce. I'm not suggesting that you should or shouldn't stay in what you believe is a bad marriage. I am saying that your finances will feel the shock of divorce, and that shock will have lasting ramifications.

Still, if you've gone through a divorce, don't give up hope of reaching a seven-figure portfolio. It will be more difficult, but it can be done. Just ask Samantha Gish.

Samantha, seventy, never made more than $30,000 during her working career. Yet, Samantha managed to overcome a divorce to build an investment portfolio worth more than $1 million. How did she do it?

- She decided that "I now had nothing to lose. The only person I was responsible for was me, and to jump in and do it."
- She read books, took a few courses at the local university and senior center, and began setting aside a little every week.
- After her house was paid off, she began investing her house payment to buy stocks.
- She contributed the maximum in her 401(k).

"If you wait until you think you can afford to invest, you will never do it," says Samantha. "There will always be things that have to be done. Make investing part of that process, and you will not even miss the money after the first month or two."

Job-hopping. It's estimated that the average graduate from high school or college will have thirteen different employers during his or her working life, or a new one every three years or so. Frequent job-hopping creates a variety of shocks to your finances:

- A new job may cause you to curtail a regular investment program until you get a better handle on your new monthly cash flows.
- You may be insecure about your new post. Insecurity could cause you to back off your investment program until you see how the new job pans out.
- A new job may mean forgoing retirement benefits at your old job. If people are changing jobs on average once every three or four years, chances are they are not sticking around long enough to be fully vested in the company profit sharing/ pension plan. At many companies, full vesting of a retirement program, such as a 401(k) plan, takes five years or more. That means every job change leaves retirement money on the table.
- Frequent job-hopping, and the accompanying need to transport the 401(k) money from your old employer to either your new employer's plan or a self-directed IRA, increases the likelihood that you'll spend the money rather than find it a new tax-deferred home. According to the Washington-based Employee Benefit Research Institute, when they leave a job, about 70 percent of Americans remove the funds from their tax-sheltered status. Raiding your 401(k) when you change jobs not only interrupts your investment program but exposes you to potentially steep taxes and penalties.
- Some companies do not permit new hires to join the pension program in their first year of service. Delaying contributions to a 401(k) plan for a year or more until you're eligible has an adverse effect on long-term results. Even worse, your new employer may not even offer a 401(k) plan, which eliminates you from participating in the best investment vehicle around.
- Job-hopping, depending on the location of the new job, may also mean a new home, which leads to yet another potential shock to your finances.
- A new job may require you to move to an area of the country with a much higher standard of living.

Some people make job-hopping work to their advantage. Their salaries increase sharply. They accrue more stock options. Nevertheless, when evaluating a new job, remember that a number of opportunity costs need to be considered.

Do our millionaire investors have happy feet? No. On average, the millionaire investors I surveyed have had three different jobs during their careers; they have been at their most recent job nearly twenty years.

Children. Don't get me wrong. I'm not advocating zero population growth. And there's no disputing the fact that children are truly a blessing. But there's also no denying the fact that kids cost money. Lots of it.

Diapers.
Bottles.
Shoes.
Food.
Soccer.
Compact discs.
Dance lessons.
Braces.
Glasses.
Textbooks.
Gas money.
Auto insurance.
College tuition.
Wedding.
Graduate school.
A loan for a starter home.
Gifts for the grandkids.
And on . . . and on . . . and on . . .

According to a U.S. Department of Agriculture 1998 survey, you'll spend an average of $5,170 on a child for the first two years

THE EXCEPTION TO THE RULE

CHERI KALENIAN HAS TAKEN JOB-HOPPING TO AN ART FORM.
After graduating from high school in California, Cheri
took a job with a software company in 1991. After
working at the firm for four years, and picking up a
moderate amount of stock options along the way, Cheri
left to join another software company. In 1995, less
than one year after Cheri joined the firm, the company
went public, just as Cheri had hoped. Cheri, who held
stock options prior to the public offering, made "eighty
times her money" on the stock. Sensing it was time to
move on, Cheri, after doing research, went to work for
an Internet auction house. The company had already
gone public, but the stock was extremely depressed.
Cheri sensed an opportunity and began accumulating
the stock. Cheri's instincts paid off, as the stock tripled
in her first eight months of employment. Where is
Cheri today? After leaving the Internet auction company in 1998, she hooked up with a closely held medical supply company. Still shy of her thirtieth
birthday—and without a college degree—Cheri figures
that she has made "several hundred thousand dollars"
from option gains and stock deals.

SOURCE: QUENTIN HARDY,
THE WALL STREET JOURNAL, AUGUST 10, 1998

of his or her life. And it only goes up from there. According to the
same survey, you'll spend nearly $7,000 for a child from ages fifteen
to seventeen. By some estimates, a baby born today will cost parents
about $104,000 by age seventeen and $600,000 (including school-
ing and wedding) by the time he or she reaches age twenty-five.

Six hundred thousand dollars. And that's after-tax dollars.

And if you have four or five children . . . well, building a seven-figure portfolio becomes extremely difficult.

Keep in mind that the out-of-pocket cost is only part of the real cost of raising a kid. Think how much that money you spend on Biff or Buffie would grow if invested. Let's say, on average, you spend $6,000 per year on a child for the first twenty years. Keep in mind that your kid won't get anywhere near Harvard Square for that kind of money, but let's be conservative. Had you invested that $6,000 per year for twenty years and earned 11 percent per year on your money, your investment would grow to approximately *$430,000.*

Obviously, I'm not suggesting your kids are financial black holes. The ugly truth, however, is that kids limit your ability to build financial wealth.

If you have four or five kids, you still shouldn't abandon your hope for a seven-figure investment portfolio. Kip Summer, a dentist in Ohio, raised four children and still managed to build an investment portfolio of $1.7 million. Felix Rose and Nathan Finch, two of our everyday millionaire investors, each raised *eight* children and still built at least seven-figure portfolios. So it can be done. Still, it's no coincidence that our millionaire investors have, on average, less than two children.

A new home. I recently purchased a new home. I needed more space and found a home I truly love. Unfortunately, my new home cost a bit more than my previous home. That's not unusual. Most home purchases are "move up" rather than "move down." What I'm discovering, however, is that I've become a bit more cautious with my monthly investment program until I get a better handle on the costs I'll incur with my new home. It's not just the bigger monthly mortgage payment.

What will my new utility expenses be?

What other overhead expenses will I incur with this new home?

How stable are the property taxes in my new area?

Buying a new home is stepping into the great unknown. (Have

you ever seen the movie *The Money Pit?*) Financial shocks come fast and furious. New roofs. Finished basements. New furniture. Indeed, a new home is the quintessential example of the "negative compounding" that takes place with big-ticket purchases. Simply put, a new home leads to *a lot* of new expenses.

And don't kid yourself that your new home represents an excellent investment. Home values, except for select areas of the country, haven't come close to matching the appreciation of stocks over the last two decades. Don't think you'll get a big return on your home expenditures. Given the demographic shift that's occurring in this country, demand for single-family homes is likely to decline as baby boomers downscale their housing needs. Most home owners will be lucky if their homes appreciate 4 to 5 percent per year over the next twenty years. In fact, I wouldn't be surprised if home values are flat to lower in many parts of the country over the next decade.

Medical/long-term care costs. According to a 1998 Merrill Lynch survey, only about half of current preretirees feel "extremely" or "somewhat" prepared to meet the costs of long-term care. This percentage is actually lower than a decade ago.

More than 40 percent of individuals turning sixty-five years old will spend some time in a long-term care facility. One in five will spend five years or longer in a nursing home.

You should be concerned about long-term care costs. They can be huge. Today, nursing-home care can cost more than $80,000 per year. Medical bills can be huge as well. Even with adequate insurance, a serious malady could cost you thousands of dollars. According to the National Council on Aging, long-term care expenses drive about 70 percent of senior-citizen families into federal poverty levels within four months of beginning institutionalized care.

I know there isn't much you can do to avoid many illnesses. But let's face it—we could do a lot more to improve our general health.

We don't exercise enough.

We don't eat right.

We don't get enough rest.

We are too stressed out.

We don't make being healthy a priority in our lives until it's too late.

Now, yes, you could do all of these things, and it still may not make a difference. But smart people play the percentages. And the percentages say that taking care of yourself physically and mentally should translate into a longer and healthier life.

Besides making a healthier you a priority, here are some other items to consider:

- Most Americans are woefully underinsured when it comes to disability. Unfortunately, after age forty, your likelihood of becoming disabled is three times greater than the likelihood of death. If you have no disability insurance, you are making a big mistake.

- When choosing a new employer, make sure the health insurance coverage is adequate for you and your family. Chasing a bigger salary, but a salary that comes with lousy insurance, may be penny-wise but pound-foolish in the end.

- Consider a long-term care policy, also known as nursing home insurance. When comparing policies, Dean Davis, a vice president at A. G. Edwards brokerage firm, suggests you consider the following items:

  1. **Home health-care option.** The policy should provide some benefit in case you want care given in your home.

  2. **Inflation protection.** According to the National Center for Health Statistics, the average age that someone enters a nursing home is seventy-nine. You'll probably buy long-term care insurance in your fifties or sixties. The cost of

nursing homes can escalate between the time you buy the insurance and when you actually need it. Make sure the policy has some protection against inflation.

3. **A reasonable daily benefit.** The average cost of nursing homes ranges from $95 to $200 per day. Your long-term care policy should offer a daily benefit that at least matches the high end of these averages.

4. **An acceptable benefit period.** Since the average stay in a nursing home is 2½ years, your benefit period should cover at least 3 years.

5. **A reasonable "elimination" period.** An elimination period is the time period when you pay for care out of your own pocket. A typical elimination period is ninety days.

6. **A solid insurer.** Don't necessarily jump at the cheapest long-term care policy. The insurance company backing the policy could be financially weak. How can you assess the financial strength of insurers? Check out the insurers' ratings with the major ratings services, such as A. M. Best (www.ambest.com) and Moody's (www.moodys.com).

Caring for parents, adult children, grandchildren. Many households are crowded these days. It's not unusual for parents to be caring for adult children. It's not unusual for parents to be caring for their parents. It's not even unusual for grandparents to be caring for grandchildren. Indeed, according to the Census Bureau, some 4 million grandparents live with and care for grandchildren under age eighteen. That number is up 77 percent since 1970. More than 5 percent of all children live in such situations.

The upshot is that once kids leave home, they may not be gone forever. And with people living longer, don't assume your parents won't need financial assistance at some point.

How do you protect yourself from these shocks?

- Teach your children and their children about investing. If you turn youngsters on to investing, you will change their lives. You will set them on a path to financial independence that will make it less likely that your assistance will be needed down the road. You can have a huge impact on your children's financial IQ. Indeed, more than two thirds of our everyday millionaire investors said that their parents were either "important" or "very important" in developing their discipline and expertise in investing. One thing is certain—kids need your help when it comes to investing. According to a 1997 survey of U.S. high school students, only 14 percent of the respondents correctly chose stocks as the best investment for long-term growth.

- Equip your children with the best education possible. Education levels correlate strongly with future earnings potential. According to the Digest of Education Statistics (1996), the median annual income of a worker with a bachelor's degree is 56 percent more than one with a high school diploma; a worker with a master's degree has a median annual income nearly double that of a worker with a high school diploma. It should be no surprise that some 85 percent of our everyday millionaire investors have at least a college undergraduate degree.

- Instill in your children and their children the importance of values. Integrity. Honesty. Lawfulness. I know this is much easier said than done. Still, many of today's households are affected dramatically by divorce, teen pregnancy, child abuse, and incarceration of the parents. If you cut down on these problems, you cut down on the likelihood that you'll be caring for children and grandchildren during retirement.

- Explore long-term-care insurance options with your parents and grandparents *before* such insurance is needed. I'm uncomfortable saying this, but it's true—protecting your parents' and grandparents' wealth protects your inheritance. And given the paltry savings rate in this country—according to a recent telephone poll commissioned by Strong Funds, nearly 18 percent of respondents said they save *nothing*—it seems an awful lot of people are banking on an inheritance to bail them out.

Lawsuits. The unfortunate truth is that the more wealth you create, the more prone you are to a lawsuit.

Don't think it can't happen to you. All it takes is one ill-advised right turn. Or a few too many drinks by one of your party guests who drives when he shouldn't.

Your life could change in an instant.

Accidents happen. Unfortunately, someone often pays dearly when accidents occur.

That person could be you.

A major judgment against you could undo decades of wealth building. Fortunately, you can protect yourself to some extent from such calamity. It's called "umbrella insurance."

An umbrella insurance policy picks up where your traditional homeowner's and auto insurance policies end. Umbrella insurance is cheap. You should be able to purchase a $1 million umbrella policy for about $20 per month.

If you have accumulated any wealth, you owe it to yourself to look into an umbrella insurance policy. I'm not a big insurance guy. But this is one insurance policy that you can't afford not to have.

CONCLUSION

One out of five of our millionaire investors is divorced. Many have more than two kids. Several have had five or more jobs.

Five of our everyday millionaire investors even declared bankruptcy.

It is possible to absorb shocks to your finances and still build a seven-figure portfolio. But the task will be much more difficult. Millionaire investors know the dangers of financial shocks and do their best to avoid or limit them.

You should do the same.

The millionaire investor profiled in this chapter is Ned Streeter. I chose Ned because he has absorbed several shocks to his finances.

Ned has four children.

He's been divorced.

He's held six different jobs.

Despite these shocks, Ned, who is in his sixties and resides in the Southeast, has built an investment portfolio worth $4.5 million.

Another reason I'm profiling Ned is that his investment philosophy is near and dear to my heart. "Buy as if you were never going to sell," says Ned.

Ned's largest holdings include blue chips Bristol-Myers Squibb, Coca-Cola, AT&T, and Intel, stocks arguably you could buy and hold forever.

What I also like about Ned's investment style is that he is focused on growth. Even at age sixty-four he has the bulk of his assets in stocks.

NAME: Ned Streeter

AGE: 64

HOME: Southeast

MARITAL STATUS: Married (been divorced)

CHILDREN: 4

EDUCATION: College (advanced degree) graduate

OCCUPATION: Retired

CURRENT INCOME: $100,000

HOW MANY DIFFERENT JOBS SINCE AGE 25? 6

HOW IMPORTANT WERE YOUR PARENTS IN DEVELOPING YOUR DISCIPLINE AND EXPERTISE IN INVESTING? Very important

AT WHAT AGE DID YOU START INVESTING? 28

WHAT IS THE SIZE OF YOUR ENTIRE INVESTMENT PORTFOLIO? $4.5 million

HOW MANY INDIVIDUAL STOCKS DO YOU OWN? 32

NAME YOUR 5 LARGEST HOLDINGS: Bristol-Myers Squibb, Coca-Cola, AT&T, Intel, Bank of America

HOW MANY INDIVIDUAL MUTUAL FUNDS DO YOU OWN? 0

HOW MANY INDIVIDUAL BONDS DO YOU HAVE? 12

DO YOU RECEIVE ADVICE ON YOUR INVESTMENTS FROM AN OUTSIDE SOURCE? No

WHAT TYPE OF BROKER DO YOU USE? Traditional discount broker

DO YOU INVEST ONLINE? Yes

WHAT ARE YOUR LONG-TERM GOALS? Secure assets for retirement, comfortable living, and leave something to heirs and charities.

WHERE DID YOU GET THE MONEY TO START INVESTING? We saved it from our salaries.

WERE THERE ANY SPECIFIC EVENTS, LIFE-CHANGING MOMENTS, ETC., THAT SPURRED YOU TO BEGIN INVESTING? Both of our parents were of little financial means and had to scrape for everything they ever got. We wanted to make sure that we would be better off than they were.

HAVE YOU INHERITED WHAT YOU THOUGHT WAS A LARGE SUM OF MONEY? No

DID YOU START INVESTING WITH A SPECIFIC PLAN IN MIND? Our initial goal was to save up to 15 percent of our annual income. We met or exceeded this goal every year.

HOW DID YOU EDUCATE YOURSELF ABOUT INVESTING? DID YOU FIND THE EDUCATION PROCESS DIFFICULT? FUN? I had long discussions with my broker, who later became a friend. I used financial advisers who were disasters. I fired them (2), as I knew that I could do better. I began the process of education, learning, researching, and forcing myself to do our investing. Once I made up my mind to take over our financial lives, it became less difficult and very interesting. In hindsight, I have had fun, along with a few perceived heartaches.

DID YOU HAVE ANY SPECIAL EXPERTISE IN INVESTING WHEN YOU STARTED? No

HOW MUCH DO YOU SPEND PER YEAR ON INVESTMENT RESEARCH RESOURCES? $501 to $1000 per year

HOW MANY HOURS PER WEEK DO YOU DEVOTE TO YOUR INVESTMENTS AND INVEST-
  MENT STRATEGIES? 15

ON AVERAGE, HOW LONG DO YOU HOLD AN INVESTMENT BEFORE SELLING? 5 years

DO YOU "MARKET TIME"? Yes

HOW IMPORTANT ARE TAXES IN THE INVESTMENT PROCESS? Very important

HAVE YOU EVER FOLLOWED A HOT TIP? No

DO YOU BELIEVE IT IS POSSIBLE TO BEAT THE MARKET ON A CONSISTENT BASIS? Yes

WHAT DO YOU THINK ARE SOME OF THE GREATEST MYTHS OF INVESTING? You must
  have a broker. You must have a financial adviser. You can only be
  safe investing in mutual funds.

WHAT IS THE BIGGEST BENEFIT OF A 7-FIGURE PORTFOLIO? Flexibility to make
  many investments, with some cushion for setbacks.

IF YOU COULD GIVE JUST ONE PIECE OF ADVICE TO INDIVIDUAL INVESTORS, WHAT
  WOULD THAT PIECE OF ADVICE BE? Buy as if you were never going to
  sell.

IF YOU WOULD, PLEASE SHARE WITH ME YOUR FAVORITE INVESTMENT STORY: Having
  the courage to fire the expensive investment advisers who were
  so proud of keeping our invested assets at or near break-even.
  This led to my taking over all of our investments. I was most
  proud when asked by my broker friend how I stood and was able
  to tell him that in most cases our accounts were up several hundred percent.

11

YOU CAN DO BETTER

Knowledge is power. The greater your depth of knowledge
with regard to investing, the greater your chances for success.
—GIO MALLARD, NEW YORK,
$1.1 MILLION INVESTMENT PORTFOLIO

Of all the everyday millionaire investors in this book, my favorite is
Gio Mallard.

Gio doesn't have the most money. Gio doesn't have the best stories. So why do I like Gio so much? Because he's a regular guy who
decided that he could do better—and did.

As you know by now, our millionaires were not all created
equally. A few had big head starts because of inheritances. Others
had high-paying jobs and could afford to invest aggressively.

And then there are millionaires such as Gio.

Gio has never made more than $46,000 in any year of his life.
He had no inheritance. He has plenty of financial responsibilities,
including a wife and a child with a learning disability.

Yet, Gio never accepted the notion that he didn't have what it
took to build a seven-figure portfolio.

Things didn't happen overnight. Gio, who is fifty-five, has been
investing for twenty-eight years. He watched his pennies. For his efforts, he now has more than $1 million.

I like Gio because he is everyman. He is the person who works in the cubicle next to you. He is the person you run into at the grocery store. He's the person who lives next door.

Gio is *you*.

I also like Gio because he was a smart investor. He focused on quality. He maxed out his 401(k) plan. He bought stock and stock equity funds. He owns no bonds. He kept transaction costs to a minimum by owning index funds.

In short, he embraced the eight steps laid out in this book.

Gio, in his own way, has done much better than many of our millionaires. In fact, if Gio's income were in the $80,000 to $100,000 range, he probably would challenge our wealthiest millionaires.

I know this is going to be hard for you to believe, but it's absolutely true—*you* can do better than many of our millionaire investors.

This chapter shows you how.

FINE-TUNING THE EIGHT STEPS

You might recall that at the beginning of this book I mentioned that you didn't have to follow all of these eight steps in order to build a seven-figure portfolio. Indeed, many of our millionaire investors made plenty of mistakes over the years and still managed to accumulate great wealth. And then there were investors, such as Gio, who followed virtually all of the eight steps and were much better off for having done so.

I want to concentrate on what the "best of the best" of our millionaire investors do and how you can fine-tune the eight-step strategy for maximum profits.

DON'T OVERDIVERSIFY

One area in which you can do better than our typical millionaire investor is portfolio diversification. On average, our millionaire in-

THIS COUPLE CERTAINLY DID BETTER THAN YOUR AVERAGE MILLIONAIRE

DONALD AND MILDRED OTHMER WERE NOT YOUR GARDEN-variety millionaires. When they died—he in 1995 and she in April 1998—the value of their estate was $750 *million*.

Now don't think that the Othmers came from huge wealth. Donald was a professor of chemical engineering at Polytechnic University in Brooklyn. Mildred was a teacher and a buyer for a dress store. So from where did all that money come? Successful investing over a period of many years.

The Othmers also received some sage advice and counsel early in their investment careers from a guy named Warren Buffett.

The Othmers knew young Warren when they all lived in Omaha. When Warren started his investment partnership in the early 1960s, both Donald and Mildred invested $25,000. In 1970, each received shares in Berkshire Hathaway, the publicly traded company that was the successor to Warren's partnership. The Othmers received shares valued at $42 per share in Berkshire Hathaway in 1970. Today, each Berkshire Hathaway share is valued at $54,500. While some family members withdrew money, the Othmers were patient investors, adding money from time to time.

"They just rode along," Buffett says, adding that the growing investment "never changed their lives."

SOURCE: KAREN ARENSON, *THE NEW YORK TIMES*, JULY 13, 1998

vestors hold forty-four individual stocks, nine individual bonds, and seven mutual funds. That's too many investments, in my opinion.

Overdiversifying leads to several problems. Having many investments makes it difficult to track your holdings for tax purposes. Your record keeping becomes onerous.

Having too many investments also means you are not leveraging your best investment ideas. Most investors probably have ten or fifteen good investment ideas. When you own forty or fifty stocks, you water down your best investment ideas with a lot of mediocre ones.

It is very easy to have too many stocks and funds, especially if you do a lot of reading and research. What happens is that you keep finding interesting stocks and funds to own. So you start collecting them, like stamps or baseball cards. I know, I've been there. I currently have about twenty-four stocks. I'm probably pushing the upper limit of what you should have in a portfolio. Indeed, you can have a nicely diversified portfolio with fifteen to twenty stocks, especially if you balance your stock holdings with mutual funds.

What I found interesting is that the millionaire investors who had many investments knew that they had too many. Take Pat Kingston. Pat owns seventy stocks and nine mutual funds. "I am so diversified as to border on the ridiculous," says Pat. "I am my own mutual fund." Interestingly, when I asked Pat how many investments were needed in order to be properly diversified, he replied, "Twenty-five to thirty."

With an investment portfolio of $1.2 million, Pat has certainly been a successful investor. But one wonders how much better off Pat would be had he not overdiversified.

My friend Gio is a good example of the power of leveraging your best investment ideas. He has eight stocks and balances out these holdings with sixteen mutual funds. Admittedly, Gio probably doesn't need sixteen mutual funds to round out his portfolio. Still, he has kept down the overall number of investments to a manageable twenty-four.

INVESTOR, KNOW THYSELF

Roughly one out of every two millionaires said that he or she doesn't believe individuals can consistently beat the market. Yet, many of these same investors own individual stocks instead of plunking all of their money into index funds that match the market.

What's wrong with this picture?

Actually, nothing may be wrong with this picture. I'm keenly aware of the difficulty of beating the market on a regular basis. Yet, I own individual stocks. Why? Because, for me (as well as for many people), stocks are fun. It's fun to analyze data and place your bet on individual stocks. I don't get the same thrill investing in funds.

For many of our everyday millionaires, stock picking is their primary hobby. They like the search for market-beating stocks.

I do think it is a mistake to assume that you will be able to beat the pants off the market over the long term. You face tall odds in doing so. Does that mean you shouldn't try beating the market by actively managing your funds? That's precisely what some experts would say, that you're much better off investing exclusively in index funds representing different sectors of the equity markets.

I take a different approach. Since I find stock picking interesting, I do it. But I also hedge my bets by owning index funds.

If you want to invest in individual stocks because it appeals to your sense of adventure and to your analytical side, go for it. But provide ballast to your portfolio by including quality large-company mutual funds or index funds that mimic popular indexes.

And if you're someone who wants a seven-figure portfolio but would rather play lots of golf than analyze balance sheets, index mutual funds and low-expense, large-company funds are no-brainers for you.

MUST-HAVE STOCKS IN MUST-HAVE INDUSTRIES

In Chapter 6, I promised I'd give you specific stock recommendations.

Here goes.

On average, our millionaire investors had enough good stocks in their portfolios to produce excellent results.

But how well could you do if your portfolio had several big winners?

I think one way to stock a portfolio with future winners is to find industry sectors that have the best long-term prospects, and buy the leaders in those sectors.

Now I don't have all the right answers when it comes to stock selection. Furthermore, I've already acknowledged the difficulty of picking stocks that consistently beat the market. Having said that, I still believe I can make your portfolio more productive by steering you toward what I believe are "must-have" stocks in "must-have" industry groups.

The following "must-have" stocks are in industries that should be represented in every portfolio. Please note that I've restricted my recommendations to stocks that offer dividend reinvestment plans, so any investor—even those without a broker—can buy these stocks. Also note that I've included a separate section pinpointing the most fee-friendly DRIPs among our "must-have" industries.

The accompanying table provides a complete listing of all "must-have" stocks. To obtain DRIP information and enrollment forms, call their toll-free numbers.

• FINANCIAL SERVICES

Given the growth of baby boomers, who are now entering their prime earning years, as well as the proliferation of retirement vehicles, the financial-services industry should show above-average growth over the next several years. A number of ways exist to play the growth of this sector. Regional banks offer interesting choices because of their growth prospects and takeover appeal. Broad-based financial-services companies, such as **AEGON NV, American Express** and **Morgan Stanley Dean Witter,** should do well, too. Specialty finance companies, such as **Finova,** should see demand for their business remain strong as long as interest rates remain under wraps.

Best of the bunch: This is a tough one given that there are many quality financial-services firms that offer DRIPs/direct-purchase plans. Two stocks I own are **Regions Financial** and **Popular.** Regions Financial is a leading regional bank in the Southeast. Popular is the bank holding company for Banco Popular, a regional bank serving Hispanic communities in Puerto Rico and parts of the United States. Popular is especially interesting as a demographic play. The Hispanic community is among the fastest-growing ethnic groups in the country. Popular provides a way to tap into this growth. I'm also partial to **Charles Schwab.**

Best investor-friendly DRIP: Popular, Regions Financial, Morgan Stanley, and Finova have no-fee direct-purchase plans that allow investors to make their initial purchases directly. Schwab has a no-fee traditional DRIP that requires ownership of at least one share.

• ENTERTAINMENT/MEDIA

Spending on entertainment and leisure is expected to grow nicely over the next several years due to demographics. These stocks often sell at steep P-E ratios, so buying them on the cheap is rare. Still, investors should not be afraid to pay up for quality in this sector.

Best of the bunch: For best of the bunch, it's really a dead heat between **Disney** and **Tribune.** But since I have to pick just one, I'm leaning toward Tribune given its broad base of entertainment/media businesses.

Best investor-friendly DRIP: While Disney, Tribune, and **Sony** offer direct-purchase plans for first-time buyers, all of them have fees. **Gannett** requires ownership of at least one share in order to enroll, but its DRIP has no fees.

• INFORMATION/BUSINESS SERVICES

Information is king in the business world. Those companies that have data that consumers and businesses need oftentimes have a license to mint money by repackaging data into a variety of high-margin products. Also, with outsourcing likely to remain a growing trend in the business world, investors cannot ignore companies providing services to businesses. If I had to pick my top three industry groups to own, this sector would be in that select group. All of these stocks have attractive earnings-growth potential for the next ten years.

Best of the bunch: I like a lot of stocks in this group. I especially like **Equifax,** which offers credit-information services, and **Paychex,** a provider of payroll-processing services.

Best investor-friendly DRIP: Equifax and **Reuters** offer direct-purchase plans, but both have fees. Paychex, and **Block (H&R)** have no-fee DRIPS that require ownership of at least one share.

• HEALTH CARE

This industry would be another of my top three. If you invest for long-term growth, it's essential that you own a health-care stock. Granted, these stocks are always expensive, so you'll not likely buy at bargain prices. However, don't wait until your favorite health-care stock pulls back before buying—you may never get in the game. Rather, buy it now and dollar-cost average into these shares. Ten years from now, you'll be glad you did.

Best of the bunch: This may be the toughest "best of the bunch" to pick. Still, since I promised just one, I'm going with **Merck.** The company has the financial and research firepower to continue to churn out blockbuster drugs. I also like **Elan,** an Ireland-based company that is one of my favorite foreign firms.

Best investor-friendly DRIP: **Johnson & Johnson** and **Abbott Laboratories** have no-fee plans, but they require ownership of one share. **Pfizer** has an extremely friendly direct-purchase plan for first-time buyers. The plan has no enrollment fee and no purchase fees. **Bristol-Myers Squibb** and **Guidant** are great companies, but their plans are a bit fee-heavy.

• RETAILING

Admittedly, I don't think retailing necessarily needs to be the first industry group you buy when building a portfolio. However, because of the number of attractive companies in this group, you couldn't go wrong including a quality stock from this economically sensitive sector.

Best of the bunch: I own **Walgreen,** the drugstore giant, and feel it is a premier holding. **Ahold NV,** the Netherlands-based supermarket chain with extensive operations in the United States, is an interesting choice for investors who want an international play in this group. **Wal-Mart Stores** and **Home Depot** are also solid choices.

Best investor-friendly DRIP: All of the stocks in this group allow investors to make their initial purchase directly. That's the good news. The bad news is that all of them also charge fees. Home Depot's fees are a bit lower than the others, so I'll give it the nod.

• CONSUMER PRODUCTS/SERVICES

I like the stocks in this group for their dependable earnings streams, strong brand names, and solid track records.

Best of the bunch: I know it's a stretch to put **General Electric** in the consumer products/services group, but it didn't seem to fit any better elsewhere. And GE should fit somewhere when you're talking about "must-have" stocks. It's my favorite in this group. I own **McDonald's, PepsiCo,** and **Procter & Gamble** and like them for long-term growth.

Best investor-friendly DRIP: **PepsiCo** doesn't permit initial purchases directly (GE does), but PepsiCo has a no-fee plan (GE doesn't). Investors should note that PepsiCo requires ownership of at least five shares in order to enroll in the plan.

• TECHNOLOGY

I'll be the first to admit that I don't understand the businesses of a lot of these companies. I do understand, however, that ours is an economy increasingly driven by technology. You can't be a long-term growth investor without having representation in the technology sector. The bad news is DRIP investors don't have a lot of choices when it comes to technology stocks. I personally own **Oracle, Microsoft, Cisco Systems,** and **Sun Microsystems** and recommend these stocks for long-term growth. Unfortunately, none of these companies offers a dividend reinvestment plan. The good news is the small number of technology DRIPs was even smaller a few years ago, so there has been some growth. My guess is that over the next four years, you'll see many of the well-known players in the technology sector offer direct-purchase plans.

Best of the bunch: I own **Intel** and feel comfortable with this semiconductor giant. You should, too. **International Business Machines** and **Hewlett-Packard** also are worthwhile portfolio choices.

Best investor-friendly DRIP: Although you need one share in order to join Intel's DRIP, it is a no-fee plan.

• TELECOMMUNICATIONS

This group represents the third of my top three industry favorites. Given the growing demand for transporting voice and data on a global scale, the telecommunications sector has huge growth possibilities. I think the safest way to go are the telecommunications-equipment stocks. It still is up in the air who ultimately will be the dominant carriers of voice and data, but all carriers will need to expand their systems over the next decade and beyond. The need to upgrade systems plays into the hands of companies that provide the telecommunications backbones.

Best of the bunch: I'm a huge fan of **Lucent Technologies.** I own the stock and regard it as one of my core long-term holdings. Don't worry that the stock always seems too high. Buy it now and add to it on a regular basis. **Nokia,** based in Finland, is an interesting overseas play in the telecommunications-equipment field. SBC **Communications** is a solid company. In addition to Lucent, I own **Motorola** and **AT&T** among telecommunications stocks.

Best investor-friendly DRIP: **BellSouth,** a leading regional Bell company, allows initial investment directly and has a fee-friendly plan. Lucent's fees are rather modest as well.

• ENERGY

Like the retailing sector, energy stocks are not necessarily the first place I'd look when starting a portfolio. At some point, however, it's a good idea to balance a portfolio with an energy stock. These stocks offer solid diversification—it's not unusual for energy stocks to move counter to the market trend—while providing a portfolio with above-average income.

Best of the bunch: I own **Exxon** and believe it's the clear-cut investment choice among energy stocks. Other solid holdings in the group are **BP Amoco** and **Chevron.**

Best investor-friendly DRIP: Once again, Exxon wins. The company permits initial purchases directly. There are no fees on the buy side. The company also offers automatic monthly investment services and an IRA option, including the Roth IRA. BP Amoco also has an extremely fee-friendly plan.

MUST HAVE DRIPS IN MUST HAVE INDUSTRY GROUPS

Financial Services

Company Name/Stock Symbol	Company Phone	800 Phone	Website
AEGON NV (NYSE: AEG)		(800) 808–8010	www.aegon.com
American Express (NYSE: AXP)	(212) 640–5692	(800) 842–7629	www.american express.com
Finova Group (NYSE: FNV)	(602) 207–2821	(800) 734–6682	www.finova.com
Morgan Stanley (NYSE: MWD)	(212) 761–4000	(800) 622–2393	www.deanwitter discover.com

Company Name/Stock Symbol	Company Phone	800 Phone	Website
Popular (NASDAQ: BPOP)	(787) 765–9800	(787) 759–7740	www.bancopopular.com
Regions Finan. (NASDAQ: RGBK)	(205) 326–7090	(800) 922–3468	www.regionsbank.com
Schwab (Charles) (NYSE: SCH)	(415) 627–7000	(800) 670–4763	www.schwab.com

Entertainment/Media

Company Name/Stock Symbol	Company Phone	800 Phone	Website
Disney (Walt) Co. (NYSE: DIS)	(818) 553–7200	(800) 948–2222	www.disney.com
Gannett Co. (NYSE: GCI)	(703) 284–6000	(800) 778–3299	www.gannett.com
Sony (NYSE: SNE)		(800) 749–1687	www.sony.com
Tribune Company (NYSE: TRB)	(312) 222–9100	(800) 924–1490	www.tribune.com

Information/Business Services

Company Name/Stock Symbol	Company Phone	800 Phone	Website
Block (H&R) (NYSE: HRB)	(816) 753–6900	(800) 456–9852	www.hrblock.com
Equifax (NYSE: EFX)	(404) 885–8961	(800) 462–9853	www.equifax.com
Paychex (NASDAQ: PAYX)	(716) 385–6666	(800) 937–5449	www.paychex.com
Reuters (NASDAQ: RTRSY)		(800) 749–1687	www.reuters.com

Health Care

Company Name/Stock Symbol	Company Phone	800 Phone	Website
Abbott Laboratories (NYSE: ABT)	(847) 937–3923	(888) 332–2268	www.abbott.com
Bristol-Myers (NYSE: BMY)	(212) 546–4000	(800) 356–2026	www.bms.com
Elan (NYSE: ELN)		(888) 269–2377	www.elan.ie
Guidant (NYSE: GDT)	(317) 971–2000	(800) 537–1677	www.guidant.com
Johnson & Johnson (NYSE: JNJ)	(732) 524–0400	(800) 328–9033	www.jnj.com
Merck & Co. (NYSE: MRK)	(908) 423–1000	(800) 613–2104	www.merck.com
Pfizer (NYSE: PFE)	(212) 573–2323	(800) 733–9393	www.pfizer.com

Retailing

Company Name/Stock Symbol	Company Phone	800 Phone	Website
Ahold NV (NYSE: AHO)		(888) 269–2377	www.ahold.com
Home Depot (NYSE: HD)	(770) 433–8211	(800) 928–0380	www.homedepot.com
Wal-Mart Stores (NYSE: WMT)	(501) 273–4000	(800) 438–6278	www.walmart.com
Walgreen (NYSE: WAG)	(847) 940–2500	(800) 286–9178	www.walgreen.com

Consumer Products/Services

Company Name/Stock Symbol	Company Phone	800 Phone	Website
Coca-Cola (NYSE: KO)	(800) 265–3747	(800) 446–2617	www.cocacola.com
General Electric (NYSE: GE)	(203) 373–2816	(800) 786–2543	www.ge.com
McDonald's (NYSE: MCD)	(630) 623–3000	(800) 228–9623	www.mcdonalds.com
PepsiCo (NYSE: PEP)	(914) 253–3055	(800) 226–0083	www.pepsico.com
Philip Morris (NYSE: MO)	(212) 880–5000	(800) 442–0077	www.philipmorris.com
Procter & Gamble (NYSE: PG)	(513) 983–1100	(800) 742–6253	www.pg.com
Unilever (NYSE: UN)		(800) 749–1687	www.unilever.com

Technology

Company Name/Stock Symbol	Company Phone	800 Phone	Website
Hewlett-Packard (NYSE: HWP)	(650) 857–1501	(800) 286–5977	www.hp.com
Intel (NASDAQ: INTC)	(408) 765–8080	(800) 298–0146	www.intel.com
IBM (NYSE: IBM)	(914) 499–1900	(888) 421–8860	www.ibm.com

Telecommunications

Company Name/Stock Symbol	Company Phone	800 Phone	Website
AT&T (NYSE: T)	(212) 387–5400	(800) 348–8288	www.att.com
BellSouth (NYSE: BLS)	(404) 249–2000	(888) 266–6778	www.bellsouth.com
Lucent Technologies (NYSE: LU)	(908) 582–8500	(888) 582–3686	www.lucent.com

Company Name/Stock Symbol	Company Phone	800 Phone	Website
Motorola (NYSE: MOT)	(847) 576–5000	(800) 704–4098	www.mot.com
Nokia (NYSE: NOK)		(800) 749–1687	www.nokia.com
SBC Comm. (NYSE: SBC)	(210) 821–4105	(888) 836–5062	www.sbc.com

Energy

Company Name/Stock Symbol	Company Phone	800 Phone	Website
BP Amoco (NYSE: BPA)	(312) 856–6111	(888) 638–5672	www.amoco.com
Chevron (NYSE: CHV)	(925) 842–1000	(800) 286–9178	www.chevron.com
Exxon Mobil (NYSE: XON)	(972) 444–1000	(800) 252–1800	www.exxon.com

CONCLUSION

This chapter covers several ways to refine the eight-step plan laid out in this book.

Don't overdiversify.

Know your strengths, weaknesses, and interests as an investor and invest accordingly, either in individual stocks, index funds, or a combination of the two.

If you invest in stocks, focus on leaders in "must-have" industries.

What I like about these concepts are that they are simple and straightforward.

Do you have to follow these refinements in order to reach seven figures? Probably not.

Will following them improve your odds of becoming a millionaire investor?

You bet.

The millionaire profiled in this chapter is—you guessed it—Gio Mallard. While you already know quite a bit about Mr. Mallard, his profile offers much useful information for would-be millionaires.

NAME: Gio Mallard

AGE: 55

HOME: New York

MARITAL STATUS: Married (has been divorced)

CHILDREN: 1

EDUCATION: College (advanced degree) graduate

OCCUPATION: Probation officer

HIGHEST INCOME: $46,000

HOW MANY DIFFERENT JOBS SINCE AGE 25? 6

DO YOU HAVE AN ANNUAL HOUSEHOLD BUDGET THAT YOU FOLLOW? No

WOULD YOU CONSIDER YOUR PARENTS TO BE FRUGAL? Yes

HOW IMPORTANT WERE YOUR PARENTS IN DEVELOPING YOUR DISCIPLINE AND EXPERTISE IN INVESTING? Important

AT WHAT AGE DID YOU START INVESTING? 27

HOW MANY YEARS HAVE YOU BEEN INVESTING? 28

WHAT IS THE SIZE OF YOUR ENTIRE INVESTMENT PORTFOLIO? $1.1 million

WHAT IS THE BREAKDOWN OF THESE ASSETS? Mutual funds (30 percent), IRA & 457 plan (40 percent), individual stocks (30 percent)

HOW MANY INDIVIDUAL STOCKS DO YOU OWN? 8

NAME YOUR 5 LARGEST HOLDINGS: Glaxo Wellcome, MCI WorldCom, Dow Chemical, Apple Computer, Merck

HOW MANY INDIVIDUAL MUTUAL FUNDS DO YOU OWN? 16

NAME YOUR BIGGEST FUND HOLDINGS: American Century Ultra, Vanguard 500 Index, Janus Olympus, Strong Growth, Janus Mercury

HOW MANY INDIVIDUAL BONDS DO YOU HAVE? 0

HAVE YOU EVER PURCHASED STOCK/INDEX OPTIONS? No

HAVE YOU EVER BOUGHT STOCK/INDEX FUTURES? No

DO YOU OWN GOLD OR PRECIOUS METALS? No

HAVE YOU EVER SOLD STOCK SHORT? No

DO YOU RECEIVE ADVICE ON YOUR INVESTMENTS FROM AN OUTSIDE SOURCE? Yes

WHAT TYPE OF BROKER DO YOU USE? Traditional discount

ARE YOU A MEMBER OF AN INVESTMENT CLUB? No

DO YOU INVEST ONLINE? No

WHAT ARE THE PLANS FOR YOUR ESTATE? To gift my estate to my son, who is learning disabled.

DID YOU HAVE ANY SPECIFIC INVESTMENT GOALS IN MIND WHEN YOU STARTED INVESTING? Yes, financial security prior to age 65.

WHAT ARE YOUR SHORT-TERM GOALS? Continue to invest in an aggressive manner.

WHAT ARE YOUR LONG-TERM GOALS? To build wealth that will exceed $2 million and to provide financial security for my son.

WHAT HURDLES, IF ANY, DID YOU OVERCOME TO BEGIN INVESTING? I had to overcome fear of making errors and gain confidence in my own ability.

HOW, PSYCHOLOGICALLY SPEAKING, DID YOU DEAL WITH THE NOTION OF PUTTING OFF CONSUMPTION TO SAVE FOR A BETTER FINANCIAL FUTURE? When my son was classified as learning disabled, I was aware that his future potential earnings would be limited, so it was a given that I put off consumption.

WHERE DID YOU GET THE MONEY TO START INVESTING? My personal savings and earnings from positions I had held.

WERE THERE ANY SPECIFIC EVENTS, LIFE-CHANGING MOMENTS, ETC., THAT SPURRED YOU TO BEGIN INVESTING? I realized in the mid-1980s that the social contract between employer and employee had changed. It was then that I began investing in earnest.

HAVE YOU INHERITED WHAT YOU THOUGHT WAS A LARGE SUM OF MONEY? No

DID YOU START INVESTING WITH A SPECIFIC PLAN IN MIND? Yes, maximize any plan (investment) offered to me by my employer, or any vehicle such as IRAs, despite the fact the amount is no longer deducted from my gross income.

HOW DID YOU EDUCATE YOURSELF ABOUT INVESTING? DID YOU FIND THE EDUCATION PROCESS DIFFICULT? FUN? Reading every possible book and publication that dealt with personal investing. Radio programs, Bob Brinker and Bill Flanagan. Subscriptions to *DRIP Investor, MarketTimer,* and various magazines. The educational process was fun!

DID YOU HAVE ANY SPECIAL EXPERTISE IN INVESTING WHEN YOU STARTED? None

HOW MUCH DO YOU SPEND PER YEAR ON INVESTMENT RESEARCH RESOURCES? $251 to $500 per year

DO YOU USE A COMPUTER TO KEEP TRACK OF YOUR INVESTMENTS? No

HOW MANY HOURS PER WEEK DO YOU DEVOTE TO YOUR INVESTMENTS AND INVESTMENT STRATEGIES? Approximately 10 hours

WHAT CRITERIA DO YOU USE TO PICK STOCKS/MUTUAL FUNDS? High beta funds for IRAs, so that capital gains will not create taxable events. Index funds for those which do not have the protected status of an IRA or pension plan. Low beta funds tend to create fewer taxable events. Three-year performance data. Emphasis placed upon purchasing blue-chip stocks. Stocks that are health-care related.

HOW OFTEN DO YOU BUY INVESTMENTS? Monthly

ON AVERAGE, HOW LONG DO YOU HOLD AN INVESTMENT BEFORE SELLING? 10 years or longer

DO YOU "MARKET TIME"? No

DOES YOUR INVESTMENT APPROACH DIFFER DEPENDING ON WHETHER THE MARKET IS CLASSIFIED AS A "BEAR" OR "BULL" MARKET? No

HOW IMPORTANT ARE TAXES IN THE INVESTMENT PROCESS? Important

WHAT HAVE BEEN YOUR BEST-PERFORMING STOCKS? Glaxo Wellcome, MCI WorldCom, Dow Chemical

WHAT HAVE BEEN YOUR WORST-PERFORMING STOCKS? Coca-Cola, Centocor, Apple Computer

WHAT WERE SOME OF YOUR BIGGEST INVESTMENT MISTAKES? The purchase of Dome Petroleum, American Century Heritage Fund, and Tandon Computer

DO YOU INVEST IN WHAT YOU KNOW? Yes

HOW WOULD YOU BEST DESCRIBE YOUR INVESTMENT APPROACH? Very aggressive. Unafraid of any short-term corrections in the market. Using corrections in the market as buying opportunities. Very slow to sell any holdings. Avoid active trading. Take a "buy and hold" approach.

DO YOU THINK INDIVIDUAL INVESTORS ARE DISADVANTAGED IN THE FINANCIAL MAR-

KETS RELATIVE TO LARGE INVESTORS? Yes, large investors usually have greater access to many outlets of data, etc., and obtain professional input.

DO YOU BELIEVE IT IS POSSIBLE TO BEAT THE MARKET ON A CONSISTENT BASIS? Yes

WHAT IS YOUR RISK TOLERANCE? Above-average tolerance for risk

HOW MANY INVESTMENTS DO YOU BELIEVE ARE NECESSARY TO BE PROPERLY DIVERSIFIED? Approximately 10

WHAT DO YOU THINK ARE SOME OF THE GREATEST MYTHS OF INVESTING? Investing is limited to the wealthy only. You can time the market. Dollar-cost averaging does not work. Brokers are essential. Day trading provides instant wealth. Index funds are boring. Buy and hold strategy is noncreative.

WHAT IS YOUR GREATEST FEAR AS AN INVESTOR? I fear that I have become too aggressive with regard to my attitude toward investing. Needless to say, when a protracted downturn in the market eventually arrives, I will be forced to turn to bond index funds, etc.

WHAT IS THE BIGGEST BENEFIT OF A 7-FIGURE PORTFOLIO? Peace of mind. I do not plan to retire from my present occupation until I am approximately sixty-seven years old. However, my portfolio size provides me with a degree of security that my son will have a solid financial foundation as he enters adulthood. My wife and I lead noncomplex lives and never intended to fully use the portfolio capital-income. If my son did not have the many needs he has, the portfolio would have been gifted to the church.

DO YOU HAVE ANY FINAL THOUGHTS? I have found investing to be a fun-filled, rewarding experience. It has become my hobby. My extensive reading, listening, research, and thought process in selection of stocks and mutual funds to purchase provides me with mental stimulation. Needless to say, I am not always correct. But I am unable to resist the challenge that investing provides me.

12

In Their Own Words

A fear I had while doing this book was that I would not be able to include all of the rich material provided by our everyday millionaire investors. That's why I decided to include a separate section showcasing their wit and wisdom. The following are what I consider some of the more insightful, useful, interesting, or simply amusing comments made by our millionaires. Remember that the individuals making these comments are not financial planners, stockbrokers, fund managers, or other professional investors. These are comments made by ordinary people—people much like you—who have no agenda other than to tell you what they believe and what has worked for them.

Please share your favorite personal investment story.

My favorite story is about a cousin on the Italian side of the family. She was an elderly widow, living in tight circumstances in the farmhouse she and her husband had had for fifty-six years until his death. He'd made a living for them, put the children through school, and saved money in the bank. But she was in bad financial circumstances. We were trying to figure out how to help her, since she, of course, wouldn't take money from any of us. So we had offered to go through her investments: a small grape farm, passbook savings account, and something called "eebayemahs." Her husband had learned about them during his WWII service and bought a few every now and then if he had money left over after selling the grape harvest. We eventually discovered, by going through cigar boxes, coffee cans, and the dining room paneling, that "eebayemahs" was her Italian pronunciation of "IBMs." What with splits, dividends, and all that, she had 100,000 of them.

I started by using a financial planner. She certainly intimidated me using terminology I did not understand. After three years of doing what she recommended, I began to say "NO!" to her. She wrote me a letter terminating our relationship. My response, "Thank God!"

October 19, 1987—the day of the huge drop—myself, my wife, daughter, and son were on a plane between London and Dallas. I was aware of the drop, but not that it was such a decline. Within the next few days we added to our portfolio as much as our finances would allow. It was one of the few times I tried to time the market, and it proved to be quite successful.

I attended a wedding and began a conversation with one of the groomsmen. He said he was a Wall Street investor. He asked if I would introduce him to a lady at the wedding, and I did. To thank me, he gave me a stock tip. In a short period of time, the stock went to $18. Then it was reported that the product the company made may have caused a death. The stock is now selling around $3.00. Oh, the wedding couple's marriage also crashed!

After holding mutual funds for a number of years, I hired a money manager in a wrap account at a large brokerage firm. After a couple of years with 15 percent to 20 percent return and lots of turnover, I asked the broker to tell the manager not to sell Cisco. When he thought it time to sell, I would keep the stock in a second account. The manager replied by firing me as his customer. Since then Cisco has gone up by twenty times.

A friend that I work with was telling me about a phone call he had from his brother-in-law. He asked him if he still had the shares of Microsoft they had both bought back in 1987. The brother-in-law had sold his after a couple of years for a decent profit, but my friend didn't even remember buying them. They had each bought 100 shares. My friend looked through his papers in his safe (which he obviously seldom does) and sure enough found the certificate. Twelve years and eight splits later he now has 14,400 shares worth over $1 million. Last year alone he had over a $500,000 gain. The smartest thing he ever did was to do nothing. He already had over $1 million in assets, mostly *from real estate, but wow! So much for day traders. I am sure if he had those shares at a brokerage firm, he would have been diversified right out of his best profits.*

Buying five shares of Philip Morris in the 1940s. Never selling, now owning nearly 3,000 shares through splits only.

I used to listen to advice from my broker until I realized I know much more about my industry segment than their analysts did. That's when I shifted my investing to focus on my industry winners. As these investments started to pay off, my broker began asking me for recommendations.

A tip that worked. My son told me of a hightech NASDAQ company, which he deals with, that was to announce a new product (software that my son said would be a breakthrough). I purchased many shares and watched the stock double in two and a half months, then split two for one and double again in two more months.

As a twenty-four-year-old graduate accounting student, I purchased my first share of stock. I really didn't have the money to be investing in stocks, but I thought I knew what I was doing and wanted to try investing on my own. I was concerned because I couldn't afford to lose the money, and the stock I invested in was in the technology area and far from a blue-chip industry leader. I was lucky and the stock did very well. After doubling in about twenty months, I sold it. Although I made money I didn't enjoy the risk I was taking at that time. I learned from that experience that the reward isn't worth the risk if you are psychologically uncomfortable with the risk you are taking. From then on I have always judged risk before reward in my investment decisions. I sleep very comfortably at night.

Taking my IRA in 1993 that was invested in fixed income and conservative investments and buying a depressed drug company stock. My IRA grew from $55,000 to over $250,000 by 1999. Switching from tax-free bonds to buying stocks in 1994–95. *Started with $400,000 that has grown to $2,250,000 with regular investing. I have been completely out of debt (including house payment) since 1992.*

I told my mother she made a bad investment in IBM and Bristol-Myers in 1992. What did I know? Mother knows best.

About thirty-five years ago I stopped to watch a ticker tape with an elderly gentleman. We struck up a conversation, and he asked me how I was doing with my investments. I proudly told him how much I had invested in the market. I asked him how much he had invested. He stated, "Young man, if you know exactly how much you have at a given point in time, you don't have much." As the years passed, I realized exactly what he meant and have conducted myself accordingly.

Many years ago, my wife and I became godparents to our friends' baby boy. For a baptism gift we gave him $100 worth of stock in a DRIP account. No additional amounts were added over the years, other than dividends. When he finished high school, he liquidated the DRIP account and had several thousands of dollars to apply to his college expenses.

For each of my children, I saved $1.00 a week from birth for twenty-one years. Once a year I added to a mutual fund. They each still have $75,000.

My grandfather, who was born about 1870, was involved in a business venture in Atlanta with his brother-in-law, who tricked him out of some money. He resolved to get along but never do business with him again. A few years later the brother-in-law offered him the chance to get in on the ground floor of Coca-Cola. My grandfather declined and was also heard to say, "Who would want that old fizzy stuff anyway?" When his brother-in-law's daughter died recently, his $110 million estate went to two colleges. The daughter, my first cousin once removed, left me $25,000, which was generous of her. I bought Coca-Cola stock. It has already split once.

I started investing in DRIPs in 1992 just as a sideline to my investment port-folio with a broker. The more I invested, the better I liked the concept. I never sold any of the stocks and reinvested all of the dividends. Over the next seven years I turned this sideline into a portfolio of over 115 stocks worth over $350,000.

My daughter and son were both in our investment club. My daughter heard about a stock on CNBC, passed it on to her brother, who was to present in the near future. He checked it out and presented it to the club. The club bought it, I bought it, and my daughter bought it (unfortunately my son didn't have money to invest at the time). This investment turned out to be EMC—our club's best performer, my best performer, and my daughter's best performer.

I bought 125 shares of Home Depot for $16 per share several years ago and never bought another share. We have several thousands now. Didn't know much about the stock, but my husband liked working with his hands.

My friend recently told me of his father-in-law who is seventy-eight and is quite wealthy (approximately $20 million) who made all of his money in the stock market. In our discussions he told me that he purchased fifty shares of Merck around 1945 and left it as if it didn't exist. In response, I said, "Well, I'll bet that's a tidy sum today." "Yes," he replied. "He has around 12,000 shares." This is without adding $1.00 over time. Talk about the time value of money!

I was out playing golf in October 1987 when the market crashed. When I came home in late afternoon my wife rushed out to tell me about the market crash. "If you had been home we could have sold half of our investments," she said excitably. My answer was "I don't want to sell half of our investments." It took a period of time to convince her that I was right, but I did not sell any investments. It came out great.

When I was nine or ten, I first learned about stocks from an army retired major. He had accumulated an immense amount of top-quality issues. He used to strut up and down in front of a small group of kids my age and whack his tall boots with a riding crop. I am probably the only person out of six or eight that ever took him seriously. So when other kids were learning about football and baseball, I was learning about stocks. P.S. I learned about football, too.

When the Clintons came out with their health care plan, the pharmaceuticals went in the toilet. I purchased as much Johnson & Johnson, Merck, Abbott, and Bristol-Myers Squibb as I could afford. Three to four years later, they doubled or better. I sold half, reinvested the proceeds, and the remainder are in the portfolio growing at no cost to me.

What hurdles did you overcome to begin investing?

Convincing myself that I was just as capable of doing this—or at least, of learning how to do it—as anybody else. Fortunately, even though I was young in the 1970s, I was quite suspicious of people who had a lot of flash but didn't seem to have much substance.

Reluctance of brokers to want to deal with small (at the time) investors. They did not have the sense to realize someone could build a larger portfolio from small beginnings.

Earlier fears of losing 100 percent of my investment, which happened when I stupidly invested in options when I was twenty-one. I lost over $3,000 in less than a year. The good news is that hard lessons are lasting lessons.

I started out with extremely limited knowledge about financial matters, investing in the stock market, etc. Having been a housewife, I gave little thought to saving for the future—I always figured my husband (an attorney) would make good decisions about savings and investments. Was I ever sur-

prised when I discovered that he had little time or inclination to learn the many nuances of stock picking!

In the fifties and sixties we were raising a family; trying to find money to invest for the future without harming the family lifestyle. In the mid-fifties, I used an income tax refund and invested those few hundreds of dollars into utilities that had dividend reinvestment programs.

I had been saving but had no knowledge of investing. I really didn't know where to start. My biggest hurdle was learning my broker was not my friend. I was very naive.

Lack of knowledge and lack of experience. Personal effort gets you over the first hurdle, experience just comes naturally. Remember to jump one hurdle and gain experience one hurdle at a time. Rome wasn't built in a day.

Being afraid of the stock market.

The biggest problem is not having a mentor or adviser. Since I believe that brokers have their best interests and the interests of their company at heart, I had to learn what I know from reading investment guides, newsletters, and books. By doing so over the years, I have developed my own investment philosophy.

Finding the self-control to save money for investment rather than spending it on myself.

Convincing my wife to take risks.

Single parenthood, and the thought that saved fixed money would be better than the volatile world of investing.

First in both families to invest. Wife considered it throwing money away, so we have been very conservative and maintained adequate cash funds.

I had to overcome the fear of making errors and gain confidence in my own ability.

Complete lack of knowledge; fear of losing money (was told by parents that investing in the stock market was just legalized gambling); learning investment business terminology.

What specific events or life-changing moments spurred you to begin investing?

I met my Great-Uncle Kenny. He was my grandfather's youngest brother. He'd gone to Los Angeles at age sixteen with $200 in his pocket, and in his seventies was a self-made multimillionaire. I met Uncle Kenny at just the right age for his stories to make an impact.

I used to work in a building (1961) that had a Bache & Co. (brokerage firm) office one floor below my office. Started stopping in the Bache office to watch ticker tape. Been hooked ever since.

In ninth grade, I discovered the miracle of compound interest.

Age thirty-two, no dough, heavy debt, no prospects. Terrifying!

When the last child left for college, my wife and I realized we could do a lot of things for ourselves if we had the money. We decided we did not want to work until death.

From 1989–95 I had to manage the affairs of my aunt, who had a stroke. I had power of attorney and had to manage her investments to offset her nursing-home expenses. I had professional advice—accounting, legal, and a broker—who helped a lot in my education. Ultimately, the low returns and high costs took a toll. I believed I could do better on my own. I have.

It was the realization that we might need lots more money for retirement than what we already had put aside. For a while, I felt really scared about our financial future.

I inherited some money from my maternal grandfather. A cousin, who was a broker, guided me in how to invest. One suggestion was Philip Morris in the 1940s. I still own it.

I tried TV get-rich-quick infomercials twenty years ago but failed. I learned a lesson—no easy, quick money!

I suddenly realized that I was aging and not saving for retirement.

My wife and I came from humble circumstances and wanted to attain a more comfortable lifestyle.

One of my dental school patients was an insurance agent. He taught me the value of time in investments.

My father has always invested. At twenty, I thought he was foolish. At thirty, like Twain, I was amazed how much more sensible he'd gotten. Naturally, but mostly unconsciously, I began following his example.

My niece married a man whose father retired from Exxon. When he talked about how he traveled on dividends, I wanted to do the same.

Most friends and relatives didn't invest. I did not want to be short of money like them.

I knew by the late '70s or early '80s that family farming operations were going down the tubes. I knew that I had to invest some place else to obtain a decent retirement.

My uncle's early retirement and seeing how he enjoyed life before his death helped me start.

Marriage. We needed to take care of ourselves—no one was going to do it for us.

I'm a child of the Depression and saw my parents struggle to keep a roof over our heads.

My aunt explained buying and selling stocks when I was five years old. She is a multimillionaire and gives my children money every year in different stocks.

I think saving was built in my mind when you start marriage with $5.00 to your name and have it tough for a while. I think you learn to save as you grow and make more money, then you try to teach others that value.

My father died broke at sixty-five and left my mother to raise nine children. I was just fifteen at the time and our well-to-do household just went upside down in front of me.

Besides the Depression years, probably the one event that really encouraged us to save/invest was the death of my father-in-law. He had what back then would be considered a good job making good money. He had the opportunity of taking a smaller pension and his wife continuing to receive a small pension after his death. He chose to take the full benefit because he thought his older sister, who was considered to be fairly well off for those times, would die before him and he would get what she had. It didn't work out that way—he died first, leaving his widow with practically nothing. We helped her out monthly. She lived with us for five years before her death. My husband said he would see to it that I would never be left in that position. And we did!

During WWII I had Uncle Sam buy a $10 war bond each month out of my $50-a-month gross pay. I held on to them for many years after the war. When

I cashed them in I realized I had lost money on every one of them when I took inflation into account. It was then I began to understand that any investment must at least keep pace with inflation. I decided that stock in the companies in this country was the best and easiest solution.

My father died at forty-eight when I was twenty-two. He was saving for an early retirement, working two full-time jobs. Decided there must be a happy medium.

Got a new boss who really got me thinking of the future and interested in investing.

How, psychologically speaking, did you deal with the notion of putting off consumption to save for a better financial future?

Direct payroll deposit. Never saw it.

I have always been an excellent saver and have never had to scrimp for money, even when I had very little. My husband is the same way. Currently we are very comfortable financially but we live way below our income and max out our savings every year. Even though we live below our income, we do not suffer any hardships or pangs of denial. We are extremely fortunate.

I grew up on a farm. One becomes accustomed to deferring gratification.

I never had the desire to have a lot of things. Just a few good quality possessions and a great adventure now and then.

I thought I would predecease my wife, and I did not want her to be dependent upon our four children nor have to live in semipoverty. This was a driving force!

I don't think we really "put off" consumption. I think that both my wife and I came from the same family background (dirt-poor) and we bought what we needed but did not go overboard. We never bought food, clothing, or household furnishings on time. We did without until we had the money to buy. While saving we accumulated interest and as you know, when interest starts to compound, you either get out of the way or get run over.

It really wasn't all that difficult for us. Our desires for material items were not as important to us as was our desire for good personal/family relationships and experiences. The best things in life really are free. The prospects of a comfortable retirement without financial worries are psychologically comforting to us.

I always kept the goal in mind. Also, after my parents lost everything in Cuba, I wanted to work toward a secure financial future.

We set up a budget which my wife and I both agreed to every year. This was not without disputing the allocation but we always agreed before the start of the year and then held to that budget throughout the year. This avoided fights over money through the year and provided savings for higher education and for our retirement. Without this budgeting and our investment success, I would not have been able to take early retirement (age fifty-three).

The goal of early retirement made it easy to discipline ourselves to save as much as possible without "doing without." Also no children, living in the same house for twenty-six years, and a willingness to take risks in equities during a great market run.

I have long believed that Social Security will not be viable when I retire. Also, I have heard/read about people with insufficient means to live and retire. An underlying fear of poverty is also a strong motivator (due to upbringing).

I have never sweat on small expenses such as for a show, movie, or dinner. But I have always been deliberate and frugal on big-ticket items like a car, and as such always bought used cars.

Got a divorce and only had one person spending my money.

I grew up in a rather poor family, economically, and saw how my father spent every dime we had and then some so he was always in debt. I vowed that I would not do that. I had an older sister who also spent every penny she made, so I had no real role models. My mother was frugal, but she had to take care of the everyday living expenses. We paid our own school expenses; i.e., books, etc., when we were in high school.

What were some of your biggest investing mistakes?

Letting brokers convince me to sell just because profit had been made. Selling too soon or for the wrong reasons.

The only hot tip I ever acted on was about 1967 and involved Rite-Aid. My broker claimed it was going to double in price. I bought a few shares, it went up ten points, and then started back down. I put in a stop-loss order to preserve a 20 percent profit. I was stopped out and later the stock went up 400 percent.

I bought IBM on three occasions. Once at $96 and sold at $83. Once at $74 and sold at $64. Once at $66 and sold at $48. When it got to $44, I was ready to buy again but decided I didn't want to get burned again. Since then it has gone up and split two for one and now sells for upward of $175 ($350 pre-split). A very humbling experience. Makes you wonder if we ever really learn anything about this business.

Following tips without doing my own research.

I was convinced by an insurance agent I had used for six to seven years that two limited partnerships he was representing were great future tax saving investments. My wife and I needed to get together something over $20,000 in funds to invest within forty-eight hours. Because I trusted him from the past, I did not have the experience to know no investment is worth a forty-eight-hour panic. Eventually, we lost all our capital in both these ventures. My entire dental education back in those days cost me less. This was my postgraduate class in buyer beware.

When young, with $500 saved during service in WWII, I was faced with choice of buying Polaroid or joining a maternal uncle in an oil-well venture. It was great fun getting all those reports about drilling and great expectations until the final report of only dry holes and out of funds. Great lesson! For years I watched Polaroid climb/split/climb/split and finally quit whipping myself. Today, I never look back at what could have been; only integrate the experience and look ahead.

Our main mistake has been to hold too many different stocks. In our old age we are active in only six to eight stocks each. We are better adjusted in investing when we just keep adding to the six or eight stocks we each choose to hold.

Attempting to time the market and taking a conservative approach initially driven by fear.

Investing in something I didn't really understand.

Investing in real estate investment trusts.

My biggest mistake has always been timing. I make an investment decision and then drag my feet before executing it, for no particular reason.

Not putting enough money into stocks I bought because of fear of losing money; keeping funds in money-market accounts.

Selling reflexively on bad news.

Buying silver futures. Investing in penny mining stocks.

Using whole life insurance as an investment.

Trying to get rich quick in the beginning. Playing the commodity market in 1955.

Selling Intel for a 2,000 percent gain. If I had waited five weeks longer, I would have had an 8,000 percent gain.

Scotch whiskey.

What do you think are some of the greatest myths of investing?
You can time the market.

Your stockbroker is working for you. You can't invest enough to make a difference.

That only rich people can do it. That you need a broker.

The "genius investor" myth is still rampant. Granted some of these people are very intelligent, but there's a lot of hard work and recognizing opportunities involved. I've actually had people asking me for advice. I give it them, but they're obviously disappointed. The "quick killing" myth; all that advertising for get rich schemes and systems on television really does convince people that with a few hundred dollars today, by the end of the year they'll be millionaires.

And, the myth that you must have money to invest money. It really doesn't take a lot to get started. The important thing is to get started.

The theory that all investors have access to all information at the same time is bunk! There is insider information.

Current hot funds and stocks will stay that way. Value doesn't count. Value will be recognized in the short term. Mutual fund managers are savvy and knowledgeable. You can trust blue-chip stocks. Funds with sales loads perform better. Government securities are good investments.

It's so difficult.

That you must have an excess of funds to invest. That you can get rich overnight or soon after investing.

That you need help. That investing is complicated. That it's okay to borrow from your 401(k). That retired people should stick to fixed-income investments.

Mutual funds are better investments than individual stocks.

Stocks are risky. Banks are guaranteed. Social Security is secure. Government can help in anything.

It takes a lot of money to start an investment program. You have to watch the market closely every day to be a good investor. It's a way to get rich fast.

Small caps outperform the market.

You can get rich day trading.

That the market can continue to return 15 percent to 20 percent and up ad infinitum. That last year's winners will automatically do the same this year.

Bonds are safe, and equities are risky.

That the overall economy matters. That the Fed matters.

You need to be an active trader in order to make money in the stock market.

That men are better investors than women.

That the way to invest is to wait until you really have the money and then do it in large amounts.

It is too late to start. I just do not have the cash to invest. Social Security will take care of me.

You can't become a millionaire by investing in common stocks. The stockbrokers and big mutual fund companies have more advantages than the small individual investor.

In today's environment, the market always goes up. That size and age of a corporation are assurance that it will always be successful. That yesterday's financial performance is a valid indicator of future performance.

That choosing a managed fund is better than indexing.

That the market never goes down. It is different this time.

The market is too high (I heard that ten years ago).

You can't beat the market.

Everybody is making a killing but me.

The need to diversify globally.

If you could give just one piece of advice to individual investors, what would that be?

Start now. The longer compounding works for you the better off you are.

Start early, invest regularly, and reinvest dividends.

Keep the faith! If you've got stock in a well-managed company with strong earnings growth, have patience that the stock price will eventually reflect the quality of that company.

Work as hard investing as at a job.

Buy quality, everyday companies. Plan on not selling.

Always pay yourself first (whether 401(k), direct purchase plan, etc.) Otherwise you will always be waiting for tomorrow to start investing.

Stick with companies you know and really understand so you can sell if the fundamentals change for the worse.

If you are a consumer, trust that you can understand a business and its product. It's very easy to pick a great company. Invest in it over time to smooth out the valuation issues.

Time, patience, and perserverance are your allies. Mistakes are inevitable, learn from them and move on. Experience is knowledge; use it wisely.

Stay out of debt. You need money to play the game. Without savings or money you can't play.

Go to work for a company with a good 401(k) or similar plan.

Buy and hold blue chips.

Don't be concerned about big moves in the market in either direction. If the market goes up it's great. If it goes down, you are buying more stock at a cheaper price.

Be focused in your commitment to bite the bullet and make appropriate contributions for the first twenty years. Climb the hill early and ride the wave you create.

Stay away from penny stocks. Make your first purchases good blue-chip companies.

Don't look back and second-guess yourself. You won't always be right.

Join a good investment club.

Accumulate good stocks when they are down 30 percent to 50 percent from their highs and then hang on for the long pull. Don't adopt a strategy of trading. Employ a broker who strongly endorses the above.

Live within 90 percent of your take-home income. Invest the rest of it each month equally in a basket of diversified stocks and mutual funds.

Think of investing as a bill you are paying to yourself.

Let your money work hard for you, so you don't work hard for your money!

Set your goals, think quality, invest regularly only in quality investments.

When you have decided to buy a stock, based upon research, advice, etc., act rather than wait for a better price.

Sell only when you are convinced another investment is superior.

The best advice I can give is to make the investing process like exercise. Learn to like it. Learn to make investing the same way.

Even if you can only save $5.00 a week, that's $5.00 more that you will have to invest than if you spent it. Anyone, at any income level, can save something if they analyze what they spend money on.

Final Thought

The thing I like most about investing, believe it or not, is not the money (as much as I do like that) but the intellectual work. I enjoy figuring out that I should buy Wal-Mart rather than Sears (which I did, when it was in the high teens) and Disney rather than Warner (also before the big run-up). Investing and the research involved take you places and introduce you to people and things you never knew about—and they're all quite interesting. I enjoy it greatly. And I do like the money, too.

I believe the individual investor has the potential to take charge of his or her own financial destiny. It takes much time and effort, but it can provide empowerment. It doesn't have to be overwhelming. On the contrary, it can be totally fulfilling.

I just think that we need to educate our young people on the power of compounding and time, and the wisdom of investing in America's finest companies. There is no reason that everyone working should not be financially comfy in their old age.

Investing, like success, is a journey, not a destination. There is always a cause and an effect for every investing result. It is important to analyze the past results for the future performance. An investor will eventually become what he thinks about—a loser or a winner!

We owe it to our children to show them the many benefits of getting started early.

I am now trying to teach my children about investing and its importance. Try and tell them about the ups and downs of Wall Street; that the value of your investments will go up if you wait long enough and have nerve. Often think of my dad's portfolio that started with a few million and shot up to $12 million. He is a very good model.

Start your children and grandchildren investing either in a DRIP or a mutual fund and use it as an educational opportunity. Our adult children owned a mutual fund when they were six or seven. They have continued to invest. Our two-year-old and one-year-old grandchildren receive stock for birthdays, etc., instead of toys from us so that their college education will be partially paid for.

Investing is not just about amassing money; it is also about enjoying the money you earn. I go to Oxford, England, every summer for three weeks to study subjects which interest me. My husband and I love to travel to France and elsewhere. We want a comfortable retirement, but we also enjoy life now because of successful investing.

Keep your eye on your goals. Know why you are sacrificing and do not take unnecessary risk. A few years ago, I realized I was right on track and ahead of schedule. I moved a significant amount of my 401(k) money from the growth equity account to the fixed-dollar account paying about 8.5% a year. Hindsight tells me that I would have more money if I had stayed in stocks. However, I did not have any reason to continue to take the risk.

Resist temptation to sell good companies just because their stock prices have risen sharply. If basic outlook for the company remains strong, hang on indefinitely. Taxes and brokerage fees make it unlikely that switching to other stocks will be profitable.

Investing in stock is the only way to acquire wealth for many working Americans. It is a state of mind that takes discipline and goal setting. It is also fun and allows people to benefit from the efforts of many.

Be charitable and reward selected beneficiaries, charities, and people before it's too late.

Investors need to understand that the greatest risk is not being in the market when it's falling, but being out of the market when it's rising. Investors must understand that stocks are a safe bet, but only if you stay invested long enough to ride out the corrections.

Investing is not gambling. Anyone who treats it as a gamble cannot be successful. A good investment will pay off in the long run. You must have patience.

Just do it.

APPENDIX

The following is a list of all U.S. and foreign companies that allow investors to buy even their initial shares directly. Each listing includes the minimum initial investment as well as the telephone number to call for further information and a plan brochure.

If you are interested in additional information on DRIPs and direct-purchase plans, let me plug my newsletters, *DRIP Investor* (800-233-5922) and *No-Load Stock Insider* (800-233-5922); and my books, *Buying Stocks Without a Broker, No-Load Stocks,* and *The Individual Investor Revolution.* You may also obtain information and enrollment materials for many direct purchase plans at **www. enrolldirect.com.** If you prefer the telephone, you may obtain enrollment information for many direct-purchase plans by calling the **Direct Purchase Plan Clearinghouse** at 800-774-4117. In the interest of full disclosure, I have business relationships with the Clearinghouse as well as www.enrolldirect.com.

U.S. FIRMS WHICH PERMIT INITIAL PURCHASES DIRECTLY

ADC Telecomm. ($500)	800-774-4117
Aetna ($500)	800-955-4741
AFLAC ($750)	800-227-4756
AGL Resources ($250)	800-774-4117
Air Products & Chemicals ($500)	888-694-9458
Alleg. Teledyne ($1,000)	800-842-7629

Alliant Energy ($250)	800-356-5343
Allstate ($500)	800-448-7007
American Elec. Power ($250)	800-955-4740
American Express ($1,000)	800-842-7629
Amway Asia Pacific ($250)	800-727-7033
Arch Chemicals ($500)	800-955-4735
Arrow Financial ($300)	518-745-1000
Ascent Entertainment ($100)	800-727-7033
Associates First Capital ($1,000)	888-297-6879
Atmos Energy ($200)	800-774-4117
Avery Dennison ($500)	800-649-2291
Bank of America ($1,000)	800-642-9855
Bank of NY ($1,000)	800-727-7033
Bard (C.R.) ($250)	800-828-1639
Becton, Dickinson ($250)	800-955-4743
Bedford Properties ($1,000)	800-774-5476
Bell Atlantic ($1,000)	800-631-2355
BellSouth ($500)	888-887-2965
Blyth Industries ($250)	877-424-1968
Bob Evans Farms ($100)	800-272-7675
Borg-Warner Auto. ($500)	800-774-4117
Boston Beer ($500)	888-266-6780
Bowne & Co. ($500)	800-524-4458
Bradley Real Estate ($100)	888-697-7873
BRE Properties ($500)	800-774-4117
California Water Service ($500)	800-337-3503
Campbell Soup ($500)	800-649-2160
Capstead Mortgage ($250)	800-969-6715
Caraustar Inds. ($250)	800-524-4458
Carpenter Technology ($500)	800-822-9828

Caterpillar ($500)	800-955-4749
Central & South West ($250)	800-774-4117
Central Hudson G&E (NY) ($100)	888-280-3848
Chevron ($250)	800-774-4117
Chock Full O'Nuts ($100)	888-200-3161
CILCORP ($250)	800-774-4117
CMS Energy ($500)	800-774-4117
Coastal ($250)	800-788-2500
Community Bank Sys. ($500)	800-842-7629
Compaq Computer ($250)	888-218-4373
Conectiv ($500)	800-365-6495
Consolidated Freightways ($100)	800-727-7033
Cross Timbers Oil ($500)	800-774-4117
Crown Am. Realty Tr. ($100)	800-774-4117
CSX ($500)	800-774-4117
Curtiss-Wright ($2,000)	888-266-6793
CVS ($100)	877-287-7526
Darden Restaurants ($1,000)	800-829-8432
Dayton Hudson ($500)	888-268-0203
Deere & Co. ($500)	800-268-7369
Disney (Walt) ($1,000)	800-948-2222
Dollar General ($50)	888-266-6785
Dominion Resources (VA) ($250)	800-552-4034
Dow Jones & Co. ($1,000)	800-842-7629
DQE ($105)	800-247-0400
DTE Energy ($100)	800-774-4117
Duke Energy ($250)	800-488-3853
Duke Realty ($250)	800-774-4117
Eastern Co. ($250)	800-633-3455
Eastman Kodak ($150)	800-253-6057

Energen ($250)	800-774-4117
Enova ($250)	800-307-7343
Enron ($250)	800-662-7662
Entergy ($1,000)	800-225-1721
Equifax ($500)	888-887-2971
Equitable Companies ($500)	800-437-8736
Equity Residential ($250)	800-337-5666
Essex Property ($100)	800-945-8245
Exxon Mobil ($250)	800-252-1800
Fannie Mae ($250)	888-289-3266
FDX Corp. ($1,000)	800-524-3120
Fed One Bancorp ($250)	800-742-7540
Finova Group ($500)	800-774-4117
First Commonwealth Fin'l ($500)	800-727-7033
FirstEnergy ($250)	800-736-3402
First Financial Holdings ($250)	800-998-9151
Food Lion ($250)	888-232-9530
Ford Motor ($1,000)	800-955-4791
Frontier Insurance ($100)	888-200-3162
GenCorp ($500)	800-727-7033
General Electric ($250)	800-786-2543
General Growth Prop. ($200)	800-774-4117
Gillette ($1,000)	800-643-6989
Glenborough Realty ($250)	800-266-6785
Glimcher Realty ($100)	800-738-4931
Goodyear ($250)	800-453-2440
GreenPoint Financial ($2,000)	800-842-7629
Guidant ($250)	800-537-1677
Harland (John H.) ($500)	800-649-2202
Hawaiian Electric Inds. ($250)	808-543-5662

Hershey Foods ($500)	800-842-7629
Hillenbrand Inds. ($250)	800-774-4117
Home Depot ($250)	800-774-4117
Home Properties ($2,000)	800-774-4117
IBM ($500)	888-421-8860
Illinova ($250)	800-750-7011
Interchange Fin'l Svcs. ($100)	201-703-2265
Intimate Brands ($500)	800-955-4745
Investors Financial ($250)	888-333-5336
IPALCO Enterprises ($250)	800-774-4117
ITT Industries ($500)	800-254-2823
Johnson Controls ($50)	800-524-6220
Justin Industries ($500)	800-727-7033
Kaman ($250)	800-842-7629
Kellwood ($100)	314-576-3100
Kerr-McGee ($750)	800-395-2662
KeySpan ($250)	800-482-3638
Lear ($250)	800-727-7033
Lehman Brothers ($50)	800-824-5707
Libbey ($100)	800-727-7033
Liberty Property Trust ($1,000)	800-944-2214
Lilly (Eli) ($1,000)	800-451-2134
Longs Drug Stores ($500)	888-213-0886
Lucent Technologies ($1,000)	800-774-4117
Macerich ($250)	800-567-0169
Madison Gas & Electric ($50)	800-356-6423
Mallinckrodt ($500)	800-446-2617
Mattel ($500)	888-909-9922
McCormick & Co. ($250)	800-424-5855
McDonald's ($1,000)	800-774-4117

McGraw-Hill ($500)	888-201-5538
MCN Energy ($250)	800-955-4793
MDU Resources ($50)	701-222-7991
Meadowbrook Insurance ($250)	800-649-2579
Mellon Bank ($500)	800-842-7629
Mercantile Bancorp. ($500)	800-774-4117
Merck ($350)	800-774-4117
Meritor Automotive ($500)	800-483-2277
Met-Pro ($1,000)	800-278-4353
Michaels Stores ($500)	800-577-4676
MidAmerican Energy ($250)	800-247-5211
MidSouth Bancorp ($1,000)	800-842-7629
Minnesota P&L ($250)	800-774-4117
Morgan Stanley ($1,000)	800-228-0829
Motorola ($500)	800-774-4117
National Service Inds. ($600)	888-836-5069
NationsBank ($1,000)	800-642-9855
Nationwide Financial Svcs. ($500)	800-409-7514
New England Business Svc. ($250)	800-736-3001
Newport ($100)	888-200-3169
NorthWestern ($500)	800-677-6716
OGE Energy ($250)	800-774-4117
Old National Bancorp ($500)	800-774-4117
Oneok ($100)	800-395-2662
Owens Corning ($1,000)	800-472-2210
Pan Pacific Retail Prop. ($250)	800-524-4458
Penney (J.C.) ($250)	800-565-2576
Peoples Energy ($250)	800-774-4117
Pfizer ($500)	800-733-9393
Pharmacia & Upjohn ($250)	800-774-4117

Phelps Dodge ($1,000)	800-842-7629
Philadelphia Suburban ($500)	800-774-4117
Phillips Petroleum ($500)	888-887-2968
Piedmont Natural Gas ($250)	800-774-4117
Pier 1 Imports ($500)	800-842-7629
Pinnacle West (AZ) ($50)	800-774-4117
Popular ($100)	787-756-3908
Procter & Gamble ($250)	800-764-7483
ProLogis Trust ($200)	800-956-3378
Providian Financial ($500)	800-482-8690
Public Service Enterprise ($250)	800-242-0813
Public Service of NC ($250)	800-774-4117
Public Service of New Mex. ($50)	800-545-4425
Quaker Oats ($500)	800-774-4117
Quanex ($250)	800-278-4353
Questar ($250)	800-729-6788
Reader's Digest ($1,000)	800-242-4653
Redwood Trust ($500)	800-774-4117
Regions Financial ($500)	800-922-3468
Reliant Energy ($250)	800-231-6406
Roadway Express ($250)	800-774-4117
Robbins & Myers ($500)	800-622-6757
Rockwell Int'l ($1,000)	800-842-7629
Sanderson Farms ($500)	800-842-7629
SBC Communications ($500)	888-836-5062
SCANA ($250)	800-763-5891
Schnitzer Steel ($500)	800-727-7033
Sears, Roebuck & Co. ($500)	888-732-7788
Security Capital Pacific ($200)	800-842-7629
SEMCO Energy ($250)	800-649-1856

SIS Bancorp ($1,000)	888-877-2891
Snap-on ($500)	800-501-9474
Sonoco Products ($250)	800-864-2246
Southern Co. ($250)	800-774-4117
Southern Union ($250)	800-793-8938
South Jersey Industries ($100)	888-754-3100
Storage Trust ($250)	800-842-7629
Sunstone Hotel Inv. ($1,000)	800-774-4117
Synovus Financial ($250)	800-337-0896
Tandy ($250)	888-218-4374
Taubman Centers ($250)	800-774-4117
Tektronix ($500)	800-842-7629
Tenneco ($500)	800-519-3111
Texaco ($250)	800-283-9785
Thornburg Mortgage Asset ($500)	800-509-5586
Timken ($1,000)	888-347-2453
TNP Enterprises ($100)	800-774-4117
Total System Services ($250)	800-553-0292
Transocean Offshore ($500)	800-727-7033
Tribune ($500)	800-924-1490
TrustCo Bank of NY ($25)	518-381-3601
Tyson Foods ($250)	800-822-7096
UniSource Energy ($250)	888-269-8845
United Wisconsin Svcs. ($100)	414-276-3737
Urban Shopping Ctrs. ($500)	800-774-4117
UtiliCorp United ($250)	800-647-2789
Valspar ($1,000)	800-842-7629
Wal-Mart Stores ($250)	800-438-6278
Walgreen ($50)	800-774-4117
Warner-Lambert ($250)	888-767-7166

Weingarten Realty ($500)	888-887-2966
Wells Fargo ($250)	800-774-4117
Western Resources ($250)	800-774-4117
Westvaco ($250)	800-432-9874
Whirlpool ($1,000)	800-409-7442
Whitman ($250)	800-660-4187
WICOR ($500)	800-236-3453
Wisconsin Energy ($50)	800-558-9663
WLR Foods ($250)	540-896-7001
WPS Resources ($100)	800-236-1551
York International ($1,000)	800-774-4117

FOREIGN FIRMS WHICH PERMIT INITIAL PURCHASES DIRECTLY

ABN AMRO ($250)	800-749-1687
Adecco ($250)	800-749-1687
Admin. de Fondos ($200)	800-345-1612
AEGON N.V. ($250)	800-808-8010
Ahold N.V. ($200)	800-345-1612
Aktiebolaget Electrolux ($250)	800-749-1687
Akzo Nobel NV ($250)	800-749-1687
Amcor Limited ($250)	800-749-1687
Amway Japan ($250)	800-749-1687
Aracruz Celulose ($250)	800-749-1687
Arcadis ($200)	800-345-1612
Asia Pulp and Paper ($200)	800-345-1612
Asia Satellite Telecomm. ($250)	800-749-1687
AstraZeneca ($250)	800-749-1687
Atlas Pacific Ltd. ($200)	800-345-1612

AXA UAP ($200)	888-269-2377
Baan NV ($250)	800-749-1687
Banco Bilbao Vizcaya ($200)	800-345-1612
Banco de Galicia ($200)	800-345-1612
Banco de Santiago ($250)	800-749-1687
Banco Ganadero ($200)	800-345-1612
BanColombiano ($200)	800-345-1612
Banco Rio ($200)	800-345-1612
Banco Santander, S.A. ($250)	800-749-1687
Banco Wiese ($250)	800-749-1687
Bank of Ireland ($200)	800-345-1612
Bank of Tokyo-Mits. ($200)	800-345-1612
Barclays Bank Plc ($250)	800-749-1687
Benetton Group S.P.A. ($250)	800-749-1687
Biora AB ($200)	800-345-1612
Blue Square-Israel ($200)	800-345-1612
BOC Group ($250)	800-749-1687
Boral Ltd. ($200)	800-345-1612
BP Amoco ($250)	877-638-5672
British Airways Plc ($250)	800-749-1687
British Telecom. Plc ($250)	800-749-1687
Bufete Industrial ($200)	800-345-1612
Cadbury Schweppes Plc ($250)	800-749-1687
Canon ($250)	800-749-1687
Cantab Pharm. ($200)	800-345-1612
Carlton Comm. Plc ($250)	800-749-1687
CBT Group ($200)	800-345-1612
China Eastern Airlines ($200)	800-345-1612
China Telecom ($200)	800-345-1612

CNH Global NV ($250)	800-749-1687
Coca-Cola Femsa ($200)	800-345-1612
Compania Cerv. S.A. ($250)	800-749-1687
Consorcio G Grupo ($250)	800-749-1687
Corporacion Bancaria de Espana, S.A. Argentaria ($250)	800-749-1687
Cresud ($200)	800-345-1612
DaimlerChrysler ($200)	800-470-7418
Dassault Systemes SA ($250)	800-749-1687
De Rigo ($200)	800-345-1612
Diageo Plc ($200)	800-345-1612
Digitale Telekabel ($200)	800-345-1612
Doncasters ($200)	800-345-1612
ECsoft Group ($200)	800-345-1612
Elan ($200)	800-345-1612
Empresa Nacional De Electricidad S.A. ($250)	800-749-1687
Empresas ICA ($200)	800-345-1612
Empresas La Moderna ($200)	800-345-1612
Equant NV ($250)	800-749-1687
FAI Insurances Ltd. ($200)	800-345-1612
Fiat S.P.A. ($250)	800-749-1687
Fila ($200)	800-345-1612
Flamel Technologies ($200)	800-345-1612
Freepages Group ($200)	800-345-1612
Fresenius Medical ($250)	800-749-1687
Gallaher Group ($200)	800-345-1612
General Cable ($200)	800-345-1612
Great Central Mines ($200)	800-345-1612

Groupe AB ($200)	800-345-1612
Grupo Casa Autrey, S.A. de C.V. ($250)	800-749-1687
Grupo Elektra ($200)	800-345-1612
Grupo IMSA ($200)	800-345-1612
Grupo Indus'l Durango ($200)	800-345-1612
Grupo Iusacell ($200)	800-345-1612
Grupo Tribasa ($200)	800-345-1612
Guangshen Rail. Co. ($250)	800-749-1687
Harmony ($200)	800-345-1612
Huntingdon Life Sciences ($200)	800-345-1612
Imperial Chem. Ind. ($250)	800-749-1687
INA ($200)	800-345-1612
Industrias Bachoco ($200)	800-345-1612
Industrie Natuzzi SPA ($200)	800-345-1612
ING Groep ($250)	800-749-1687
IRSA Inversiones ($200)	800-345-1612
ISPAT Int'l ($200)	800-345-1612
Israel Land Devel. ($200)	800-345-1612
Istituto Mobiliare Italiano S.P.A. ($250)	800-749-1687
Koor Industries ($200)	800-345-1612
Lihir Gold Ltd. ($200)	800-345-1612
London Int'l ($200)	800-345-1612
LucasVarity ($250)	800-749-1687
Luxottica Group ($200)	800-345-1612
Macronix Int'l ($200)	800-345-1612
Maderas y Sintecticos Sociedad Anonima ($200)	800-345-1612
Makita ($200)	800-345-1612
Matav ($200)	800-345-1612
Matsushita Electric Inds. ($250)	800-749-1687

Mavesa ($200)	800-345-1612
Medeva Plc ($200)	800-345-1612
Micro Focus Group ($200)	800-345-1612
Mid-States ($200)	800-345-1612
National Westminster Bank Plc ($250)	800-749-1687
NEC ($200)	800-345-1612
Nera A.S. ($200)	800-345-1612
Netcom Systems ($200)	800-345-1612
NFC Plc ($200)	800-345-1612
Nice Systems Ltd. ($200)	800-345-1612
Nippon Tele. & Tele. ($250)	800-749-1687
Nokia ($250)	800-483-9010
Norsk Hydro A.S. ($250)	800-749-1687
Novo-Nordisk A.S. ($250)	800-749-1687
Oce NV ($250)	800-749-1687
OLS Asia ($200)	800-345-1612
Orange ($200)	888-269-2377
OzEMail Ltd. ($200)	800-345-1612
Pacific Dunlop Ltd. ($250)	800-749-1687
Pepsi-Gemex ($200)	800-345-1612
Petsec Energy ($200)	800-345-1612
Pioneer Electronics ($250)	800-808-8010
Portugal Telecom ($200)	800-345-1612
P.T. Pasifik Satelit ($200)	800-345-1612
Rank Group Plc ($250)	800-749-1687
Repsol S.A. ($200)	800-345-1612
Reuters Group Plc ($250)	800-749-1687
Ricoh Company Ltd. ($200)	800-345-1612
Royal Bank of Scotland ($200)	800-345-1612
Royal Dutch Petroleum ($250)	800-749-1687

Santos Ltd. ($250)	800-749-1687
SCOR ($200)	800-345-1612
Select Appointments ($200)	800-345-1612
Select Software Tools ($200)	800-345-1612
Senetek Plc ($200)	800-345-1612
SGS-Thomson Microelectronics ($200)	800-345-1612
Signet Group Plc ($200)	800-345-1612
Smallworld ($200)	800-345-1612
SmithKline Beecham ($200)	800-345-1612
Sony Corp. ($250)	800-749-1687
Supermercados Unimarc ($200)	800-345-1612
Super-Sol ($250)	800-749-1687
TAG Heuer ($250)	800-749-1687
TDK Corp. ($250)	800-749-1687
Telecom Argentina STET-France Telecom S.A. ($250)	800-749-1687
Telecommunicacoes Brasileiras ($200)	800-345-1612
Telefonica del Peru S.A. ($250)	800-749-1687
Telefonos de Mexico S.A. de C.V. Series L ($250)	800-749-1687
Telex-Chile (Empresas) ($200)	800-345-1612
Thorn Plc ($250)	800-749-1687
Tricom ($200)	800-345-1612
Tubos de Acero de Mexico, S.A. ($250)	800-749-1687
TV Azteca ($200)	800-345-1612
Unilever NV ($250)	800-749-1687
Unilever Plc ($250)	800-749-1687
Valmet ($200)	800-345-1612
Vimpel Comm. ($200)	800-345-1612
Vodafone Group Plc ($200)	800-345-1612

Westpac Banking ($250)   800-749-1687

Wharf Holdings ($200)   800-345-1612

WMC Holdings ($200)   800-345-1612

Xeikon ($200)   800-345-1612

YPF Sociedad Anonima ($200)   800-345-1612

BIBLIOGRAPHY

Chapter 1

Akron Beacon Journal, July 3, 1995, "Retirement Will Be Easier, But Inflation Still Takes a Hit," by Humberto Cruz.

The Arizona Republic, July 29, 1997, "Bull Market Helps Create Large Group of Middle-Class Rich," by Kathy Bergen.

Business Week, June 28, 1999.

The Charlotte Observer, May 24, 1998, "Shareholder Nation's Army of Investors Marches On," by John Talton.

Detroit Free Press, July 15, 1996, "Come Learn the Secrets of Eccentric Millionaires," by Jane Birnbaum.

Fortune, July 5, 1999.

Investor's Business Daily, July 15, 1999.

The Millionaire Next Door (Longstreet Press, 24th printing, 1998), by Thomas J. Stanley, Ph.D., and William D. Danko, Ph.D.

Morgan Stanley Dean Witter, January 27, 1999, "U.S. Strategy: Wealth Versus Money," by Peter Canelo.

The Wall Street Journal, July 28, 1999.

Worth, September 1999, "How America Got Rich," by Walter Russell Mead.

Chapter 2

www.lifeinsurancebrokers.com/lifee.html

Akron Beacon Journal, May 31, 1998, "Junior Partner Knows His Stuff," by Peter Alan Harper.

The Detroit News, June 30, 1998, "Nielsen Poll Shows Kids Watch an Average 3 Hours of Television Daily," by Tim Kiska.

Investor's Business Daily, June 18, 1998.

Investor's Business Daily, October 15, 1998.

Investor's Business Daily, November 5, 1998.

Investor's Business Daily, November 12, 1998.

Investor's Business Daily, November 24, 1998.

Investor's Business Daily, July 20, 1999.

The Wall Street Journal, June 30, 1999.

Why Smart People Make Big Money Mistakes—and How to Correct Them (Simon & Schuster, 1999), by Gary Belsky and Thomas Gilovich.

Chapter 3

Investor's Business Daily, February 16, 1999.

Investor's Business Daily, April 26, 1999.

Investor's Business Daily, August 31, 1999.

Your Nest Egg, August 17, 1998, by Robert Law.

Chapter 4

Are Your Goals and Values In Line? (www.topachievement.com), by Kimberly Goodwin.

Becoming a Goal Detective (www.topachievement.com), by Kevin L. Polk, Ph.D.

Creating S.M.A.R.T. Goals (www.topachievement.com), by Paul J. Meyer, "Attitude Is Everything."

Dog Teaches Master Tricks (www.topachievement.com), by Don Coggan.

Goal Setting Your Way to Top Achievement! (www.topachievement.com), by Gene Donohue.

Investor's Business Daily, March 22, 1999.

Money, June 1997.

The Principle of Success (www.topachievement.com), by Craig Lock.

The 7 Steps to Creating Powerful Written Goals! (www.top achievement.com), by Gene Donohue.

The Top 10 Best Ideas for Setting Goals (www.topachievement.com), by Hilton Johnson.

The Top 10 Conditions for Creating a Compelling Outcome (www.topachievement.com), by Robert Knowlton.

Chapter 5

Akron Beacon Journal, May 22, 1997, "What's a Million Mean to a Guy Who Has Around 400 of Them?" by Anne Gearan.

Financial Dimensions, Spring 1999.

Investor's Business Daily, January 6, 1999.

Investor's Business Daily, February 17, 1999.

Investor's Business Daily, March 22, 1999.

Investor's Business Daily, May 7, 1999.

Investor's Business Daily, June 29, 1999.

Investor's Business Daily, July 27, 1999.

Investor's Business Daily, July 28, 1999.

Money, 1998, "Five Secrets from a Real Long-Term Investor," by Duff McDonald.

Stock, Bonds, Bills, and Inflation, 1999 Yearbook (Ibbotson Associates, 1999).

Stocks for the Long Run (McGraw-Hill, 2d ed., 1998), by Jeremy J. Siegel.

The Wall Street Journal, March 17, 1999, "Stock Prices Are Still Far Too Low," by James K. Glassman.

Chapter 6

Contra Costa Times, August 26, 1996, "Young Fogies Retire at 40 with a Small Fortune, A Dose of Frugality," by Anita Sharpe.

Individual Investor, 1999.

The Outlook, "Directory of Dividend Reinvestment Plans" (McGraw-Hill, 1999 Edition), by Standard & Poor's.

Chapter 7

Investor's Business Daily, November 17, 1998.

Investor's Business Daily, March 24, 1999.

Investor's Business Daily, June 16, 1999.

Investor's Business Daily, June 23, 1999.

Investor's Business Daily, July 21, 1999.

Investor's Business Daily, August 5, 1999.

Mutual Fund News Service, February 19, 1999, "Yes, Dividends Do Still Matter, Says Pioneer."

Philadelphia Inquirer, August 1, 1997, "Hospital Gets $18 Million."

The Outlook, August 4, 1999, by Standard & Poor's.

"The Slight Edge Philosophy" (www.topachievement.com/slightedge. html), by Jeff Olson.

Your Money, January 5, 1999, "How to Make $1 Million," by David Rynecki.

Chapter 8

The Baltimore Sun, December 23, 1996, "Coke Millions Fortify a Town."

Business Week, January 18, 1999, "Day of Reckoning for Day-Trading Firms," by Geoffrey Smith.

DRIP Investor, November 1998, "Just Because You Can, Doesn't Mean You Should," by Charles B. Carlson.

Investment News, November 23, 1998.

Investor's Business Daily, August 3, 1995.

Investor's Business Daily, February 13, 1998.

Investor's Business Daily, October 29, 1998.

Investor's Business Daily, November 30, 1998.

Investor's Business Daily, June 22, 1999.

Investor's Business Daily, August 10, 1999.

Investor's Business Daily, August 25, 1999.

The Miami Herald, January 5, 1997, "If Only Miami Had Invested in Coca-Cola," by Adam Levy.

The New York Times, July 18, 1999, "In Day Trading, Less Thrill and More Chill," by Diana B. Henriques.

SmartMoney, August 1999, "Day Trading Is for Losers," by Roger Lowenstein.

The Wall Street Journal, October 21, 1998.

The Wall Street Journal, November 30, 1998.

The Wall Street Journal, May 4, 1999.

The Wall Street Journal, August 2, 1999, "Day Trading Can Lead to Big Losses, Dangerous Illusions, Specialists Warn," by Rebecca Buckman and Ruth Simon.

The Wall Street Journal, August 3, 1999, "Day Trading and Its Dangers," by Burton G. Malkiel.

The Wall Street Journal, August 9, 1999, "Probe of Day-Trading Firms Finds 75% of Surveyed Accounts in the Red," by Rebecca Buckman.

The Wall Street Journal, August 10, 1999, "Day-Trading Firms Rebuked by Group of State Regulators Over Marketing," by Michael Schroeder.

Chapter 9

Better Investing, January 1999, "Contributing to Your Retirement Plan at Work," by Alexandra Armstrong.

Better Investing, August 1999, "Withdrawing Money from Your 403(b) Retirement Plan," by Alexandra Armstrong.

The Individual Investor Revolution (McGraw-Hill, 1998), by Charles B. Carlson.

Investor's Business Daily, February 2, 1999.

Investor's Business Daily, March 23, 1999.

Investor's Business Daily, July 30, 1999.

Investor's Business Daily, August 12, 1999.

Investor's Business Daily, August 26, 1999.

On Investing, Fall 1999.

Profit Sharing/401(k) Council of America, October 2, 1998, "41st Annual Survey of Profit Sharing and 401(k) Plans Released."

Profit Sharing/401(k) Council of America, June 17, 1999, "401(k) Day an Occasion for 55 Million Participants to Celebrate."

SmartMoney, August 1999.

The Wall Street Journal, June 29, 1999.

The Wall Street Journal, August 3, 1999.

The Wall Street Journal, August 12, 1999.

The Wall Street Journal, August 27, 1999.

Worth, September 1999, "Season of the Witch" by Nick Pachetti.

Chapter 10

Divorce, Dollars & Debt: Financial Risks Involved (www.divorcesource. com).

Investment News, June 28, 1999.

Investor's Business Daily, June 30, 1998.

Investor's Business Daily, April 21, 1999.

Investor's Business Daily, July 2, 1999.

The Merrill Lynch Retirement & Financial Planning Survey of Employees, 1998.

More Than an Education, an Investment (www.strayer.edu).

Morningstar, July 9, 1999, "Advice for the Soon-to-Be-Divorced," by Susan Dziubinski.

Physical Activity Is a Family Value, Dr. Koop Says, May 2, 1996 (www.shapeup.org).

The Gary Post-Tribune, August 26, 1999.

Self-Employed Coverage—Disability (www.amfam.com).

Time, July 12, 1999.
The Wall Street Journal, August 10, 1998.
The Wall Street Journal, May 24, 1999.

Chapter 11
The New York Times, July 13, 1998.

INDEX

ABOUT THE AUTHOR

CHARLES B. CARLSON, CFA, is the author of the books *Buying Stocks Without a Broker* (350,000 copies in print) and *No-Load Stocks,* and editor of the investment newsletters *DRIP Investor* and *No-Load Stock Insider,* reaching nearly 40,000 subscribers. He is also coportfolio manager for the Strong Dow 30 Value no-load mutual fund. Carlson earned his MBA from the University of Chicago, and his comments appear regularly in the top business press, from *Forbes* to *The New York Times* to *USA Today.* He lives in Valparaiso, Indiana.